Now a
Major Motion Picture

Genre and Beyond
A Film Studies Series
Series Editor: Leonard Leff, Oklahoma State University

Genre and Beyond offers fresh perspectives on conceptions of film as well as cinema's role in a changing world. Books in the series explore often overlooked or unconventional genres as well as more traditional themes. These engaging texts have the rigor that scholars demand and the creativity and accessibility that students and interested readers expect.

Now a Major Motion Picture

Film Adaptations of Literature and Drama

Christine Geraghty

ROWMAN & LITTLEFIELD PUBLISHERS, INC.
Lanham • Boulder • New York • Toronto • Plymouth, UK

ROWMAN & LITTLEFIELD PUBLISHERS, INC.

Published in the United States of America
by Rowman & Littlefield Publishers, Inc.
A wholly owned subsidiary of The Rowman & Littlefield Publishing Group, Inc.
4501 Forbes Boulevard, Suite 200, Lanham, Maryland 20706
www.rowmanlittlefield.com

Estover Road, Plymouth PL6 7PY, United Kingdom

British Library Cataloguing in Publication Information Available

Library of Congress Cataloging-in-Publication Data
Geraghty, Christine.
 Now a major motion picture : film adaptations of literature and drama /
Christine Geraghty.
   p.   cm. — (Genre and beyond)
 Filmography: p.
 Includes bibliographical references and index.
 ISBN-13: 978-0-7425-3820-7 (cloth : alk. paper)
 ISBN-10: 0-7425-3820-6 (cloth : alk. paper)
 ISBN-13: 978-0-7425-3821-4 (pbk. : alk. paper)
 ISBN-10: 0-7425-3821-4 (pbk. : alk. paper)
 1. Film adaptations—History and criticism. I. Title.
 PN1997.85.G47 2008
 791.43'6—dc22

                                                                2007017433

Printed in the United States of America

∞™ The paper used in this publication meets the minimum requirements of
American National Standard for Information Sciences—Permanence of Paper
for Printed Library Materials, ANSI/NISO Z39.48-1992.

Contents

Acknowledgments

This book could not have been completed without the research leave funded by the UK Arts and Humanities Research Council, and I acknowledge its support with gratitude. Thanks also to the University of Glasgow for matching this period of research leave and to Dr. Dimitris Eleftheriotis, who acted as head of department during my absence. I would like also to thank Jeanette Berrie for supporting my work as head of department, throughout the time of writing, in such a generous and effective way.

I would like to thank my colleagues in the Theatre, Film, and Television Studies Department who have helped to shape the work presented here. Their commitment to the intertwining of research and teaching is exemplary, and their critical engagement with textual and contextual work continually demonstrates the importance of textual analysis in illuminating our understanding of what film and television can offer. I am very grateful to Charlotte Brunsdon, Karen Lury, and David Lusted, who read chapters at various stages of writing, and to research seminars at London Metropolitan University, University of Glasgow, University of St. Andrews, and University of Stirling at which I presented material from this research. I regret that I was not always able to follow up on the points raised in those discussions, but the many valuable comments made and the interest shown in this research was enormously encouraging. My thanks also to Anna Marks for initial help with the referencing and to Elke Weissmann for completing the process by finalizing the bibliography and filmography; her cheerful efficiency was a great boost at a late stage in the project.

I was able to use the resources of the British Film Institute and the Billy Rose Collection at the New York Public Library of the Performing Arts. My thanks to staff members there for their help and to my dear friends, Lynne, Neil, and Chess, for their hospitality during my stay in New York.

Finally, I particularly thank Paul Marks for his perceptive comments at important stages in the writing and for his unwavering encouragement and support. As always, this book is dedicated to him with love and thanks.

Introduction

It is traditional for books about screen adaptations to begin with a discussion of adaptation theory, the body of work normally deemed to have started with George Bluestone's 1957 book, *Novels into Film*.[1] This book does not do so partly because there are now excellent accounts of these debates in, for instance, Sarah Cardwell's *Adaptation Revisited* and Kamilla Elliott's *Rethinking the Novel/Film Debate*.[2] In addition, starting with Bluestone and moving through some of the other key works on film adaptation seems too readily to lead to methods of analysis that rely on comparisons between original source and film and make judgments that are rooted implicitly or explicitly in the concept of fidelity. As Thomas Leitch expresses it in his splendid polemic, "Twelve Fallacies in Contemporary Adaptation Theory," the central question of such analysis is "in what ways does and should an intertext resemble its precursor text in another medium?"[3] Almost inevitably, this approach leads to the conclusion, sometimes in sorrow, sometimes in anger, that "'It wasn't like that in the book.'"[4] It is widely recognized that it is time to move on, and this book endeavors to do so by suggesting other ways of approaching adaptations.

In seeking to analyze the relationship between source and adaptation, adaptation theory has been surprisingly judgmental, often making pronouncements that depend on ideas about medium specificity, "what novels can do that films can't (and vice versa)" to quote the title of one influential article.[5] The search for a generalized model for adaptation can quickly disintegrate into a list of do and don'ts, a set of requirements and prohibitions. So, it is ruled that, among other things, novels are verbal and use words while films are visual and rely on images; novels can express internal knowledge of a character, but screen adaptations have to imply feelings or motivations from a character's actions since the camera is best suited to the objective recording of physical appearances; films can only use the present tense; voice-overs are noncinematic; and cinema and television rely on realism while literature requires the reader's imagination. Even critics who have challenged this approach can fall into this prescriptive mode and find themselves pronouncing, as Deborah Cartmell and Imelda Whelehan do of a *Harry Potter* adaptation, that "any film that prioritises transposition over interpretation is unlikely to recognise the pitfalls . . . and will, moreover, spectacularly fail."[6] Such theoretical writing sometimes resembles the advice offered in handbooks to potential screenwriters, with their rules about, for example, the "five elements that can make an adaptation work."[7] These prescriptions often rely, more or less overtly, on a hierarchy of judgment that brings together and privileges literature, reading, and authorship over screen, viewing, and mass production. Robert Stam calls this "iconophobia [a] deeply rooted prejudice against the visual arts."[8] A literary background certainly lies behind the tendency of many theorists, as Brian McFarlane recognizes, to restrict their analysis to narrative and theme, ignoring aspects that are fundamental to film analysis such as genre, mise-en-scène, editing, acting, stars, and sound.

Numerous critics including James Naremore, Dudley Andrew, and Stam have pointed to the cul-de-sac into which much adaptation theory leads, although as examples in this book will show, it is proving surprisingly difficult to get out of it. Most influential perhaps has been the work of Robert Stam, who has used post-structuralism to challenge the notion that adaptations involve a one-way interaction with a single source. Stam places a trenchant emphasis not on what cinema lacks in relation to print but rather on its multitrack qualities; the "linguistic energy of literary writing turns into the audio-visual-kinetic-performative energy of the adaptation," he writes.[9] He argues that, read intertextually, source texts are themselves formed through a dense network of textual relationships. Because of this, adaptations no longer depend on a single source but are "caught up in an ongoing whirl of intertextual reference and transformation, of texts generating other texts in an endless process of recycling, transformation and transmutation, with no clear point of origin."[10] This range of sources makes ascribing cultural value more difficult and challenges the sweeping judgments made about low cultural forms such as Hollywood films or indeed comics and genre novels. Stam stresses the multicultural dialogue that can take place across different versions of classic novels such as *Robinson Crusoe*. And just as texts develop from a network of sources that have no single author, they too can have a plurality of meanings, depending on the textual skills and the contextual positioning of the reader.

This emphasis on the reader is helpful but suggests that the perennial question of faithfulness is not a matter for textual analysis but rather for work on reception. Faithfulness matters if it matters to the viewer. Many reviewers and critics (and there will be numerous examples of this practice in this book) put themselves into the role of the viewer who has not only read the book but also wants the film to be faithful to it. But this is not the only position. As McFarlane points out, "the precursor literary work is only an aspect of the film's intertextuality, of more or less importance according to the viewer's acquaintance with the antecedent work."[11] There are many films based on previous sources that go unacknowledged as adaptations: the book is not well-known, the film does not draw attention to its status as an adaptation, and the publicity machinery ignores the original source. Faithfulness is not an issue, and the film in a very real sense is not an adaptation. Catherine Grant makes an important point when she proposes that adaptations should be understood as part of the reception process: "The most important act that films and their surrounding discourses need to perform in order to communicate unequivocally their status as adaptations is to [make their audiences] *recall* the adapted work, or the cultural memory of it. There is no such thing . . . as a 'secret' adaptation."[12] When this work is done, the film can be known as an adaptation by people who have not read the original, those who have read it and did not like it, those who have read it and cannot remember it, and any number of other permutations. Any single cinema or television audience will include people in different positions, and it would seem logical to look at the audience rather than the text to discover what those positions are and to measure the importance of faithfulness in particular cases. Reception work in this area has been limited, though we can see its potential in, for instance, Jacqueline Bobo's study of black women's responses to Spielberg's version of *The Color Purple* (1985). By considering the responses of black women to this controversial adaptation, she was able to explore how her respondents reinterpreted the question of faithfulness to the book in a very different way from the black male critics who had condemned the film.[13] Such direct work with audiences will be taken further in the major research being conducted by Martin Barker and others on *The Lord of the Rings: The Return of the King* (Jackson, 2003).[14]

Stam's work brings adaptation studies, as Naremore comments, "more into line with both contemporary theory and contemporary filmmaking" and has been influential in suggesting that the proper object of study should not be the relationship between source and adaptation but rather "the study of the adaptation's intertextual universe" and, in this way, moving from a metaphor of "reflection" to one of "refraction."[15] The emphasis on intertextuality does lead Stam to suggest that adaptations are merely extreme examples of what is at play in any kind of text: "Virtually all films, not only adaptations, remakes, and sequels, are mediated through intertextuality and writing."[16] By trying to bring adaptation theory into a broader account based on cultural theory, Stam runs the risk of underplaying the particular features of adaptations that I wish to explore in this book. The much-quoted emphasis on the ceaseless whirl of references underplays the processes, particularly those associated with generic framing and film reviewing, which provide a framework by which adaptations are recognized and understood. The openness of Stam's approach is indeed productive, but it might lead to textual accounts that deliberately seek to escape the interpretative and social processes that work to pin down meaning at a particular point. This not only makes analysis almost impossible, given the number and fleetingness of possible associations and connections between texts, but also does not necessarily help our study of adaptations. While I contest the relationship with an original source as the main criterion for judging adaptations, I still want to explore the particular ways in which adaptations make their own meanings.

This book therefore does not argue "from page to screen," and my emphasis is not on the process of adaptation. Instead, I focus on the films themselves and the work of "recall," which Grant suggests is essential for an adaptation. This work of recall positions an adaptation precisely as an adaptation, and studying it involves both textual and contextual analysis. The adaptation might draw attention to its literary origins in its presentation of its own material, but the act of comparison invited by an adaptation might also draw on memories, understandings, and associations with other versions of the original, in a variety of media. In many cases, some of this referencing will be made explicit in the publicity material and reviews, which ensure that the audience is alert to the fact of adaptation. I draw on such material for my analyses of individual films, and in chapter 2, reviewing practices are specifically examined as the main way in which the films under discussion were assessed as adaptations. Such contextual material is not limited to the initial publicity. The production of new versions maintains an interest in the older ones, so that the 2005 film of *Pride and Prejudice* (Wright) revived references to the BBC's 1995 television version, while a controversial adaptation of *The Last of the Mohicans* (Mann, 1992) can be drawn into discussions about U.S. history well after its initial release.

In marking the similarities between adaptations and other fiction films, Stam makes the point that all films "adapt a script" and, in this sense, can be considered adaptations.[17] Again, this underestimates the way in which adaptations might differ from other fiction films because they emphasize rather than hide the performance that is involved in putting a script on screen. This applies not just to the story but also to other elements such as characterization, costume, and setting; in each case, the differences between source and film or between different versions of the same source create a gap in which we can see the act of making fiction. In their emphasis on repetition and difference, adaptations are not unique; cinema and television continually present what is familiar (generic iconography, stars, character, stories, formats) in new contexts. Adaptations are, though, distinctive in the way in which they make this process an overt part of the pleasure of viewing. One striking example of this relates to acting. Adaptations not only present different actors in the same role but also present acting in a different way. Very often, star performances in cinema are deemed to rely on actors simply being themselves, but adaptations draw attention to what Stam calls "a tension between the characters as constructed and projected during our reading, and the embodied actors/characters witnessed on screen."[18] The gap between character and actor allows for a performance to be seen, a fact that helps to explain why so many acting Oscars have been awarded to performances in adaptations. But this awareness of a gap, between what is being referred to in the work of recall involved in the adaptation and what we see on screen, can also, as we shall see, be discussed in relation to other elements—in the rendering of landscape, for instance, or the use of costumes.

Screen adaptations are not confined to a particular kind of genre, though academic analysis often focuses on the classic adaptations. This book brings together analyses of very different kinds of films, but it does not expect them to be representative. Since there is no one model for creating or analyzing an adaptation, there cannot be a particular sample of films that will illustrate how being an adaptation affects our understanding of particular works. All the films and television programs discussed here have a connection with a previous source, but that need not be what they are best known for. This book does not comment on the faithfulness or otherwise of the adaptations it looks at and does not take comparison with the source as its main method, although comparison between different screen adaptations of the same source is a valuable approach, used particularly in chapter 1. Instead, the analysis focuses on the films and television programs themselves: examining how the fact of adaptation is referred to or used in the text; looking at how such references interact with other factors such as genre, editing, and acting; looking at the reviewing context, which often provides the framework for treating a film as an adaptation; and assessing the critical debates that have been generated by particular adaptations. The judgments I make about individual films or television programs are not based on how they work as adaptations but rather on how they work in themselves and in this context. Detailed textual and, in some cases, contextual analysis is important in this approach, although space restrictions mean that not all of these approaches can be used on any one film. Instead, the studies offered here allow us to look at particular instances of screen adaptations that have been chosen both for their own interest and for the way in which they illustrate particular points.

Chapter 1 looks at classic adaptations through an analysis of some of the adaptations made from the novels of Charles Dickens and Jane Austen. It focuses in particular on the handling of narrative and character and suggests that even in this familiar mode of adaptation there are considerable variations in how the classic adaptation works. In particular, the chapter looks at the different patterns of dealing with narrative and characterization in classic adaptations, patterns that depend not just on the source but also on the screen genres that they deploy. *Oliver Twist* provides an early example of the problems caused by faithfulness, while a discussion of three adaptations of *Pride and Prejudice* takes further the question of genres. By contrast, chapter 2 focuses less on the adaptations themselves and much more on the contextual framework of film reviewing, which provides an often disparaging commentary on what are usually presented as impossible projects—the filming of works by, for instance, Marcel Proust and Virginia Woolf, writers whose reputation rests not on narrative and characterization but rather on intellectual debate and modernist experimentation. The framework here is the art film, and I look at how the perceived difficulties of such adaptations are understood through discourses of authorship, audience, and film style. In chapter 3, I look at films that have been by contrast comparatively well received as film adaptations—the plays of Tennessee Williams. This chapter concentrates on detailed analysis of three films based on Williams's plays in the context of the changes in the film industry in 1950s Hollywood. Drawing on the work of André Bazin, I examine how theatrical space is transformed and referenced in these screen adaptations and look at the way in which the handling of acting and star image is crucial to the generic crossover of the family melodrama and the 1950s adult film.

The following two chapters look at adaptations with sources that might be considered less respectable. Edna Ferber and Pearl S. Buck provided Hollywood with blockbuster novels that might now be categorized as "a good read" and that were made into highly prestigious films in the 1930s. Chapter 4 looks at how authorship, genre, and the studio system contributed to films of their novels that combined action and adventure with stories of romance and family. The chapter analyzes how this combination of epic stories and family sagas was used to present particular historical events set in the United States (Ferber) or in the world outside (Buck) and suggests that the feminism of the two authors was an important factor in their translation into successful Hollywood films. Once again, genre provides an important element for discussion, and particular attention is paid to the question of romance and happy endings. Chapter 5 examines two films that can be described as modern or revisionist westerns, one based on a classic novel—*The Last of the Mohicans*—and the other on a short story—*Brokeback Mountain*. This chapter looks at these films in terms of critical writing about the western as a genre and its representation of masculinity. It focuses in particular on two aspects important to the study of adaptations—the creation of a viewing position in relation to the overall narrative and the depiction of landscape. This discussion is set in the context of particular claims about faithfulness made by the makers and illustrates again how fidelity, used rather differently in the publicity for both films, is not a given but rather a highly problematic construction.

Screen adaptations are normally discussed in terms of their literary sources. The final chapter looks at something rather different. Settings, particularly historical settings, are often a crucial factor in adaptations, combining spectacle and realism in their promise of authenticity. Following on from the discussion of landscape, this chapter looks at the adaptation of a setting, in this case, the use of New York. The chapter comments on film's creation of space through editing, art design, and mise-en-scène. It looks at the way in which the setting of the nineteenth-century city is contrived from studio sets in *The Heiress* (Wyler, 1949) and location shooting in *The House of Mirth* (Davies, 2000) and concludes by considering the meaning for cinema of the elaborate sets of *Gangs of New York* (Scorsese, 2002). This chapter crystallizes a thread running through the book: the notion that the transformative move made by adaptations is not just from words to image, the common shift discussed in work on adaptations. The shift also concerns space and landscapes. Following the discussions of Dickens's London in chapter 1, the epic landscapes of chapter 4, and the landscapes of the western in chapter 5, a focus on the way in which the streets and houses of New York are transformed and reimagined for the screen gives a new insight into the analysis of screen adaptations.

My starting point in these analyses is that film and television adaptations are autonomous works in their own right. I take up Cardwell's challenge that "adaptations are rarely studied for themselves" and also accept her caution that in any adaptation there is likely to be "a considerable proportion of the filmic text which is not explicable in terms of the source book."[19] One particularly important element that is often not explicable in terms of the source is the impact of genre, particularly that of melodrama. For many critics of adaptations, as we shall see in a number of examples, genre is associated with the industrialization of Hollywood, the commercial imperatives that require the use of formats, imposed happy endings, and the simplification of complex themes into melodrama. In film studies, too, genre is the source of debate. Steve Neale, in particular, points out that the use in film theory of generic categories like "film noir" or "family melodrama" has no justification in terms of industry use in the 1940s and 1950s and provides little purchase in understanding the knowledge that audiences bring with them to the cinema.[20]

Genre is a term that works in a number of ways. It can be used to describe the relationship between industry, audience, and text in which a generic term like a horror film or a western becomes the means by which the industry sells a film. It is therefore a way in which a film can be promoted and categorized but also indicates how it can claim difference; a particular film might belong to a genre, but it is also a distinctive contribution to its further development. Although genre might be used as a way of selling the film, fan activity in criticizing generic claims and assigning films to new or different categories indicates that genres are neither owned by the industry nor imposed on audiences: "To accept the premises of a genre is to agree to play within a special set of rules and thus to participate in a community precisely *not* coterminous with society at large."[21] But genre is also a tool of critical analysis, a way of grouping together films that seem to have common features and making arguments about them that do not necessarily relate to the conscious practices of the audience. Thomas Schatz, for instance, influentially distinguished between genres of social order (westerns, gangster films, detective films) and genres of social integration (musicals, screwball comedies, family melodramas), making a critical distinction at the level of analysis rather than consumption.[22] While Neale is right to criticize confusion between the industrial and critical uses of genre, it seems to me that the critical creation of generic frameworks for the purpose of analysis is not only legitimate but also can actually feed back into production in a way that arguably happened with film noir.

In much of the work that follows, I set specific adaptations into the context created by film genres. I do not see "adaptations" as a generic category in itself; the term is too broad and lacks any specific weight in terms of narrative organization, characterization, iconography, or setting. Screen adaptations involve a more fluid set of possible processes and recognitions that might work with or against generic formulations, and the process of transformation that adaptations go through means that their generic framework must be transformed in their move to the screen. The move is not from a genre-free environment (literature) to a genre-determined one (film and television) but rather between different systems and understandings about categorization. But that is not to say that film genres provide a rigidly fixed framework into which an adaptation must fit, and my purpose is to use genres to help analyze a particular film rather than set up another set of criteria, based on genre rather than source, which it must fit. I draw on genres as a tool for critical analysis and see generic features as layering on top of each other rather than setting up barriers between genres. Genre criticism has been criticized as being too vague, circular, and unscientific, and indeed the terms used in relation to particular genres are overlapping and broad. The terms "costume drama," "heritage film," "historical romance," "classic film," and "literary film" could all be used to describe the same film, and the definitions of such terms are loose and work within a particular context. Nevertheless, the classifications are used by reviewers and critics, they do have meanings within film and television criticism, and most crucially, they do emphasize differences that might be marginal but are often vital in understanding how the film makes sense.

In terms of adaptations, generic categorization is a particular feature of the context that surrounds an adaptation. Genres are associated with the formulae of mass fiction, and within the system, value judgments are often implied about particular genres; describing a film as a "heritage film" or a "melodrama," as we shall see in chapters 2 and 3, for instance, is often a hostile judgment. One of the arguments I propose is that, because generic categorization is often associated with such value judgments, adaptations are often haunted by the fear of crossing over into a less respectable genre—into the heritage film, the romance, or the western in the case of a number of films explored in this book. As a result, the adaptation is not only matched against the associations generated by its relationship with its source; generic associations from other films also accompany it on the screen. And, just as adaptations draw attention to the gap between the source and the new version they offer, so the gap between an adaptation and other examples of its genre also draws attention to the processes of transformation and performance.

In many cases, the term used to condemn an adaptation is "melodrama." In the course of this study, I will use terms like "family melodrama" or "maternal melodrama" in the context of critical analysis of particular films. But given that the term "melodramatic" is often used more generally to attack Hollywood's output, I need to say something here about my use of it, which draws on the critical work on melodrama associated with, among others, Christine Gledhill. An early study of genre fiction suggests that melodrama underpins other formulaic modes and involves "the heightening of feeling and moral conflict and multiple lines of action that work together to create a sense of the rightness of the world order."[23] Gledhill also sees melodrama as a mode and draws specifically on Peter Brooks's 1976 book, *The Melodramatic Imagination*, for her influential discussion of how the term might be used in film analysis. She identified a number of features of melodrama, which included the following: the notion of melodrama as an aesthetic response to the social upheaval in society generated by the industrial revolution; the construction of a highly polarized worldview in which good and evil are clearly delineated and in which evil threatens to overwhelm good; the personalization of good as an innocent woman and sexual seduction or rape as the vehicle of the threat; and the eventual assertion of good when the woman speaks in order to name and identify evil. The enactment of this struggle, Gledhill suggests, "draws into a public arena desires, fears, values and identities which lie beneath the surface of the publicly acknowledged world."[24] The association of melodrama with the aesthetic of excess in terms of music, editing, visual effects, and acting style arises from this attempt to articulate what is normally below the surface, so melodrama is conceived of as a "rhetorical strategy that struggles to convey charged emotional and psychic states through visual and dramatic means."[25] Gledhill and others who take this approach argue that, in terms of Hollywood cinema, melodrama is a mode that operates below the traditional genres and that, rather than just being associated with women's films that deal with the family and personal relationships, it also underpins traditionally male genres such as the western and the action film. As a result, within film theory, melodrama is seen as a mode that allows for problematic positions in relation to gender, class, race, and power to be expressed through an emphasis on what it *feels* like to have your fate determined by remote, external forces beyond your control.

The ubiquity of melodrama in Hollywood cinema puts mainstream adaptations in a doubly difficult position. Not only are they criticized for failing the original; we shall also see how they are attacked for their recourse to melodrama. This kind of criticism is often present in a throwaway comment by a film reviewer or might appear in a critical analysis that relies on a version of medium specificity to make very broad judgments about Hollywood cinema. It seems to me impossible to provide a more nuanced understanding of screen adaptations if such a dismissive attitude to melodrama is maintained. This can place me in what some readers will see as an overly defensive position toward mainstream work and Hollywood films, in particular, but in endeavoring to understand such work it seems pointless to start from a position of denunciation. And, while one of the characteristics of melodrama is an ameliorative resolution in which the victim finds a place in a reordered society, analyses of melodrama in film studies tend to emphasize the contradictions and disturbances of the processes of negotiation rather than the (often precarious) settlements of the ending.

This example of the all-too-ready dismissal of melodrama is indicative of a general attitude to Hollywood and commercial filmmaking that pervades the work even of those who challenge the hierarchies of literature and screen-based work. So, Stam, the champion of intertextuality, nevertheless appears to set limitations on the way in which "many televisual or mainstream Hollywood adaptations" operate in the whirl of transformation he proposes. They are the victims of "aesthetic mainstreaming," which Stam illustrates by referencing screenwriting manuals with their emphasis on narrative arcs and conflict resolution. The goal of such an approach, he argues, "seems to be to 'de-literalize' the text, as the novel is put through the adaptation machine," a machine that also has to take into account the need for "mass-audience legibility" and "economic censorship . . . in the name of monies spent and box-office profits required." Like many before him, Stam falls into the literature/film binary, the trap of ignoring the production contexts of literature while emphasizing those of cinema and television, of assuming that popularity means a decline in reading skills of the audience, of ignoring the social and historical context of production, and of assuming that the "machine" is automatically successful in its task and that in the process the "novel is 'cleansed' of moral ambiguity, narrative interruption, reflexive meditation."[26] He therefore criticizes Vincente Minnelli's MGM version of *Madame Bovary* (1949) for its cultivation of "an aesthetic of crescendo and excess," which is "in contradiction" to the novel but "effective in terms of mainstream entertainment norms."[27] In contrast, in studies that deal largely with mainstream film and television adaptations, I argue that generic streamlining and financial success do not necessarily mean that moral and social ambiguities are easily resolved and indeed that the commercial success of popular screen adaptations might, as Gledhill suggests, indicate that particularly difficult problems are being addressed. The tools of analysis developed in film and television studies allow us to look at popular films in a critical way, to read their incoherences and excesses for what is hidden behind them, and to explore the contradictions that they are often seeking to reconcile.

Metaphors of adaptation and transformation have been a feature of the study of film adaptations and often carry emotional weight; the dominant trope of faithfulness indeed implies the possibility of betrayal and loss. In developing the work that follows, I have found it useful to think in terms of layering and transparencies. Familiar stories and generic references fold into one another; one setting can be seen through another, and characters are created from the ghosts of actors who have played them; features from two or three genres layer over one another in an attempt to tell the story; and the respectable adaptation is haunted by its disreputable counterpart. In much adaptation theory, screen images are objective, settled, and reality bound. My analysis reveals a cinema that is much more fleeting, more conscious of artifice, engaged in making meanings that might be incoherent and contradictory and that work on a number of shifting levels. Screen adaptations have doubleness written into their makeup. Exploring what that means in the particular studies here will, I hope, make a contribution to the debate.

NOTES

1. George Bluestone, *Novels into Film* (Baltimore: Johns Hopkins University Press, 1957).

2. Sarah Cardwell, *Adaptation Revisited: Television and the Classic Novel* (Manchester, UK: Manchester University Press, 2002); and Kamilla Elliott, *Rethinking the Novel/Film Debate* (Cambridge: Cambridge University Press, 2003).

3. Thomas Leitch, "Twelve Fallacies in Contemporary Adaptation Theory," *Criticism* 45, no. 2 (Spring 2003): 168.

4. Brian McFarlane, "It Wasn't Like That in the Book," *Literature/Film Quarterly* 28, no. 3 (2000): 163.

5. Seymour Chatman, "What Novels Can Do That Films Can't (and Vice Versa)," *Critical Inquiry* 7, no. 1 (Autumn 1980): 121.

6. Deborah Cartmell and Imelda Whelehan, "*Harry Potter* and the Fidelity Debate," in *Book in Motion: Adaptation, Intertextuality, Authorship*, ed. Mireia Aragay (Amsterdam: Rodophi, 2005), 48.

7. Linda Segar, "Creating Workable Adaptations," *Creative Screenwriting* 4, no. 2 (Summer 1997): 88.

8. Robert Stam, "Introduction: The Theory and Practice of Adaptation," in *Literature and Film: A Guide to the Theory and Practice of Film Adaptation*, ed. Robert Stam and Alessandra Raengo (Oxford: Blackwell, 2004), 5.

9. Stam, "Introduction: The Theory and Practice of Adaptation," 46.

10. Robert Stam, "Beyond Fidelity: The Dialogics of Adaptation," in *Film Adaptation*, ed. James Naremore (London: Athalone Press, 2000), 66.

11. McFarlane, "It Wasn't Like That in the Book," 167.

12. Catherine Grant, "Recognising Billy Budd in *Beau Travail*: Epistemology and Hermeneutics of Auteurist 'Free' Adaptation," *Screen* 43, no. 1 (Spring 2002): 57.

13. Jacqueline Bobo, "*The Color Purple*: Black Women as Cultural Readers," in *Female Spectators Looking at Film and Television*, ed. E. Deirdre Pribram (London: Verso, 1992).

14. This research project on "The Launch and Reception of *The Lord of the Rings III*: The Role of Film Fantasy" has been funded by the UK Economic and Social Research Council (ESRC).

15. James Naremore, "Introduction: Film and the Reign of Adaptation," in *Film Adaptation*, ed. James Naremore (London: Athalone Press, 2000), 12, 23.

16. Stam, "Introduction: The Theory and Practice of Adaptation," 45.

17. Stam, "Introduction: The Theory and Practice of Adaptation," 45.

18. Stam, "Introduction: The Theory and Practice of Adaptation," 23.

19. Cardwell, *Adaptation Revisited*, 69, 62.

20. Steve Neale, *Genre and Hollywood* (London: Routledge, 2000), 151–204.

21. Rick Altman, *Film/Genre* (London: British Film Institute Publications, 1999), 158.

22. Thomas Schatz, *Hollywood Genres* (New York: Random House, 1981), 34–35.

23. John G. Cawelti, *Adventure, Mystery, and Romance* (Chicago: University of Chicago Press, 1977), 45.

24. Christine Gledhill, "The Melodramatic Field: An Investigation," in *Home Is Where the Heart Is*, ed. Christine Gledhill (London: British Film Institute Publications, 1987), 33.

25. John Mercer and Martin Shingler, *Melodrama: Genre, Style, Sensibility* (London: Wallflower, 2004), 97.

26. Stam, "Introduction: The Theory and Practice of Adaptation," 43.

27. Robert Stam, *Literature through Film: Realism Magic and the Art of Adaptation* (Oxford: Blackwell, 2005), 173.

1

Narrative and Characterization in Classic Adaptations

David Copperfield, Oliver Twist, *and* Pride and Prejudice

This study of adaptations begins with what is perhaps the most familiar example and one that tends to shape the debate—the adaptation of a classic, literary novel. Although we might also call a classic adaptation a literary adaptation, I have chosen to use the term "classic" because we could argue that nearly all the works I look at are literary in one way or another, even if the books they draw on are less prestigious than those discussed here. The term classic indicates the nature of the source in the canon of English literature as defined in the twentieth century and alerts us to the fact that these are adaptations that are generally strongly linked to a previous source not only by title but also by drawing on the author's name, the use of the original's illustrations, and often by an image of the book or pages from it appearing in the opening sequence. The adaptation might be accompanied by a reprinting of the novel with a cover that carries a picture from the new screen version. It is in this explicit referencing of the original that the classic adaptation distances itself most clearly from the other genres with which it has strong overlaps—the costume drama, for instance, or the historical romance. It offers a sense of being engaged with the reassuring durability of a classic: this story is already known and has been proved to work. But through the fact of it being a new version, a version made for a contemporary audience, it promises changes and transformations not only of the original source but also of the screen adaptations that have preceded it. In this way, while repetition marks such adaptations, they also allow for a more open narrative process in which it is possible to see variations in how particular incidents or characters are handled and how the familiar is updated. As the trailer for a recent *Pride and Prejudice* (Wright, 2005) put it, the film is "from the beloved author, Jane Austen" but is "the story of a modern woman."

The process of recall is therefore to the fore when a classic adaptation is offered to the audience, but the attachment to a source does not depend on having read the original novel but rather on the story being available through a range of other sources including children's abridged versions, plays, comics, radio, and musicals, as well as film and television. The ability to compare one version of a novel with another is now reinforced by the fact that these classic adaptations have increasingly been made available on video and then DVD so that it is possible to build up a collection for comparison. In some senses, this feeds into the emphasis on intertextuality discussed in the introduction since there are potentially numerous points of comparison that might be brought to bear on a new version; in 2005, Matthew MacFadyen in the role of Darcy is compared not just to a character in a novel but also to previous performances of the role by, for instance, Laurence Olivier and Colin Firth, while his status as hero is related to comparable characters in *Wuthering Heights* (Wyler, 1939) or *Bridget Jones's Diary* (Maguire, 2001). But the fact of numerous adaptations also helps to refine what is needed for a recognizable adaptation and can close down, rather than open up, interpretative possibilities. Narrative events and characters that go through a number of adaptations become streamlined and efficient through regular use; only key details are required to make them recognizable.

Classic adaptations are set in the past and so present some kind of relationship with or attitude to that past. Although there have been updated versions of the classics, most notably *Clueless* (Heckerling, 1995) that excited discussion as a Californian version of Jane Austen's *Emma*, they are relatively rare, partly perhaps because they pull away too much from the connections to previous versions and lose the cultural values associated with a classic adaptation. The writer John Romano ruefully referred to this when he ascribed the failure of a modernized *Great Expectations* (Cuarón, 1998), which updated the story to contemporary Florida and New York, "as a tribute to the literary acuity of the mass audience."[1] Precisely how classic adaptations deal with the past, what version of the past they choose, and how they represent it has been a matter of some controversy. The idylls presented by 1930s Hollywood to Depression audiences and the conservatism of the "heritage" film in the context of Thatcherite Britain are two examples of these debates.[2]

In making various versions of the past available for use, classic adaptations throw particular light on class and gender. In dealing with gender, classic adaptations often push contemporary debates about women and their position back into the past, and the figure of the heroine testing out her desire for independence is a familiar if sometimes anachronistic figure in classic adaptations.[3] The restrictions of gender are important here but so also are those of class. Because of the emphasis on the past and the adaptation's referencing of an original written in the past, class is used as a driver of narrative more than would be normally the case in much U.S. or even in contemporary British drama. Miriam Margolyes, talking about acting in Dickens adaptations, refers to the way class distinctions are written into "the rhythms of his characters and in the vocabulary," though she suggests that performing this is becoming more difficult now that such distinctions are "flattening out . . . even in England."[4] Classic adaptations are indeed often associated with a particular version of the English past, and Romano agrees with many in the audience when he suggests that "the British do period pieces better."[5] While class and gender are pushed to the fore, it is worth noting that race and ethnicity tend to be overwhelmed in the genre's association with Englishness and that postcolonial versions such as Patricia Rozema's *Mansfield Park* (1999) have proved controversial for exposing what are claimed to be the repressions of the original. Nevertheless, the canonic status of the original sources, and the (imperial) education systems that sustained them, mean that the novels can be drawn on differently outside the home territory. Hollywood and Bollywood offer different examples of how this can be done with Dickens and Austen.

In discussing how narrative and characterization are handled in classic adaptations, this chapter takes as its focus a number of the many adaptations taken from the work of Jane Austen and Charles Dickens. The two authors are not unexpected choices, but that partly is the point for they are authors who have been so consistently adapted in cinema and television that the different versions of their novels have helped to define how other classic adaptations are judged. It is worth noting that the audience's relationship with the source material for the classic adaptation has changed over time, particularly in relation to Dickens. Austen, whose reputation has depended on relatively few novels, has remained part of the literature curriculum for many English-speaking students, reinforced in the late twentieth century by the way in which gender issues have come to the fore in the teaching of literature. Dickens's popularity, however, always depended not only on the novels themselves but also on a variety of forms including magazines, plays, and public readings before his works became one of the most popular sources for early cinema.[6] Familiarity with Dickens's stories through such popular extracurricular activity might be now less assured, although numerous websites offer commentary and comment, often with an educational impetus.

Dickens and Austen go together for what they have in common—a relationship with national culture, a long history of being adapted, an emphasis on historical period, and the performance of social roles—as well as what separates them so far as screen adaptations are concerned—different forms of society and the roles played within it, a different use of narrative form and tone, and differences based on gender. These similarities and differences have helped to shape production values and audience expectations in relation to other classic adaptations. This analysis of the chosen examples looks at narrative structure and the organization of place and time; characterization and issues around stars and performance; and the handling of visual spectacle, including costume and décor. This will set up some of the key approaches that will operate in the rest of the book but will also show that even within this restricted format there are differences in how these screen adaptations work. Some of the chosen examples relate very clearly to their source while still accommodating considerable transformation, but I have also included versions that illustrate how far the boundaries can be stretched. The approach here is a comparative one, setting different versions alongside each other; it works with the grain of Brian McFarlane's observation that some "narrative elements . . . function independently of medium"[7] and are, in this way, more readily transferable. My discussion of various versions of *David Copperfield* concentrates on the creation of classic status and on narrative and characterization; the section on *Oliver Twist* analyzes why and how generic flexibility is such a strong feature of the adaptations of this novel; and the discussion of adaptations of *Pride and Prejudice* focuses on how the emphasis on femininity and the generic requirements of romance are handled in terms of characterization, costume, and setting. The interaction between shared narrative elements and the similarities and differences traceable to generic framings is an important element throughout.

DAVID COPPERFIELD AND THE STORY OF A WRITER

The association between Dickens and cinema is strong, and indeed many critics have identified him as one of a number of nineteenth-century authors who prefigure the invention of cinema. In the case of Dickens, Sergei Eisenstein influentially made this identification and traced the development of montage through Dickens and D. W. Griffith. Others though, particularly Grahame Smith, have made a case for Dickens as a precursor of cinema that goes beyond montage and associates him with a change in consciousness exemplified in the novels' subject matter (urban life, the interaction of personal and public life, the impact of technologies) and technique (the movement of the prose, the structural imagery, the techniques of visualization that include the pan and the close-up as well as the cut).[8] *The Death of Nancy Sykes* (Fenton/Ross, 1897) was the first of around a hundred short versions that became a staple of early cinema, and Dickens's work was also important to early radio and television. BBC radio established Sundays as the time for serial readings from classic novels and serial dramas based on them, with Dickens as a popular source, and the same practice was followed when television was established, with Sunday teatime providing a secure space for the classic adaptation.[9]

Dickens's *David Copperfield* and *Oliver Twist* have been popular sources of adaptations for mainstream viewing. Both, although not novels for children, have been seen as novels important for children to know about, and both have a strong narrative line centered on the eponymous hero. As Jeffrey Richards has argued, adaptations of later novels such as *Bleak House* and *Our Mutual Friend* have offered darker accounts, but *David Copperfield* and *Oliver Twist* are deemed reliable sources of more straightforward pleasures. Even a necessarily limited account of some of their adaptations demonstrates how flexibly they work in different contexts. This section looks at four versions of *David Copperfield*: MGM's 1935 film, directed by George Cukor, which for many critics has remained a definitive account; an NBC television version of 1969; and two television versions that sought to revive, at the end of the 1990s, a novel that had rather lost its position as a favorite adaptation. This emphasis on television versions reflects the way in which Dickens with his long serial narratives and multilayered worlds has been a favorite source for television.[10]

The 1935 version established that Hollywood could produce a version of Dickens that was a classic in its own right. Although questions of faithfulness have not disappeared, the film has largely been accepted as molding the novel into its own terms as a Hollywood product. The film is not a transparent means of getting to the novel but rather a presentation of it treated with the full panoply of a premiere. The way in which it does this sets out a model for an adaptation of a particular kind. *The Personal History, Adventures, Experiences, and Observations of David Copperfield, the Younger*, to give the full and elaborate title, sets out to bestow on cinema the respectability and middle-class popularity associated with the novel, but it does so from a position of strength. Here the literary classic meets the prestige melodrama, and Hollywood makes no apologies for its strategies. Richards describes both *David Copperfield* and *A Tale of Two Cities* (Conway, 1935) as "classical products of Hollywood in its heyday, polished, vivid, life enhancing dramas, on which all the departments of the studio were working together at the top of their form and in which handpicked casts triumphantly realized Dickens' teeming casts of characters."[11] What is clear is that these production-line qualities that gave such a sheen to the film were combined with other elements that relied on the novel's reputation to weave together literary source, cultural value, and national identity. As Jeffrey Sconce discusses, Selznick's publicity machine emphasized the importance of the novel as a childhood favorite in his own home, positioning himself as a reader who shared the audience's wish to see a respectful adaptation. This was to be achieved by reinforcing the Englishness associated with Dickens through the use of British actors who were selected in a highly public campaign in which the Dickens Fellowship was invited to participate.[12] Although the film was shot entirely in Hollywood, locations and settings were researched in England, and the question of faithfulness was a major selling point.

The later versions make similar claims to notions of Britishness and cultural value. The 1969 version, directed by Delbert Mann, had a special presentation on NBC. It ran for 120 minutes and featured Michael Redgrave, Laurence Olivier, and Ralph Richardson among an almost entirely British cast. The 1999 coproduction directed by Simon Curtis ran for 179 minutes and was shown over Christmas on BBC1 in two episodes and in the United States also over two nights on *Masterpiece Theatre*. Its cast was again entirely British and included Maggie Smith and Ian McKellen, honored actors from the British stage. It was shot on location in England on sites including Norfolk and London. Christmas 2000 saw another U.S. television version from Hallmark, directed by Peter Medak, "a diverting alternative" one critic suggested, "to the competing versions of *A Christmas Carol* that fill the television schedules."[13] Its 180 minutes were spread over three episodes. This version was more geared to U.S. production values with *Seinfeld*'s Michael Richards and film star Sally Field taking key roles, but it still had a strong British emphasis in its use of actors such as Eileen Atkins and Nigel Davenport, its location shooting in Ireland (standing in for the English countryside), and music provided by the Academy of St. Martin in the Fields, London. These television adaptations are therefore presented as special events for television and sell themselves as culturally valuable by linking themselves not only to the original source but also to the notion of an enduring classic with appropriate scenery and music. Represented in DVD format, they are flagged as "a family classic that spans the ages" (1969), "Dickens' most enduring novel" (1999), and "Charles Dickens' timeless tale" (2000).

Since the source deals with the creation of a novelist, *David Copperfield* offers the possibility of a direct referencing of the literary process, and all these adaptations take this as a starting point, though they handle it in different ways. All start with the first words of the novel: "Whether I shall turn out to be the hero of my own life, or whether that station will be held by anybody else, these pages must show." The sentence sets up an enigma in the novel that works differently in the adaptations that have come into being precisely because David Copperfield *has* become a recognizable hero. The adaptations either have to accept that settled status and celebrate it or set up rather different narrative questions for the viewer. The MGM version offers the most settled account. The opening titles that feature theater curtains and Christmas carols establish strong associations with Dickens himself: an epigraph signed by Dickens reminds us that *David Copperfield* was his "favourite child," and the first words of the novel appear in print on the page of the completed novel *David Copperfield*. The credit illustrations refer to those of "Phiz" that were used as important references for set design and costume.[14] So, from the beginning, it is established that the book has been written and successfully brought into print. There is no voice-over, and only a few titles are used to indicate a change of location. The story is not being written; it has already been written, and David's career as a novelist is smoothly integrated into the later stages of the story. In this version, David is not articled to the law at his aunt's expense, his first book is published before his marriage to Dora, and the integration of his writing into the home is encapsulated in a scene in which Dora finds a supportive role in holding the pens for him as he writes. The difficulties in his story arise from his personal life, but his professional position as a novelist is never in doubt.

The 1999 BBC version comes the closest of the television versions to this settled referencing of the literary process as the basis of the hero's success. In this version, the start of the novel is voiced over the opening scene of the burial of David's father. The voice-over brings a third actor to the playing of David alongside the two required for the roles of child and adult. This weighty, reflective voice provides a continuing commentary at key points such as the child's last glimpse of his mother from Barkis's cart, David's reflections on the second year of his marriage to Dora, and his final commentary on those who have been lost. This reflectiveness reminds us that the life we are being shown is also the matter for a novel, and as David becomes established as a writer (the scene of Dora and the pens is used here too), the adaptation moves to combine David as a hero with his creator Dickens. The ending of this version therefore uses the novel's device of returning to the beginning. Another baby is born, this time a girl whom David proudly presents to Aunt Betsey. David is now, like Dickens, a successful novelist, living in a large house and the head of a growing family.

The other two versions handle this narrative of literary success rather differently though both still call on the process of writing (or not writing) as a thread through the story. The 1969 version establishes its status as an adaptation by reworking the novel's illustrations for the opening credits. In the first scene, the adult David writes while the opening lines of the novel are heard in a voice-over by the actor. This time though the words appear to fail as an opening, for David crumples up the paper and throws it away. It is established that David is a successful novelist since we are shown the title page of his novel *Salem House*, and the structure of the adaptation, through regular use of the voice-over and an emphasis on the interweaving of past and present, emphasizes how the story of David could be written. Most of the present of the adaptation takes place at Yarmouth as David with the help of Agnes and Traddles reflects on his life, continually hearing voices and seeing ghostly figures as flashbacks take us back into the past. But critically, David is unable to write, and the story centers on how this block might be cured; can he forgive himself for the harm he feels he has done by introducing Steerforth to Emily or for being unkind to Dora? This certainly helps to make this David a more troubled and indeed vacillating hero who spends much of his time wandering on the deserted beach. It is only when he accepts Agnes's advice to learn from the past that he can become a writer again; the voice-over repeats the opening lines of the novel but this time in strong tones and with a rising inflection, which indicates that the crisis is over and the novel can now be written. The unsatisfactoriness of the 1969 version can at least in part be ascribed to the fact that the question posed is unconvincing. Since we know that the novel was successfully written (for otherwise there would be no adaptation), David's crisis lacks conviction and renders him a somewhat unenterprising hero.

The Hallmark 2000 version solves the problem differently by inventing a different enigma associated with the act of writing. This version combines the literary referencing of the classic adaptation with the cause-and-effect pattern of the Hollywood film. It contains many episodes familiar from earlier adaptations, but it transforms the act of writing the book into one of revenge. The book is written for a reason—to expose the Murdstones' villainy—and the narrative drive is thereby tightened. In this version, the opening scenes that take place as the credits roll through are unfamiliar. A man strides through the formal gardens and elaborate rooms of what appears to be a grand hotel and is apparently involved in an altercation with an older man and woman who are taking tea with a young girl and her chaperone, though the words of their exchange cannot be heard. The man walks away to his room and starts writing at his desk— only then do we hear the familiar words of the opening lines of the novel, but the questions raised by the opening scenes are not fully resolved by this. The voice-over continues to remind us of the process of writing as do scenes that return to the act of writing in the hotel. The villainy of the Murdstones is rendered not only by their treatment of David as a child but also by the reappearance of Miss Murdstone as Dora's governess who betrays the lovers to Dora's father. But it is only at the end, when the first scenes are repeated, that we are given the information to explain both the opening and the act of writing. The older man and woman are the Murdstones, working on another victim; over the teacups, David accuses them of murder and tells them "I'll write it." In this version, becoming a hero through success as a novelist is paralleled by taking action as a hero to expose the evil represented by the Murdstones. Certainly, this offers a more dynamic hero than the sufferer of writer's block portrayed in the 1969 version, and the pulling of the story line into a single thread of revenge also has the effect of making David a hero whose writing involves action rather than reflection.

Alongside the need to represent the motif of writing, *David Copperfield* offers a further narrative problem when it is visually represented, the shift from the child to the adult David, which has to be handled through a change of actor. The problems poised by this are reinforced by the fact that the child's story has an emotional coherence that the adult's lacks. This is particularly striking in the 1935 MGM version in which the boy's story draws on the resources of silent film melodrama to engage our emotional identification with the mother and child. This version establishes many of the visual motifs for the telling of Davy's story—the storms on the dark night of his birth, the country cottage and the churchyard with its gravestones, and the slow-moving cart journeying through the countryside. This use of telling imagery underpins the intensity of the Oedipal relationship between mother and child; the dyad of mother and child is supported by Peggotty as a third party (all three cry together after an argument) in contrast to Murdstone, who splits them up by usurping the boy's place in his mother's bed. Clara is characterized as possessing an extreme sensibility, which is communicated to her son through dance, touch, and embrace. She cannot accept rejection or withdrawal; as she tells Murdstone, "I must have affection," and that affection is most deeply found in her relationship with her son.

This emotional sensitivity is passed on to David, and the film adopts the child's viewpoint so that his extreme emotional experiences are expressed through the editing and montage characteristic of silent cinema. So, his distress at failing at his homework is rendered in a sequence that cuts together his frightened eyes with close-ups of Murdstone's cane flexed against his hand, Murdstone's eyes, and the sharp needles of Miss Murdstone's sewing. When Davy is locked in his room, the close-up of the key in the lock outside the room carries melodramatic weight reinforced by the cut to Davy inside, lying in distress on the floor. It is significant that the episode of Davy's exclusion from his mother and his mother's death are condensed into a continuous episode that has the quality of a dream sequence. The child sees himself in the reflected window as he hears whispers about his mother's "great pain"; the locked door opens so that the boy in his white nightdress can venture onto the dark staircase; and black somber figures in the hall ignore his hysterical cries until Peggotty unfolds him in her embrace and gives him a detailed account of his mother's deathbed, of how she spoke of "my pretty darling" and said "tell him that his mother blessed him." The delivery of this speech in musical tones in a higher register than usual reinforces its emotional invitation to identify with the boy's vulnerability. By contrast, the second part of the film, which deals with the adult David, although it contains Dora's reprise of his mother's sensibility and the melodramatic complications of the Steerforth/Emily story, takes a more distanced position from the events that are observed as material for the writer.

The 1935 film, therefore, uses the still-resonant silent cinema traditions of editing and performance alongside psychoanalytic references to play up intense feeling; Clara's maternal feelings are endorsed, and, while David must grow up, the process does not sully the image of his delicate and playful mother. Later versions do not have this option and have to find other ways of handling the different registers of David's story. The 1969 *David Copperfield* offers a therapeutic account in which childhood experiences are subjected to adult scrutiny. The narrative framing devices discussed above emphasize that the early scenes must serve the overall drive of the adult David's move to release. This version allows no time to establish the idyllic life of maternal love before the Murdstones' arrival. The first flashback shows his mother's funeral, and the story of his childhood starts with the arrival of the Murdstones into the household, quickly followed by the beating/biting episode. Instead of acknowledging the emotional intensity of this aspect of the story, as the 1935 film does, this sixties version judges the relationship as psychologically inappropriate, setting Clara alongside Steerforth and Dora; "All my life," the adult David reflects, "I've loved and hated the careless, irresponsible world of Steerforth and Dora, yes and even of my mother," the people who "fall to pieces when you touch them." Agnes is the mature opposite of such people, and she urges him to talk because it is "better to expose a wound to the open air." In the end, David allies himself with her strength, summoning up a final image of his mother with himself on her knee only to reject it: "It's not enough to be talented Steerforth or beautiful Dora or even simply loving . . . mother." This rejection of his childish relationships not only removes the writer's block but also permits the mature relationship with Agnes promised by the final image of his reconciliation with her back in Dover. This adaptation therefore allies a narrative of writing with a narrative of psychological understanding that, however, works against a convincing or engaging account of childish fears and loss.

The 1999 and 2000 versions take a less critical view of the mother/son relationship and are less concerned to offer a modern reading of it. They are closer to the book and to the 1935 film, using some of the latter's devices to generate emotional feeling. The wise voice-over of the 1999 BBC version introduces the section on childhood by commenting, "I grew up in the certainty that my beautiful mother loved only me," and we are shown Peggotty supporting them both. Murdstone's appearance in the idyllic cottage garden is the more threatening since his dark bulk is contrasted with its light and color. Clara has some of the characteristics of the 1935 version; she is playful, quick to feel, and delicate. This version uses Clara's devotion to the second baby to show us again the strength of her maternal love. In general, though, the presentation of separation and death lacks the hysterical intensity of the earlier film since it is working within the regime of television adaptation rather than that of early cinema. This Clara is more resilient and is in control of her own home until Murdstone appears; she is unlucky in this relationship rather than fated. This characterization is reinforced by a restrained performance style and a quiet, relatively unexpressive voice, which is used in quite long speeches in which she attempts to challenge Murdstone. The events that lead to the parting and death are more logically laid out, and there is none of the compression that elided David's punishment with the disappearance of his mother. The boy's isolation after the beating is consoled by the discovery of his father's books, reminding us of the broader narrative of success as a writer. There are moments, though, in which feeling is strongly communicated in, for example, the kiss David and Peggotty exchange through the wooden door of his imprisonment or the farewell to his mother in which the movement of the cart carrying David causes her figure, holding up the baby, to recede both into the distance and the past. Such moments are moving but are positioned within the overall sense of memory and renewal that the narrator communicates: "So I lost her," reflects the voice-over. "So I saw her afterwards in my sleep."

The 2000 version offers a more broad-brush approach in which there is an emphasis on the physicality of feeling. Images have a literal quality here that recalls the Sirkian melodramas of fifties Hollywood. The "sunlight" David recalls of his early years is put on the screen while huge apples in the childhood garden refer to the Garden of Eden. Murdstone literally becomes a shadow that falls between mother and son onto the grave of Davy's father, while Jane Murdstone's character is represented by a close-up of the metallic snap of her mesh purse. In this version, both Clara and Davy look younger than in the BBC version, and after the marriage, Clara is immediately rendered tearful and almost incapable of speech. When Davy is sent away to school, he has to be dragged out of her arms, and our final view of Clara is of her tearful face trapped in the diamond panes of the cottage window. The emphasis here is on the child's experience of Murdstone's cruelty, conveyed by a greater number of shots from David's viewpoint and the way in which the narrative is organized. When Murdstone loses control as he beats the boy, the image returns to the adult David writing in the present, but boy's cries and the sound of the cane continues on the soundtrack. David stops writing and moves to the window, shaking, and the voice-over comments, "He beat me then as if he'd have beaten me to death." A similar emphasis on the physical expression of the child's experience occurs when, at the end of Peggotty's description of his mother's death, David and the camera move into hug her. In this version, the narrator is shown reliving his experiences as he writes and the mise-en-scène and camerawork emphasize an engagement with that process rather than the more distanced reflection of the BBC adaptation.

All adaptations have to make decisions about how to make changes from the original source. In *David Copperfield*, we have an example of a relatively stable story line in which the literary antecedents can be naturally referenced. But we have also seen how different narrative frameworks and aesthetic devices can effect changes in significance and emotional register. This can be related to social factors outside the text. The 1935 film emphasizes David's ability to mediate between classes and restore harmony in the manner of other Hollywood films during the Depression, while in 1969 David's need to unburden himself of the past can be linked to developing ideologies of the self in the 1960s. Other changes relate to the conventions established as appropriate for audiences at any one point. The conventions of editing and montage taken from silent cinema are no longer available to television audiences, which might, however, be felt to require the suspense engendered by the revenge story in the 2000 version.

Dickens's flexible serial narratives lend themselves to this kind of treatment. Many versions of *David Copperfield* follow the 1935 film by cutting out the story of Steerforth, his mother, and Rosa Dartle, while Traddles, if he appears at all, is deprived of his own story. Such excisions do not threaten the legitimacy of the relationship between adaptation and source, which is based instead on a series of visual and verbal motifs that are linked to character rather than narrative; it is the appearance of these elements that reinforces what DeBona calls "the quintessence of 'Dickensness.'"[15] This has the virtue of economy since the events themselves might be quite brief—a sentence or an image—and they allow a showcase for a particular performance. So, *David Copperfield* has numerous key phrases, among them "Barkis is willing"; Mr. Micawber's pronouncements on annual income and Mrs. Micawber's assertion that she "never will desert Mr. Micawber"; Steerforth's plea to "always think of me at my best"; Aunt Betsey's detestation of donkeys; and Jane Murdstone's dislike of boys. Micawber's advice about income, for instance, occurs in the 1935 film, as it does in the novel, before he boards the coach away from London after being freed from prison. In the 2000 version, it is first said in prison and then reprised when he gets on the coach. And in the 1969 and 1999 versions, Micawber offers the advice when he first takes David home from the bottling factory. The words therefore have no narrative function to which they need be tied but serve to identify a required character and offer a marker as to how the actor playing that character is approaching the performance. For in a classic adaptation, repetition of such lines draws attention to the actor who is showcased as the different element. The well-known lines combine with roles that are often quite short and lend themselves to cameo performances.

In many cases, it is a British actor who is given the spotlight afforded by these roles. The literary roots of the source can be nourished by actors who continue that connection by being identified either with the British stage or more commonly with previous classic adaptations. But again this use of national identity to enhance and endorse the final product is not managed in a uniform way. MGM notoriously exploited its British angle, and DeBona and Richards discuss the history of its use of British actors. But many of the major roles were played by experienced U.S. actors such as W. C. Fields, Lionel Barrymore, and Jessie Chambers. The "British" stars included Maureen O'Brien and Basil Rathbone, both of whom were born elsewhere, and they tended to have experience of Hollywood and, in some cases, of the U.S. stage. Like the white cliffs of Malibu, which Cukor argued were "whiter and cliffier" than the originals in Dover,[16] the British qualities seem to have been taken on and groomed into something that fits a Hollywood film. In contrast, the 1999 version, despite the coproduction credits, is presented as an English production by the BBC. It features celebrated British theater actors such as Maggie Smith alongside those chiefly known for their work in popular television drama such as Pauline Quirke. The style is an integrated television style that draws attention to certain features of performance such as Smith's markedly precise intonation when it is appropriate for the story. The importance of making the performances coherent through a consistent production register is demonstrated by the problems of the 1969 production in which a long list of British actors give performances marked by overacting and hamminess. This is particularly the case in short cameo roles such as the double act by Laurence Olivier and Richard Attenborough as Creakle and his shadow, Tungay, but it extends to Redgrave in the more substantial role of Daniel Peggotty.

These different versions of *David Copperfield* provide one model for the classic adaptation. They are relatively consistent in the handling of the basic plot, which starts with the birth and ends with marriage to Agnes; they provide consistent motifs and taglines that contribute to characterization; and they make claims to a certain cultural significance by showcasing literariness and performance. I want to extend this discussion further by an analysis of various versions of *Oliver Twist*. This novel has proved more malleable than *David Copperfield*, more open to different kinds of treatments that in some cases have pushed the adaptations into different genres, including the children's film and the musical.

GENERIC VARIATIONS AND *OLIVER TWIST*

The many and various adaptations of *Oliver Twist* provide an example of the situation in which what is being adapted is not so much the novel but rather a series of characters and vignettes that find their inspiration and source as much in previous versions as in the original source. What then is stable in the various versions of *Oliver Twist*? First, the child himself and his situation of extreme vulnerability remain central. This finds expression in key narrative events such as the opening scene. David Lean's 1948 film influentially opened with the pregnant woman finding her way to the workhouse,[17] a scene repeated in many adaptations since including Alan Bleasdale's script for the 1999 television coproduction that started at this point but then went into a flashback to explore the mother's past. The intricacies of the organization and characters at the workhouse can be simplified, but the key element of Oliver's isolation, both within the bureaucracy of the adult world and among his more hardened peers, remains. That's why the gruel scene in which Oliver is singled out is so consistently important. Very often Oliver, as in Jackie Coogan's 1922 characterization, is bullied into the drawing of lots and has to be forced into making the request for more. The child's extreme isolation is reiterated in the journey to London, which features calculated refusals of his appeals for help and the chase after the theft at the booksellers, two narrative events that are consistently used to represent respectively the indifference of the world outside the workhouse and Oliver's vulnerability in a criminal world.

The second factor that gives some stability to adaptations of *Oliver Twist* is London. London, in these screen versions, is taken from a variety of sources—the lengthy descriptions from the novel itself, the illustrations in the novel, prints such as those by Gustave Doré and the conventions built up by the films themselves. London is normally introduced through a distance shot at the end of Oliver's journey of escape; a view of the city on the misty horizon emphasizes grandeur and achievement. A second standard shot is of St. Paul's Cathedral and the City taken from the ramshackle bridge that leads to Fagin's den and emphasizes the dangers to Oliver as he plunges into the city's depths. This shot, achieved most graphically in Lean's film with its expressionist alleys and stairways, provides later versions with a ready-made reference to the mixture of classes and fortunes in London. The city is represented not just by its identifiable landmarks—St. Paul's, the river, Covent Garden, London Bridge—but also by the vigor and danger of its streets and the dramatic contrast between rich and poor. This encourages not so much a realistic representation of London but rather a symbolic one that serves two functions. It provides a literary reference—this is a version of London that is recognizable as Dickens's London without the need for the literary framings of *David Copperfield*. Although clearly it is of the past, it relates, unlike the green countryside and stately homes of other classic adaptations, to contemporary London, which opens up the possibility of making the social commentary of the book more relevant. But it is also a space that fits a particular kind of narrative action; its corners and niches are associated with the acts of spying and snatching. London is a space across which Oliver is continually spied on, kidnapped, carried, and chased; it is the activity rather than the perpetrators (different versions use the Dodger, Charlie, Noah, Monks) that is important. And indeed, when Nancy decides to help Oliver, she too is followed and spied on, becoming vulnerable to the activity made possible by the space that is London.

The starting point of the isolated child, pathetically asking for more, and a particular image of London are sufficient to identify the story as *Oliver Twist*. Beyond that there are a surprising number of variations that go well beyond the usual slicing away of the source's plot complications. There are two main reasons for this. First, there is the problem of Fagin, a portrait of a Jew that Dickens himself amended and that has caused problems for adaptations. Second, Oliver's request for "more" opens up a number of possible resolutions that are not closed down by the original in the way in which the marriage to Agnes determines the ending of the different versions of *David Copperfield*. In looking at a number of versions from the silent 1922 U.S. version to the 1999 coproduction, we can see how the freeing up of the story, forced by changing attitudes to Fagin, leads adaptations of the novel to take different directions and draw on different generic conventions.

The problem of Fagin is that the character cannot be retained as faithfulness to the source demands without raising objections to his stereotyping as a Jew and perhaps also by the end of twentieth century as someone who exploits and abuses children. Lean's 1948 version famously fell foul of this problem, and the film was cut heavily before it could be released three years later in the United States.[18] The plea that the characterization was faithful to the book and that the makeup was based on George Cruikshanks's illustrations did not persuade, although the same sources can be seen in Lon Chaney's silent version. Alec Guinness claimed that they took pains not to make the film anti-Semitic by not using the term "jew"[19] though his prominent nose, straggly beard, and distinctive vocabulary and accent certainly drew on Jewish stereotypes. The portrayal does not hold back from the viciousness of Fagin's cruelty though it also uses humor and some kindness; while it remains in many ways the definitive performance, later versions of Fagin have tended both to play down the Jewish references and to make Fagin a more sympathetic character, particularly in contrast with the unredeemable Bill Sikes.

In a way, the problem of Fagin gives adaptations of *Oliver Twist* permission to be unfaithful. The issues are raised most explicitly in George C. Scott's portrayal of Fagin in Clive Donner's 1982 *Oliver Twist*. The makeup and acting play down any stereotypical references to Jewishness, and Fagin is given a speech in which he protests that those now calling him a "filthy Jew" have previously done business with him as a "wise Jew, kind Jew." *Oliver!* (Reed, 1968), with its emphasis on music and dance, makes Ron Moody's Fagin into a deft performer with a feather in his hat and parasol in hand; as Oliver pulls the "wipes" out of his pocket, they emerge tied together as in a conjuror's trick. This association is carried further in the 1999 version in which Robert Lindsay's Fagin becomes a conjuror from Eastern Europe. Fagin's evil can also be played down by narrative twists that show him helping to resolve the mysteries of Oliver's parentage as happens in the 1982 and 1999 version as well as in the Disney ending discussed below.

Changes in the characterization of Fagin are related both to anxieties about stereotyping and to the audience being aimed at. Variation is even more marked in the portrayal of Oliver, the role he plays in the story and the fulfillment of his needs, which brings about resolution. Chaplin discovered Jackie Coogan, and his role in *The Kid* (Chaplin, 1921) established him as a child star. His Oliver is a very small boy, and Coogan plays a convincing waif in the workhouse and particularly in the dock. But he has a resilience that is apparent on his first appearance in the workhouse when he bumps into the Beadle and bounces up when thrown into the hemp. After his first stay with Mr. Brownlow, he resists being recaptured and even tries to punch Sikes. This version includes the episode in which Oliver is forced to participate in a break-in; as the intertitle suggests, Oliver "boldly tries to thwart the robbery" and so effects his own rescue. After that, Oliver is safe and the threat passes to Nancy. At the end, he is brought to the site of Sike's pursuit and strives to get out of the carriage to get up to Sikes on the roof. He is held back, and the film closes with a meeting in which Monks explains Oliver's true parentage. Oliver persuades Mr. Brownlow to let his half brother go and "bows in thanks to the man who has appraised him of this true name." Less important than the complications of the plot here is the achievement of identity and the final image of Coogan; head down, he frowns and then smiles as he repositions himself, his hands on his hips and feet apart in a confident and defiant pose of Oliver as an all-American boy. Oliver's isolation has been transformed into sturdy independence.

John Howard Davies as Oliver in 1948 was very different. He was an unknown eight-year-old with fair hair and a slim build. Taller than Coogan, he is nevertheless frail compared with the other boys in the film, particularly Anthony Newley's Artful Dodger, who is clearly a teenager.

Davies is also distinguished by his soft voice and middle-class accent, a trait that is used to mark him as soft and vulnerable in the workhouse and the streets. Oliver is consistently filmed as isolated and passive, watching what others will do. Sometimes the isolation is literally rendered, for example, when he is framed from above as an isolated figure whom the boys in the workhouse move away from as he draws the short straw. Sometimes the light is used to emphasize his white face and blond hair, distinguishing him, for instance, from the group of boys watching the pickpocketing game. Key images are of him in bed when first rescued by Mr. Brownlow. His fair hair and white face against the white sheets in the sunlight counter the dark world of the den, and as a sickly child, he is fed broth and grapes to make him strong again. In this version, the denouement returns him to the extreme vulnerability of the beginning as Sikes takes him up on the roof. When he had asked for more, the camera looked down on his pale face looking up; now, on the roof, it looks up at him holding on to the chimney, the only light figure in the darkness. The happy ending is brief, but it is clear that this Oliver has lacked not so much a name as a family and home. Returning to Pentonville with Mr. Brownlow, Oliver runs forward to hug the housekeeper, Mrs. Bedwin, and then in a continuation of this rare active gesture makes a family of the three of them by taking their hands. This is a makeshift family but one that the child constructs as he finally runs toward the shining whiteness of the house that will be his home. In 1948, this portrayal of the vulnerable child, remaking his family after the losses of war, had a particular poignancy.

In some ways, twenty years later, Carol Reed's *Oliver!* helped to establish Lean's *Oliver Twist* as a classic. *Oliver!* was the film of the stage musical but drew its setting, camera setups, and editing from the earlier film. Certainly Mark Lester's physical resemblance to Davies is strong, with his frail physique, fair skin, and bright hair. Isolating his close-ups in the same way through framing and lighting is more difficult given the use of wide-screen and color, but there certainly are points when this is achieved, for instance, when he acts as a funeral mute, against a white and black background, or when his fair head is set against the dark colors of Fagin's den. As with the 1948 version, class is also a factor in distinguishing Oliver from the large troupe of boys in the chorus, and his voice and intonation are specifically mocked in the singing of "I'd do anything." Song indeed is used to emphasize Oliver's vulnerability. His pure, frail singing marks him out from the chorus in the gusty rendition of "Food Glorious Food"; "Where is love?" is his first solo, in which his tearful face is seen in close-up in the dark cellar and his soft voice almost speaks the words. Even his happiness seems fragile; "I don't want to lose it," he sings as he celebrates the beautiful and orderly London morning that can be seen from Mr. Brownlow's balcony. In some ways, this Oliver's most vulnerable moments occur in the first part of the film in a reprise of the rooftop scenes of the 1948 film. During the chase from the bookshop, Oliver climbs up to the railway (taken straight from a Doré print) and finds himself high above the street. His slim body is silhouetted against the sky, close-ups show his trembling face, and as the train approaches, a shot from below shows his head and shoulders isolated against the grey sky. By contrast, although he is clearly in extreme peril at the end when Sikes forces him to take a rope along a high beam, the framing shows Oliver in the context of the set as a whole, and neither lighting nor editing is used to highlight his plight.

But the musical version also works to make Oliver one of the boys in a way that fits the generic demands of the musical. Though he lacks Coogan's pugnaciousness, this Oliver does not peach, does not faint in court, and lashes out at Sikes. He looks the same size and age as the Artful Dodger, and when they first meet the two quickly become friends, matching each other in the first singing of "Consider Yourself." As a musical, *Oliver!* uses its musical numbers to generate a utopian feeling of enjoyment that renders the den a much less fearsome place. Oliver takes his part in these songs, becoming one of the chorus of boys who join in "I'd Do Anything" and "Be Back Soon." This helps to explain the double ending of the film. The final shots offer a curtailed version of the 1948 ending as Mr. Brownlow leads Oliver home into the arms of Mrs. Bedwin. But this lacks the resonance of the postwar version, and the musical is effectively ended by the cheerfully pragmatic alliance of Fagin and the Artful Dodger as they dance off into the sunrise singing "crime can pay." This provides a musical resolution that confirms the status of Ron Moody and Jack Wild as stars of what has after all been a musical production.

Tony Bill's 1997 Disney version reiterates the prominence given to the Dodger in *Oliver!* Here the elements of a child's adventure story are brought to the fore, and sturdy, brown-haired Oliver is transformed into the active hero of his own tale. The mechanics of the plot are changed so that Oliver himself holds the evidence of his own parentage in the form of a locket that he steals from the workhouse and that Fagin takes from him when he reaches the den. Escaping from the workhouse, Oliver is accepted as "a pal" by the Artful Dodger, and though he is marked out by his trusting belief in goodness, the mise-en-scène frequently works to make him one of the boys who enjoy the freedom from restrictions that Fagin offers; the film's set pieces in the den, as the boys help to clothe and feed Oliver on his arrival or celebrate his first venture out to steal, are edited like musical numbers. This Oliver is excited by the teeming streets of London, learns the three rules of pickpocketing, refuses to peach, stands up to Fagin and to Sikes, and debates his future with the Artful Dodger.

The effect of this can be seen in the handling of the denouement on the roof. Sikes takes Oliver onto the roof, but his peril is hardly emphasized. Instead, Sikes falls to his death quickly, and the rest of the scene is taken up with Oliver's negotiations with Fagin to get his locket back. Fagin tries to wheedle and charm him, but Oliver is implacable and finally, with his property returned, makes his own way down from the roof. Once back on the ground, he and the Dodger say goodbye, each going their own way but swearing never to forget each other. The final shot is more traditional; Oliver is asleep, tucked into bed by Rose, but the camera moves down to show that he is still clutching the locket, a reminder that this resolution has been driven by Oliver himself. The ending of this version therefore is much more like that of a children's book in which the lost family is restored (Oliver turns out to be Mr. Brownlow's grandson) but only after a series of adventures in which the child effects his own solution while enjoying the company of other children. As in *Oliver!* genre rather than source determines the ending.

PRIDE AND PREJUDICE—FEMININITY AND THE HEROINE

We have seen that adaptations of Dickens sometimes follow the route of remaining relatively close to the plots and literary address of the novel as in various versions of *David Copperfield* or, as adaptations of *Oliver Twist* show, draw on characteristics of other genres such as the musical or the children's film to reformulate plot and character. I want to explore further the question of how the classic adaptation references and uses elements from other genres by looking at three adaptations of *Pride and Prejudice* that foreground romance. The Austen revival of the 1990s has been explained as a combination of the classic adaptation's traditional emphasis on costume, landscape, and a familiar plot with a new exploration of a more modern sensibility—that of the independent young woman facing choices in her personal life; "modern interest in gender issues" has, according to the editors of *Jane Austen on Screen*, allowed "screen writers to use her novels as valuable launching pads for filmic vehicles that track changing notions about women's roles in society."[20] Compared with the Dickens adaptations, then, there is a shift not only to a central heroine but also to an address to a female audience. But there is a further complication, for this terrain was already occupied by the romance genre in which the narrative structure is organized around the learning process that has to take place before the central couple can find harmony and love; in this negotiation, a tomboyish girl grows into her own femininity and establishes a lasting relationship with a man whose "cruelty and indifference" toward the heroine have been transformed into "tender care."[21]

The specter of romance haunts critics of Austen adaptations. Romance is seen as the opposite of Austen's ironic, witty, and complex accounts of the human heart. While the BBC sells its 1995 version on video as "this famous romance [running] its rocky course"[22] and *Bridget Jones's Diary* exploits Darcy as a silent, brooding hero, literary critics protest at the way in which more recent adaptations are, for commercial reasons, "shaped by powerful generic conventions of romance."[23] This leads, it is argued, to a narrow focus on the courtship of the central couple, a thinning out of the social world in which they are placed, and an overemphasis on physical glamour and attraction. In exploring the issues raised by the association between Austen adaptations and romances, I want to take versions that seem to exploit rather than disdain the crossover with the romance genre and that have their own strong film conventions for handling romance. This section therefore will look at MGM's 1940 *Pride and Prejudice* (Leonard), produced like the earlier *David Copperfield* by Hollywood at its most confident; at the 2005 Working Title version of the novel, made in Britain for Universal Studios; and at Gurinder Chadha's deliberately hybrid 2004 *Bride and Prejudice*. These are versions that set out to transform the novel by relocating it to different spaces, inventing new scenarios, and celebrating the romance without irony or social comment.

The 1940 version centers on Greer Garson as a determinedly vivacious Elizabeth and Laurence Olivier fresh from his portrayal of the quintessential romantic hero, Heathcliff. This *Pride and Prejudice* emphasizes comedy as well as romance and offers a coming together in which the basic suitability of the pair is always clear. "Based," as the credits tell us, "upon the dramatization of Jane Austen's novel," the film adds scenes that emphasize cinema's capacity for spectacle, including a coach chase in which Mrs. Bennet and Lady Lucas vie to be first with the news of the arrival of the eligible Mr. Bingley. There is no voice-over, and the irony of the narrative voice is largely replaced by broad comedy. And, unlike the same studio's *David Copperfield*, there is little overt referencing of the status of the original book or the literary credentials of the adaptation.

Critics have suggested that the studied Englishness of this *Pride and Prejudice* needs to be seen in the context of the grave position of Britain at war in 1940. Ellen Belton argues that the film, in its portrayal of English life, offered its audience "an emblem of a lost and lovingly remembered world," a world that is made the more desirable because it "never existed either in history or in the novels of Jane Austen."[24] But, she suggests, the film makes a link between U.S. audiences and 1940s Britain by "infusing" this imagined world "with associations and values that are understood as essentially American and democratic in character," by the demolishing of the class barrier between the potential lovers and the endorsement of the collective well-being of the family unit.[25] In this way, the film suggests that there are common values between U.S. and British society that cannot be preserved by individualism and isolationism and lends support to arguments that the United States will need to get involved in the war in defense of those values.

Within this broad understanding of how such a deliberately anachronistic film might speak to contemporary anxieties, it is worth noting how the film emphasizes femininity, endorsing its pleasures and seeking to find a way out of the problems excessive femininity can lead to. The basic plot is of course driven by the lack of men in the family (and society more generally), which explains Mrs. Bennet's interest in what she rather daringly calls "those exquisite young men" whose arrival in Meryton causes the initial disruption. The few somber moments of dialogue occur when this lack is commented on. "We have no sons," Mr. Bennet unnecessarily reminds his wife, an observation that is followed by Mrs. Bennet's shriek as she opens a door to show him their five daughters engaged in various feminine pursuits. By contrast, the film overflows with women who are sisters, friends, and rivals so that the task is to distinguish between them or else one will, like Mr. Collins at his first meeting with the Bennet family, feel "quite overpowered." Darcy in particular has to learn to discriminate properly, and this process places the romance in a social context; Darcy learns to separate Elizabeth out from the rest of her sisters and friends, as the romantic plot requires, but he also learns to recognize that she can be admitted to the social category of the "accomplished woman." At first, Darcy seems to accept the rather exclusive definition of the accomplished woman offered by Miss Bingley that, as Elizabeth points out, leads to most women, including herself, being excluded. But the fact that this is a socially negotiated category is underlined by the film's controversial use of Lady Catherine as a source of approval for Elizabeth's match with her nephew. Her comment to Darcy—"she's right for you"— endorses the individual romance that can now move to its conclusion but is also, given her status, a sign of social recognition.

But if the main narrative drive of the film is to enable Elizabeth to be separated from the other women in the film, the costume, art direction, and soundtrack all serve to suffuse the film in an atmosphere of femininity that Elizabeth shares. The film opens in a draper's shop where a detailed discussion of fabric is going on—shell pink gossamer muslin and figured damask are on display. The characters are at home in this world although Elizabeth is allowed some ironic commentary. The film continues to emphasize the dramatic costumes by Adrian, quite shamelessly going out of the correct period to emphasize wide crinolines, huge sleeves, frilled and furbelowed underwear, and extravagant hats. There is some character identification in this emphasis on costume; Elizabeth and Jane, for instance, wear rather darker colors than their sisters, and there are points (for example, when Darcy visits Elizabeth to offer his help over Lydia's disgrace) when the central couple wear matching costumes that indicate their fundamental compatibility. But, in the main, the costumes are excessive even for a historical romance and endlessly distract from the narrative in order to please the eye. So, after the crisis between Elizabeth

Laurence Olivier and Greer Garson in Pride and Prejudice *(1940). The costumes in MGM's* Pride and Prejudice *are excessive and distract from the narrative.* Source: *MGM/The Kobal Collection*

and Darcy during the party at Netherfield, the next scene begins with Elizabeth watering a window box in what appears to be a tailored dress. The dark color might be deemed to reflect her mood, but this interpretation is undermined by her deliberate pose and the extravagance of the costume. The camera moves out to reveal huge sleeves, dramatically slashed in black and white, with contrasting cuffs and a matching striped skirt and then shows Jane and Charlotte, equally elaborately dressed, attending to a group of puppies.

The puppies are also an example of the kind of accessories and activities that are deployed by the female characters in the film. In line with observations made by Darcy about women strolling around the room to show off their figures to best advantage, so the sewing, wool-winding, music-making, dancing, chasing, and teasing serve to show off the characters' extreme femininity. This might not of course be to their advantage in Darcy's sense, but it is important that Elizabeth is aligned through dialogue and mise-en-scène with this feminine activity. Elizabeth, during the conversation at Netherfield about a woman's accomplishments, declares her pleasure in "frivolous things," and though she can play the piano and the harp well (compared with Mary's musical disasters) she declares to Lady Catherine that she cannot draw. Far from being clearly separated from the problematic sisters in the family, Elizabeth is aligned with them in the various tableaux of feminine life that scatter the film, including the chaotic preparations for the move to Margate when Elizabeth feeds her mother broth while Mary and Kitty squabble over taking a music box and a parrot. The music box and the parrot contribute to the noise that accompanies this scene and indicate the importance of the soundtrack in creating the bubbling commotion and anticipation that runs through the film. Particularly striking are the sounds of the women's clothes—the swish of silks, the rustling of petticoats, the light slap of dancing shoes on the wooden floor. This provides a continuing susurration above which can be heard the giggles, gossip, and screams of laughter that punctuate the dialogue. Again, the film suggests criticism of some of this activity, but it provides a sense of the feminine liveliness and fun in a house in which the pretentiousness of Mr. Collins and the pride of Mr. Darcy are both mocked. As Belton suggests, the happy finale in which all the sisters find a man suggests a commitment to the solidarity of the family, but it also suggests a thorough endorsement of romance and femininity with Lydia, Mary, and Kitty brought into the fold with Jane and Elizabeth. Mr. Bennet imagines his own "Bennet utopia, a domestic paradise where . . . nobody shall ever even think of bonnets or teapots or gossip," but this *Pride and Prejudice* reinforces its use of romance with a commitment to artifice and to the pleasures of frivolous femininity.

Greer Garson was considerably older than the Elizabeth of the novel, and this maturity was useful in establishing the basic intellectual equality between the couple, despite their social differences. This underpinned the film's references to the screwball comedies of the 1930s in which a man and woman battle for control of the relationship and settle for an equality that acknowledges rather than overrides sexual difference. The 2005 version presents femininity in a rather different way. By making Elizabeth very young and playing on Keira Knightley's celebrity status, this adaptation indeed offers a modern young woman at the heart of a familiar narrative. In terms of looks and performance, Knightley conforms more readily to the 2005 image of a female film star than to the conventions of representing an Austen heroine. She is a very modern beauty, with the thin figure of a model, large, wide eyes, high cheekbones, and a broad, rather square mouth. The performance depends on the use of silent close-ups to show the expressiveness of her eyes and face; her mouth is often slightly open as if she is caught at the point at which emotion is being experienced but not articulated. When she does speak, Knightley adopts a light, flat tone with a modern handling of language that contrasts with the drawling of Caroline Bingley and the circumlocutions of Lady Catherine. In the early scenes, before her feelings toward Darcy begin to change, she is sharp and decisive, but under the pressure of emotion her voice becomes more breathy and tentative, a way of expressing the fact that what she is saying is often at odds with what she is feeling. In the context of a classic adaptation, with its emphasis on literary language and well-known phrases, this delivery can be understood as fresh and modern, but it runs the risk of seeming inappropriate and anachronistic.

This characterization of Elizabeth as a modern young woman is supported by other factors. This is a costume drama but not one in which the beauty and texture of the costume is foregrounded as one of the film's pleasures. The women's costumes in particular are used for characterization and contrast rather than as a feature in their own right as they are in MGM's version. So, Elizabeth and her sisters wear clothes that are often pretty but are lived-in and comfortable; their flying ribbons and flapping skirts are contrasted with the more fashionable elegance of Caroline Bingley and the simple charm of Darcy's sister, Georgiana.[26] For Knightley, in particular, the difference between costume and modern dress is consistently played down. She is rarely seen in bonnets, hats, or ribbons, and her hair often escapes from her chignon; she wears either earthy greens and browns or plain cream and white, eschewing the pastels used for young women in many costume dramas. The informality of her dress is such that at some points, dressed in a simple, collarless blouse with a dark waistcoat or in the roughly textured brown dress that featured in publicity material, she hardly seems to be in costume. Along with this goes a physical freedom of movement as Elizabeth is consistently shown walking alone in the countryside.

If looks, performance, and costume remind us that this is a modern young woman, the film, while affirming that the position of women in this society is limited and unfair, does not require Elizabeth to comment on it or live with its consequences as Emma Thompson's Elinor does in *Sense and Sensibility* (Ang, 1995).[27] It is Mrs. Bennet who consistently emphasizes the injustice of the entailment through the male line and Elizabeth's friend Charlotte who is given the strongest speech about women's position. Trying to explain to Elizabeth why she has picked up her rejected suitor, Charlotte tells the audience quite clearly what is at stake. This Elizabeth is not a heroine who is fighting for equal recognition in terms of her social position or her sexual relationships; she expects that recognition and is angry when it is withheld from her by arrogance or snobbery. In some senses then this is a postfeminist Elizabeth who hardly knows of the battles for independence being fought for or around her. The difficulties associated with her romance are to do with personality and age rather than gender.

The overt emphasis of this romance is that Elizabeth and Darcy have to learn to see each other clearly and understand that they are the same kind of people with, as Elizabeth says to her father, the same obstinate honesty. Two factors work with this. The first is the emphasis on Elizabeth's youth, which is reinforced by the extreme youthfulness of her sisters, in particular Lydia, and of Georgiana; the film tries to replace the social scandal of Lydia's running off with Wickham with a more modern disapproval of the advantage Wickham takes of two fourteen-year-old girls. Elizabeth shares some of the giggling impulsiveness of Lydia and Kitty, which can be seen in her under-the-counterpane confidences with Jane, her romantic response to Wickham's gesture of picking up her handkerchief (an accidental repetition of a trick first tried by Kitty), and in the half-suppressed giggle of shock at her first sight of Pemberley. The development of her feelings for Darcy then is accompanied by learning how to grow up. She learns to hide her feelings from others, to be more aware of the dangers of her younger sisters' behavior, and most crucially to move away from her father as she moves toward her future husband. The final scene of the film, in the UK version, is a long leave-taking of her father as she reassures him that she has found someone worthy of his assessment of her. The final shot leaves the audience with him, bereft of Elizabeth, who has moved quickly and lightly out of the room; the U.S. ending completes the transfer of the romance by closing with a scene of the married couple together.

Of course, establishing a relationship with Darcy is not just a matter of growing up. The film draws heavily on the conventions of romance in its representation of this relationship. Unlike the MGM version with its highly artificial sets and its emphasis on positioning the romance within society, these romantic conventions are strongly associated with landscape. While the different houses are careful gradated to reflect the status of their different owners, the rural landscape faithfully reflects the emotions of the heroine, sometimes in quite an extreme way. The shots of Elizabeth on the crag in Derbyshire, of the exchange between the potential lovers in the drenching rain at Pemberley, and of Darcy emerging out of the mist to claim Elizabeth in the final, hopeful dawn are all highly romantic compositions that serve to emphasize not only that this relationship is driven by fate but also that it is positioned in nature, outside society. Halfway through the film, after Bingley and Darcy have left Netherfield and Charlotte has married Collins, Elizabeth winds herself round in a swing as the camera offers her 360-degree view of the farmyard, buildings, and people that threaten to entrap her. By contrast, the relationship with Darcy, begun in the confined spaces of dances and dinners, comes to fruition in outside spaces where time and social order can be ignored. These scenes seek to elevate the relationship to a timeless romance, referencing not only the gothic traditions associated with the Brontës rather than Austen but also that reaching for extremes of feeling that had made *Titanic* (Cameron, 1997) so successful as a Hollywood romance. These romantic moments are visually heavily marked. They contrast not only with the film's emphasis on realism in its representation of family life and its use of dialogue and costume but also with the more naturalistic modes of appearance and acting with which Knightley presents this Elizabeth's version of postmodern femininity.

Both the 1940 and the 2005 versions of *Pride and Prejudice* are set in a version of the past even if the emphasis is on spectacle and emotion rather than accurate recreation. Chadha's *Bride and Prejudice* gives a contemporary setting to the story, but colorful and noisy Amritsar is as much fantasy India as MGM's Meryton Village was fantasy England. "Inspired by Jane Austen's *Pride and Prejudice*," this British film is addressed firmly to mainstream, but diverse, audiences including those in India and the Indian diaspora. The film retains many of the characters and episodes now familiar in the story, but the barrier between the couple is not so much class as national identity; the film's Elizabeth, renamed Lalita, defends India, as well as her family, in the face of what she sees as the ignorance and scorn displayed by the American Darcy.

While the romance narrative provides the central core, *Bride and Prejudice* specifically offers numerous and overt examples of intertexual referencing. A wide variety of sources is boldly drawn on, and the self-conscious referencing is reinforced by the comments made by the director in publicity for the film and in the DVD commentary in which Chadha and co-scriptwriter Paul Mayeda Berges continually reference other sources. Chadha's previous films, including the phenomenally successful *Bend It Like Beckham* (2002), had emphasized the hybrid nature of contemporary British national identity, delighting in the incongruences and complexity of multiculturalism. *Bride and Prejudice* follows this by offering itself as a hybrid that seeks to adapt Bollywood for Western tastes, presenting what Chadha describes as "Bollywood and Hollywood, tied up with a British sensibility."[28] References included a whole range of Indian and Western musicals, British television programs such as the BBC's *Goodness Gracious Me* (1998–2000) and *The Kumars at No. 42* (2001–) and Working Title comedies such as *Notting Hill* (Michell, 1997). Knowingly, in the chase at the end, the sisters interrupt a screening at London's National Film Theatre of the Indian film *Purab Aur Pachhim* (Kumar, 1970), literally translatable as "East and West."[29]

Bride and Prejudice shares some of the features that had marked the earlier versions of the story, though they are inflected through the Bollywood lens. Like MGM's *Pride and Prejudice*, the emphasis is on comedy with broad characterizations and a particularly farcical interpretation of Mr. Collins/Chetan Kohli's wooing. The emphasis on the family is also strong here, as in the other two films, and the claustrophobia, femininity, and warmth of family life is reinforced not just by the emphasis on the family in Bollywood films but also by references to the stereotype of the Indian family used as the basis of comedy in BBC radio/television programs. This affects, in particular, the role of Mrs. Bennet/Bakshi as the Indian mother who is obsessed with marrying off her daughters and defending the family's social status. The referencing of this stereotype, outside the novel and its adaptations, has the slightly unexpected effect of naturalizing Mrs. Bakshi's behavior, making it understandable in the context of an established set of representations of the Indian mother. Similarly, the dances function as a combination of spectacle and narrative organization in all three versions, but in *Bride and Prejudice* they clearly work as elements of a musical combining Bollywood music and choreography with direct references to *Grease* (Kleiser, 1978) and *West Side Story* (Wise, 1961) when the sisters tease Lalita in "No Life without Wife" or to *Oliver!* in the dance in the street market.

This provides a rather different context for the representation of the heroine. The character of Lalita fits the persona established for Austen's heroines over a number of adaptations—that of a modern, independent-minded young woman who will not be bound by the conventions of the day. But this is inflected in a number of different ways and in particular is crossed with a familiar British stereotype about a modern young Asian woman resisting the expectations of her parents and the restrictions of domestic life, a characterization found in *My Beautiful Laundrette* (Frears,

1985) and *East Is East* (O'Donnell, 1999) as well as *Bend It Like Beckham*. By positioning the heroine in this way and by taking national identity as an issue, *Bride and Prejudice* sets Lalita up as a spokesperson for her country who is ready for debate with Darcy; rather more than Knightley's Elizabeth, her disagreements with the hero arise over what she takes to be his political and social attitudes as well as his personal behavior.

But perhaps the most significant element in the presentation of this heroine is Aishwarya Rai's star status. Her fame as a former Miss World underlines her beauty, and her position as a major star of Indian cinema means that she has a star image as a very rich young woman who controls her own destiny. Her identification with an older India is reinforced by the use of landscape (mirroring the use of English countryside in British adaptations), which is celebrated, for instance, in the first scenes of the film when she rides through the green fields around Amritsar in a deliberately old-fashioned cart and in the shot that sets the famous Indian film star in front of the Golden Temple. Costume too plays its part, and throughout the film, Lalita's switching between Indian and Western dress demonstrates her position as a modern Indian woman but also allows her beauty to be displayed in different cultural modes. In addition, key devices such as the use of close-ups, slow motion, and dance, drawn on to depict the romance between Lalita and Darcy, also underline Rai's understanding of Bollywood modes, the fit between her face and body and the emphasis on fantasy in music, camerawork, and choreography.

Because of this, the representation of Lalita draws on many of the heroine's characteristics familiar from earlier versions, but the very elements that serve Lalita/Rai so well undermine the balance of the romance relationship. The romance enabled by the mature sparring and witty repartee of the MGM version and by the gothic use of nature in the 2005 adaptation allowed for the man to be established as a hero equal to, as well as finally sympathetic to, the heroine. In *Bride and Prejudice*, however, no such support is available for Martin Henderson's Darcy. Thematically, Darcy's American wealth is rendered suspect by the discourse about India; although Lalita has to learn to curb her prejudices and her tongue, the film is sympathetic to her argument that diversity should be welcomed not trampled over. Darcy's unease with Indian mores reinforces Henderson's difficulties in taking on the modes of performance demanded by Indian cinema. Henderson's star status clearly cannot match that of Rai, and his acting is awkward and uneasy for much of the time. Henderson's uneasy, unemphatic gestures when the couple comes together at the end indicate an imbalance in the pairing that the romance has difficulty in reconciling. The failure here is not due to lack of faithfulness to the original novel but to the generic conventions of romance since Rai's star status unbalances the narrative and prevents the generic resolution normally achieved through an alignment of femininity and masculinity.

Having discussed these examples in some detail, it is tempting to try to move to a more general theory of classic adaptations arising from this analysis. This approach is characteristic of adaptation theory and can be seen in the way in which Ellen Belton's excellent essay on two versions of *Pride and Prejudice* concludes with some final generalizations:

> A successful adaptation enters into a conversation with the original that ani-mates the viewers' pleasure in both works. The goal of the adaptation is not only to rediscover the prior text but also to find new ways of understanding it and to appropriate those meanings for the adaptors' own ends.[30]

But such generalizations about the viewers' pleasure or the adaptation's goal cannot be justified by the analysis that Belton provides. In terms of my examples, why should Disney's *Oliver Twist* be judged by these crite-ria rather than its success in animating the generic framework of chil-dren's fiction that sustains it? Do we not need to distinguish between those adaptations that refer distinctly to the original source and those that escape from it, as I have tried to do in my discussion of *David Copperfield* and *Oliver Twist*? Do the various versions of *Pride and Prejudice* discussed here "hold a conversation with" the original, or can they best be seen as explorations and celebrations of femininity that actually depend on the transformation of Austen's novel into a conventional romance? The films have to be judged in their own right not as readings of the original; the ex-traordinary differences in the endings of *Oliver Twist* indicate what hap-pens when the imperative of faithfulness is removed. But, if generaliza-tions are needed, it is possible to say that popular and much-adapted texts have to work with similarity and difference in a movement that refers to but does not rely on knowledge of previous versions including the origi-nal. Their status as classic adaptations gives them a flexibility that allows them to remain recognizable even when subjected to considerable change. This flexibility does not mean free-floating intertextuality, however; adap-tations that move furthest from the original are often sustained by other generic expectations that shape narrative organization, mise-en-scène, and costume. In addition, setting and place often function as spectacle, providing a space in which a story can be referenced and invoked rather than realistically represented. And, finally, visibility of artifice marks some of the most distinctive adaptations in, for instance, the dreamlike condensations of MGM's *David Copperfield*, the stylized London of various *Oliver Twists*, and the genre-shifting of Chadha's *Bride and Prejudice*. These are issues that will be pursued further in the studies that follow.

NOTES

1. John Romano, "Writing after Dickens: The Television Writer's Art," in *Dickens on Screen*, ed. John Glavin (Cambridge: Cambridge University Press, 2003), 89. See David Lusted, "Literary Adaptations and Cultural Fantasies," *Journal of Popular British Cinema* 4, (2001): 72–80, for a sympathetic account of this film and other versions of *Great Expectations* in relation to class.

2. See Jeffrey Richards, *Films and British National Identity: From Dickens to Dad's Army* (Manchester, UK: Manchester University Press, 1997), for a discussion of Dickens adaptations in this light; and Andrew Higson, *English Heritage, English Cinema: The Costume Drama in the 1980s and 1990s* (Oxford: Oxford University Press, 2003), for an account of debates about 1980s heritage films.

3. Kamilla Elliott suggests that when "filmmakers set modern politically correct views against historically correct backdrops, the effect is to authorize these modern ideologies as historically authentic" (*Rethinking the Novel/Film Debate* [Cambridge: Cambridge University Press, 2003], 177).

4. Mariam Margolyes, "Playing Dickens: Miriam Margolyes. A Conversation with John Glavin," in *Dickens on Screen*, ed. John Glavin (Cambridge: Cambridge University Press, 2003), 107.

5. Romano, "Writing after Dickens," 89.

6. See Michael Pointer, *Charles Dickens on the Screen: The Film, Television, and Video Adaptations* (Lanham, Md.: Scarecrow Press, 1996). The British Film Institute's DVD *Dickens before Sound* (2006) offers British and U.S. examples of early adaptations.

7. Brian McFarlane, *Novel to Film* (Oxford: Clarendon Press, 1996), 196.

8. Grahame Smith, *Dickens and the Dream of Cinema* (Manchester, UK: Manchester University Press, 2003).

9. See Robert Giddings and Keith Selby, *The Classic Serial on Television and Radio* (Basingstoke, UK: Palgrave, 2001), 1–30.

10. See Sarah Cardwell, *Adaptation Revisited: Television and the Classic Novel* (Manchester, UK: Manchester University Press, 2002), 77–101, for a discussion of the specificities of television for classic adaptations.

11. Richards, *Films and British National Identity*, 334.

12. Jeffrey Sconce, "Dickens, Selznick, and *South Park*," in *Dickens on Screen*, ed. John Glavin (Cambridge: Cambridge University Press, 2003), 171.

13. Bob Wake, "David Copperfield (2000)," *Culturevulture*, culturevulture.net/Television/DavidCopperfield(2).htm. Wake recommended the program "for viewers who find the yuletide season incomplete without a dose of Dickens," a comment that illustrates the strong association among Dickens, television, and Christmas.

14. Guerric DeBona, "Dickens, the Depression, and MGM's David Copperfield," in *Film Adaptation*, ed. James Naremore (London: Athalone Press, 2000), 115–16.

15. DeBona, "Dickens, the Depression, and MGM's David Copperfield," 110.

16. Quoted in Richards, *Films and British National Identity*, 335.

17. There was difficulty in finding a dramatic opening for the film to replace what was felt to be the abstract opening of the book, and it was Kay Walsh, the ac-

tress who played Nancy, who came up with the idea of the pregnant woman, struggling over the moors. See Kevin Brownlow, *David Lean* (London: Richard Cohen Books, 1996), 228–29.

18. Lean thought this made the portrayal more anti-Semitic. See Brownlow, *David Lean*, 249.

19. Quoted in Brian McFarlane, *An Autobiography of British Cinema* (London: Methuen, 1997), 261.

20. Gina Macdonald and Andrew Macdonald, "Introduction," in *Jane Austen on Screen*, ed. Gina Macdonald and Andrew Macdonald (Cambridge: Cambridge University Press, 2003), 1.

21. Janice A. Radway, *Reading the Romance: Women, Patriarchy, and Popular Literature* (Chapel Hill: University of North Carolina Press, 1984), 147. Radway's narrative model of the romance, though based on a study of novel readers, has been influential in film genre analysis.

22. Cardwell, *Adaptation Revisited*, 153.

23. Deborah Kaplan, "Mass Marketing Jane Austen: Men, Women, and Censorship in Two Film Adaptations" (1996), reprinted in *Jane Austen in Hollywood*, ed. Linda Troost and Sayre Greenfield (Lexington: University of Kentucky Press, 1998), 180.

24. Ellen Belton, "Reimagining Jane Austen: The 1940 and 1995 Film Versions of *Pride and Prejudice*," in *Jane Austen on Screen*, ed. Gina Macdonald and Andrew Macdonald (Cambridge: Cambridge University Press, 2003), 178.

25. Belton, "Reimagining Jane Austen," 180.

26. The film is set in an earlier period than the novel, and so the Empire-line dresses of the 1995 BBC adaptation are not a feature of this production.

27. See chapter 1 of Julianne Pidduck, *Contemporary Costume Film* (London: British Film Institute Publications, 2004), for a discussion of the deployment of a liberal, feminist perspective in 1990s Austen adaptations.

28. Chadha, in DVD commentary.

29. I discuss the intertextual aspects of the film more fully in "Jane Austen Meets Gurinder Chadha: Hybridity and Intertextuality in *Bride and Prejudice*," *South Asian Popular Culture* 4, no. 2 (October 2006): 163–68.

30. Belton, "Reimagining Jane Austen," 105.

2

Art Cinema, Authorship, and the Impossible Novel

Adaptations of Proust, Woolf, and Joyce

The classic adaptation has the status of an adaptation but must make sense to those who have not read the original; it might be heavily trailed and advertised as an adaptation, but it does not require exegesis or explanation, and although critics might comment on its (lack of) faithfulness, its success tends to be judged by how it works with its audience. The modernist adaptation to which we now turn could be considered as a classic adaptation, and indeed, some films that I discuss in this chapter do feature in the collection *Classics in Film and Television*.[1] Nevertheless, I consider that the way in which they handle their status as adaptations and, crucially, the impact that the critical discussions of that status have is different and requires further exploration. The adaptations I am concerned with here are films made from a particular kind of classic, the modernist novels of the first part of the twentieth century that challenged the concept of what the novel might do and who it might be addressed to. Such works often came out of a cosmopolitan, European, and literary milieu that defined itself against the bourgeois, self-contained world of national literature. Their authors include Marcel Proust, the later Henry James, James Joyce, Thomas Mann, and Virginia Woolf. The nature of their work, its relationship with what came before, and its influence on how the novel was understood is beyond this book as indeed is their relationship with the development of cinema in the 1920s and 1930s. Here, I am concerned with how they function as sources for screen adaptations.

As sources, they have a number of things in common. First of all they are perceived as "difficult." This is not a question of being difficult to adapt, which could well apply to the classic novels we have already discussed. Instead, the sources are perceived as difficult in themselves and beyond the capacity of a shared, popular culture. Second, their adaptations are much less likely to be repetitive: screen adaptations of this nature are more likely to be seen as unique events associated with a particular film director rather than another version of a well-loved classic. Third, because they are perceived as being difficult, the critical context takes on a particular resonance. Critics serve to identify an audience for this work and explain its complications in a way that is not deemed necessary for a television version of *Pride and Prejudice* or a musical of *Oliver Twist*.

This chapter therefore focuses on the cinematic culture that supports the films under discussion more than on the films themselves. By this I mean not just the critical response, though this is important, but also the audience expectations that are set up by modes of exhibition and marketing. Broadly, I want to put this kind of adaptation into the context of art cinema by using five films as the basis of the case study. I compare the critical reception of two adaptations taken from parts of Proust's *À la recherche du temps perdu* and look at what that reveals about how the modernist adaptation is positioned generically, particularly in terms of the relationship between this kind of adaptation and the specter of heritage cinema. A study of adaptations by two feminist directors then allows for a more detailed discussion of authorship as a feature of the modernist adaptation. The example of Strick's 1967 *Ulysses* concludes the chapter with the suggestion that a critical focus on adaptation might distract from other ways of looking at the film. Throughout, the emphasis is on the way in which the critical use of faithfulness as a touchstone overrides other questions of genre and authorship and leads to particular kinds of judgment.

The proposition that art cinema is or was a genre was forcibly developed by David Bordwell in the late 1970s and early 1980s and has been the subject of debate. For our purposes, the criteria Bordwell proposes are useful in clarifying some elements to be found in modernist adaptations. Bordwell, contrasting art cinema with his model of the classical Hollywood film, argues that it defined itself by "realism and authorial expressivity."[2] Three main characteristics are associated with this kind of cinema. First, there is an emphasis on narrative "verisimilitude in which the tight causality of Hollywood construction is replaced by a more tenuous linking of events."[3] This leads to films in which narratives are marked by chance and coincidence, reflecting the episodic stories of real life rather than purposeful, deadline-driven stories of Hollywood. Second, art cinema is concerned with a commitment to subjective verisimilitude, the representation of the psychological reality of a character who might be inconsistent, aimless, disturbed, or indeed mad. Space and time conform to this psychological realism as, through the use of dreams, memories, and fantasies, "art cinema presents psychological effects in search of their causes."[4] Third, art cinema draws attention to its modes of narration. The narration process is not smooth and helpful but resists, defers, and undermines our understanding of what is presented as the story. Films start in the middle of an event, and endings fail to reach resolution. Bordwell stresses the ambiguity of the art film, an ambiguity that underpins the apparent contradictions of an approach that combines realism with the stylization of overt narration. These films tell us that "life lacks the neatness of art and *this art knows it*."[5] If they have a form of resolution, it can only be temporary and contingent, the recognition by an individual of "fundamental human issues," a recognition that fits the "art film's thematic crux . . . its attempt to pronounce judgements on modern life and *la condition humaine*."[6]

Bordwell suggests that the stylistic marks of art cinema indicated the presence of an author, with the filmmaker identified as the source of this self-conscious mode of narration. In the 1979 article, this author is textual, "the overriding intelligence organising the film,"[7] but in his later version of the argument Bordwell relates this authorial voice to the extra-filmic activity used to promote the film: "The consistency of an authorial signature across an oeuvre constitutes an economically exploitable trademark."[8] The name of the director was a means of channeling audience expectations and generating pleasure. More generally, art cinema required different modes of production (different sources of funding, subsidy, protection) and exhibition (specialized cinemas, serious film magazines, festivals, film education). It was through such mechanisms that the audience could be brought together and educated, and the critical apparatus was particularly important in creating an audience since "a cinema of ambiguity required machinery to interpret it."[9] Art cinema, as Steve Neale points out, also involved a balance of the national and international. It relied on "an appeal to the 'universal' values of culture and art"[10] and so could aspire to an international audience of a particular kind. But because of its clear differences from Hollywood cinema, art cinema could also be co-opted by national cinemas trying to maintain themselves in the face of U.S. domination. In that context, the name of the author could function as a mark of artistic self-expression, funded by cultural or government organizations in the interests of promoting a national cinema. Such cinema could be commercially successful with its own national audiences, as 1960s art cinema often was, but could also garner prestige in international contexts. It could be understood both as the outcome of an intensely personal and individual struggle and as the product of educated European cultures in danger of being overwhelmed by Hollywood.

Much has changed since art cinema was described in this way. Certainly, the impact of the "new cinemas" particularly from France and Italy in the 1950s and 1960s that provided the backbone of Bordwell's argument has receded with time. Nevertheless, despite the dominance of the multiplex and the blockbuster, "an 'independent' film culture" just about survives, "existing in the arthouse spaces for white and higher social grade audiences" who use information provided by "specialist film magazines and listings produced by individual circuits" to guide their choice of film.[11] Films for these audiences often still have the characteristically difficult narratives that Bordwell describes, an emphasis on the exploration of character, and a visual organization that draws attention to itself. The films have relatively small budgets and might indeed be subsidized or protected by government support, but they claim the status of being the artistic product of an identifiable author. Audiences in the art house circuits are tightly defined by specialist exhibition practices though distributors such as the British Film Institute, Artificial Eye, and Milestones Films, which have made access to art house films via video and DVD easier. The importance of festivals in promoting such films can be seen in the way that prizes from Cannes, Berlin, and Toronto are reported on in specialist magazines and referred to in trailers and posters. And the director (now validated as an auteur as the terms established in sixties film theory have been popularized) is a key selling point and a critical means of explaining such films.

Alongside art cinema, however, there has been the rise of the "heritage film," which seemed to occupy "a kind of 'halfway house'"[12] between mainstream narrative cinema and earlier European art cinema. Films in this genre that emerged strongly in the 1980s were often based on literary sources and told stories of the upper-middle-class life in exquisite settings and with careful attention to the detail of costume and décor. Like art cinema, such films drew attention to their visual style, and the working through of narrative was less important than character and décor. Here though visual style was an overt source of pleasure as was the leisurely procession of characters, often played by actors known for their theatrical credentials; there was an emphasis on ensemble playing, and the films often offered strong roles for women. Although there were nuances and subtleties in their narratives, these films have been deemed less ambiguous and challenging than the art film. Their appeal to verisimilitude related to historical décor rather than contemporary life, and they were heavily criticized for presenting a nostalgic account of a narrowly configured past. In a British context, the genre was strongly established by Merchant and Ivory's Forster adaptations, particularly *A Room with a View* (1985) and *Howards End* (1992), and was a key element in British cinema's struggle to offer something different to national and international audiences.[13]

It is in this context that I want to look at adaptations of modernist novels, arguing that the textual marks of the art film can be seen to reinforce and complicate the process of referencing through which adaptations are often understood. First, the emphasis on faithfulness to the source is set against another type of verisimilitude characterized by the art film's deployment of a narrative that is both more lifelike and more opaque than its Hollywood equivalent. Second, the literary significance of the originals' use of words for complex purposes is set into a relationship with the art film's emphasis on fully using the possibilities of cinema in a way which is validated as artistically significant. And third, although the author of the original novel has an artistic reputation as a pillar of modern literature, art cinema adds a possible second author, the director, with his or her own markers of artistic style. All of these factors reemphasize the sense of doubleness that is a strong feature of adaptations from a well-known source, the test of one kind of work against another. In the case of the modernist adaptation, the context of the art film and the reputation of the source set up potential clashes that relate to the relationship between word and image, the accessibility of modernist art, and the relationship between author and auteur.

"PROUST IS FILMED AT LAST"

Swann in Love (Schlöndorff, 1984) is an excellent example of how the critical context of the art film positions a modernist adaptation and of the difficulty of gaining approval for such a film. The publicity that surrounded its first screenings in 1984 provides an exemplary model for the work that such a screen adaptation has to do. First, there is great emphasis on the difficulty of the project. This partly relates to the work of adaptation itself so that the publicity describes how the process of adaptation was approached. In this case, there is discussion of why this adaptation focused on one book from its lengthy source and how that one book might be considered to stand for the whole. Background publicity for the critics drew attention to the decision to focus not just on one book but to handle that by focusing on one day in Swann's life, using flashbacks to tell the story and an epilogue to provide a moral coda. Second, the difficulty of the adaptation process is compounded by the difficulty of getting the film itself made, an emphasis that underlines the film's status as an art film. Here, the publicity is able to draw on a history that draws attention to the determination of the producer, Nicole Stéphane, and the failed attempts by Luchino Visconti and by Harold Pinter and Joseph Losey, which demonstrate the impossible nature of the project. The use of this kind of material can be seen in a *New York Times* article written as the film was being made and entitled "Proust Is Filmed at Last." The journalist comments on the "missionary zeal" of Stéphane and her interest in an aspect of Proust that she claims the scholars have neglected: "the dramatic wit of his language." The article rehearses the previous failures and describes how Peter Brook pulled out of this version, leaving Volker Schlöndorff to step in to save it. The commitment of all those involved is summed up in a quotation from Jeremy Irons, the British actor playing Swann, who comments, "We eat, sleep and dream Swann." "Tension hovers over the set," the article reports. "Everyone feels an enormous burden of responsibility towards the Proust movie."[14] A headline in a London paper rather sums up the tone of all this material: "They Said It Couldn't Be Done."[15] "They" in this context refers not just to the Hollywood mainstream, traditionally seen as indifferent or hostile to European filmmaking, but also to the experts on Proust.

The publicity for the film therefore sets up the production as, what Phil Powrie calls, "an Herculean struggle,"[16] and a number of British critics used the analogy of climbing Everest to describe the director's task. "My only constraint," Schlöndorff is reported as saying, "is to be true to Proust's vision."[17] Faithfulness to the source is reflected in the use of dialogue, which a number of critics note is taken directly from the book, and it is acknowledged that the "film painstakingly realizes Proust's descriptions of places and people and gestures."[18] This notion of faithfulness to the original is linked to the need to be faithful in representing the period, a drive for verisimilitude that maintains authenticity as "a keynote" in lighting, in the casting of real French aristocrats, and in the use of valuable period jewelry.[19]

Schlöndorff's role in this discourse of verisimilitude draws attention to the way in which his status as director and auteur is set up in relation to Proust as the original author. Although his purpose is, as we have seen, to serve Proust, the director must nevertheless be ascribed sufficient status to do the job. Because of this, the publicity material draws attention to Schlöndorff's extensive career in European cinema and his expertise in literary adaptations, particularly *The Tin Drum* (1979). Powrie suggests that Schlöndorff's more radical credentials are downplayed in favor of a presentation of him as "an honest craftsman" who has, according to the *Variety* critic, "no substantial style of his own, no controlling design to impose on the material."[20] Powrie emphasizes the importance of this to the marketing of the film—"Schlondorff's *transparency* allows the supposed 'truth' of the film's textual origins to spectacularize themselves"[21]—and some critics responded favorably, commending Schlöndorff's "ferocious determination to put his material before himself."[22] But Schlöndorff himself draws attention to the double authorship of the adaptation. Despite his reverence for Proust, he knows that more is needed than transparency;

using terms familiar to adaptation theory, he comments that he is looking to find "emotional and visual equivalents to Proust's vision," and adds, "if I make a movie which Proustians celebrate for its fidelity, I will have failed as a director."[23] A number of the British critics comment that, at the press screening, Schlöndorff asked them to treat the film as they would the other offerings that week rather than insist on the comparison with Proust.

The publicity material that supported the film and that was picked up by critics therefore tries to set up the film as a monumental labor in which the elements of the art cinema (Europeanness, verisimilitude, dedication to the project, and the role of the director) are put at the service of the revered source. The film's reception was determined by how far critics were willing to use some of this material to stray, as Schlöndorff asked, beyond the traditional mode of comparison between film and source. The most hostile critics were those who insisted on this task of comparison. One striking maneuver in the response to the film was for the critic to imagine different kinds of audience members and predict their response to the film. The *New York Magazine* critic comments, "I have the feeling that the uninitiated moviegoer wandering into *Swann in Love* will be rather puzzled."[24] The critic of course is not uninitiated, and indeed a number of critics make it clear that they are familiar not just with this particular book but also with *À la recherche du temps perdu* as a whole. Pauline Kael comments that the film cannot emulate Proust's "subtle feeling for rhythms," Denby refers to a "brutal act of reduction," and Vincent Canby concludes that the film can "never escape the sense that it's some sort of mad super-synopsis."[25] In the *New York Review of Books*, Roger Shattuck took the trope of the initiated versus uninitiated viewer further and constructs his review around the (imagined) responses to the film from the "point of view of an occasional moviegoer unfamiliar with Proust," then "the thoughts of a reasonably literate film critic" who has read the first volume, and "only then shall I allow the Professor and Proust scholar to say his piece."[26] His piece is of course entirely hostile, and one can only wonder why among the imagined viewers there was no room for a regular filmgoer with a liking for European art films.

These hostile reviews do however give an indication of what the pleasures of the film might be but condemn them as inappropriate. Denby admits grudgingly that *Swann in Love* "can be enjoyed for philistine reasons, for its setting and its clothes, its air of heavyweight swank, its turbid splendour."[27] Claire Tomalin is critical of the film's handling of Proust's themes and remarks that the film only works as "a period story of a familiar type, graced with authentic Parisian settings, authentic clothes, a hint of a social message . . . and a group of recognisable stars."[28] Jill Forbes in the specialist journal *Sight and Sound* found the "decorative authenticity

. . . obtrusive."[29] These comments indicate the dangerous generic tightrope *Swann in Love* teetered on, for if the Proustian framework was played down then the film ran the risk of being pigeonholed as a heritage film. Some critics refer to this possibility but felt it had escaped: "Whenever [it] threatens to subside into the reflected elegance of costume drama, it is hoisted high on the sinewy modernism of Hans Werner Henzes' music and the grainy glow of the colour photography by Bergman's cameraman Sven Nykvist."[30] Note here how the masculine, tough adjectives ("sinewy," "grainy") are attached to the art film attributes of music and photography and rescue the film from the feminine associations of costume drama. Others were not to be diverted in this way: "For all its good intentions, *Swann in Love* is essentially a form of up-market costume drama."[31]

By contrast, the film got very positive reviews in much of the popular and middle-brow British press. This meant that the key features of the heritage film—the acting, the setting, costumes, and photography—were read in a different way. For the *Sunday Telegraph*, *Swann in Love* was "a haunting, sumptuous picture, gloriously photographed."[32] For the *Mail on Sunday*, "The whole film flares with compelling art. The glowing triumph of Jeremy Irons in that creative fire is unmistakable."[33] The *Glasgow Herald* described it as "ravishing" and "sumptuous,"[34] while for the *Sunday Express* it was "visually so eloquent and filmic you almost do not need to know what is being said to perceive its drift and enjoy its subtle satire of a self-centred upper class."[35] For these critics, the film was the product of individual creativity (of the photographer, Sven Nykvist, and of Irons as well as Schlöndorff), and the middle-brow British press was generally more willing to understand its visual beauty in the context of the stylistic preoccupations of a European art film.

We can take *Swann in Love* as an example of how the modernist adaptation is positioned in film culture. It is treated as an art film in terms of its European funding, the film circuits it will show in, the use of festivals to market it, and consequently its relationship to mainstream U.S. cinema. But it is also marked by additional elements that relate to the way in which adaptations are understood. Publicity is given to its genesis both in terms of the adaptation process and the practical difficulties in getting it made; its audience is defined by their understanding of the original novel, and the task of the critic is to advise about how faithfully the relationship between film and source has been maintained. Only when the critic moves out of that paradigm can the film be praised; in the case of *Swann in Love*, however, this involved a move into the terrain that was beginning to be occupied by heritage cinema, a move that opened up the film to accusations of indulging in nostalgia for an idealized past and the commodification of costume and sets.

The rather different reception given to the adaptation of the last book of Proust's sequence, *Time Regained* (Ruiz, 1999), both refines this model and shows how it can be adjusted in different circumstances. By the time the film arrived in cinemas in Britain and the United States, it had already been a commercial success in France, suggesting that it could be a successful art house product elsewhere. The critical response to *Time Regained* dwelt much less on the labor of the actual filmmaking, though the challenge of filming "the epic's sixth and final volume . . . the one that recapitulates and resolves all that has come before"[36] is regularly referred to. *Swann in Love* is cited among the previous attempts to film Proust and is now generally reckoned to be a failure. The discussion of the director is also rather different; whereas Schlöndorff was a European art film director, Raoul Ruiz, it was noted, though living in France, was "a footloose Chilean intellectual"[37] with a "background in leftist politics and experimental film-making."[38] The critical context for this film generally plays down elements that might characterize the film as a reverential labor of love and emphasizes the project's audacity, which is often linked to the director's origins outside Europe. It is suggested that Ruiz has "taken on Proust as one more macho dare"[39] and that the "filmmaker has not abandoned his 'underdeveloped' disrespect for European culture";[40] Ruiz himself is quoted as saying that "at the beginning, it was just an act of irresponsibility . . . *Chilean* irresponsibility."[41] There is much less emphasis here on the director as the vehicle through whom Proust's work emerges and a more balanced sense of two sensibilities being brought into a playful relationship with each other.

Time Regained did not escape the fidelity test, and again some critics went to considerable lengths to demonstrate their own familiarity with Proust. Once more, there are suggestions that the endeavor of adaptation is pointless; the sympathetic Rosenbaum writes that "even if he's met the challenge with more ingenuity and wit than one might have thought possible, one can still question whether it was ever worth thinking about."[42] There is still the same concern to categorize the viewers of the film by their knowledge of the original with a common questioning of how far the film can be followed by those unfamiliar with the book. The general agreement is that such a viewer will be in difficulties with one British reviewer for an upmarket paper stating flatly that "it is pointless to pretend that anyone unfamiliar with the original will find their bearings in *Time Regained*."[43] And the *Washington Post* staff writer complains, "I wasn't ever really sure what they [the characters] were talking about or why. . . . It's the sort of movie that can make normally well-read and intelligent viewers feel stupid."[44] For others, though, this was less of a problem. Philip French put himself in the camp of those "for whom Proust is only a half-open book" and confessed, "Not all of it is comprehensible at a first viewing to those like myself. I enjoyed it much more second time around."[45] Veteran critic Alexander Walker, in a mainstream London newspaper, didn't even suggest a second viewing but buoyantly advised audiences to immerse themselves in the film: "Open your eyes and senses to it: comprehension will follow."[46]

But if critics allow that fidelity is not the only test, the question of genre remains. Again, the heritage film is marked as a possible framework, and Rosenbaum does not think it entirely avoids this fate, asking, "Is it possible to separate its praiseworthy value from its value as a glossy, high-priced cultural object—the sort of position awarded most Merchant-Ivory productions and comparable upscale consumerist literary adaptations such as *The Wings of the Dove?*"[47] *Time Regained* does indeed adopt some of the characteristics of heritage cinema as it had been established by the late 1990s. It is set in the past, it allows for pleasure to be taken in the elaborate, authentic costumes and décor, and the beauty of its visual composition is drawn attention to in the framing of shots and the way in which the camera often moves to conceal or reveal. It certainly draws on a cast list of stars, often in the cameo roles associated with heritage cinema, who combine glamour with art house credibility. But *Time Regained* holds on much more fully to the ambiguity and subjectivity that Bordwell associates with art cinema. Its opaque narrative, its referencing of hidden social truths, and its transformation of time and space into malleable forces that manipulate the characters and are manipulated by the director were all key factors in art cinema of the 1950s and 1960s, which *Time Regained* combined with the apparently magical properties of digital cinema. Whereas *Swann in Love* had worked to smooth out narrative complications, *Time Regained* seemed not to care that the audience might be confused. In this way, the film avoided the heritage label by going back to the textual markers of the art film, what one broadsheet review called "a narrative structure founded on discontinuities, digressions, repetitions, short-circuits and surreal dislocations of time and space."[48]

For those critics who were interested in cinema, Ruiz seemed to be addressing not just Proust as a writer but also the creative force of cinema. "The pleasure it provides is the involuntary memory of cinema itself,"[49] wrote Hoberman, while a British critic commented that "the film shows how cinematic magic is at one with this sense of time captured and also fading: film itself is the Proustian vehicle of so much in our time."[50] Ruiz might be more playful in his attitude to *la condition humaine* than the art cinema Bordwell describes, but he offered its modernist textual devices. This allows the adaptation to escape the generic positioning of *Swann in Love*. "*Time Regained* is anything but a heritage movie," writes Keith Reader, because "Ruiz rewrites Proust in cinematic terms. The camera movements . . . correspond to the oscillations of the written narration between the recollected and the imagined, the past and the present."[51] Following a similar argument, Rosenbaum comments on the way in which "not only camera movements but the gliding displacements of objects and characters re-creat[e] some of the complex, winding journeys of Proust's sentences."[52] This is a more open and sophisticated approach than the critical approach that denies cinema any such possibilities by emphasizing its essential concern with realist observation, but it is worth noting that this is still a version of the fidelity approach. The heritage genre is deemed not to be cinematic, and Ruiz's approach is judged successful insofar as it equates to something first done by Proust. Not surprisingly, both reviews finish with the suggestion that the best thing would be if the film acted as a "trailer" by sending viewers back to the original.

I am not arguing that the critical emphasis on *Time Regained*'s visual style as a means of translating Proust's verbal complexity is wrong, but I am drawing attention to the way in which it is used to fend off a mode of viewing of the film as costume drama. More interesting perhaps is Romney's account, which accepts that the film has strong elements of "a classic costume drama, handsomely photographed by Ricardo Aronovich using all the resources of realistic historical design and featuring a prestigious international cast." Rather than rejecting these features because they belong to the heritage film rather than Proust, Romney suggests that Ruiz uses them cinematically to make "a costume drama of a different kind: it's a Ruiz film in the costume of costume drama, heritage film as a form of travesty."[53] Here, the heritage film, rather than being a tepid or commodified version of the literary classic, is recognized as a cinematic genre that can like any other genre be reworked and reformed.

FILMS FOR WOMEN?

In pursuing these questions further, I turn now to films by two feminist directors, Marleen Gorris's 1997 adaptation of Virginia Woolf's *Mrs. Dalloway* and Chantal Akerman's *La Captive* (2000), a film inspired by Proust's *La Prisonnière*. Here I want to look at the films themselves as well as the critical context to see how the layering of authorship and genres can work to explain the films. Akerman and Gorris are the names associated with two key works in the feminist canon—*Jeanne Dielman, 23 Quai du Commerce, 1080 Bruxelles* (1976) and *Question of Silence* (1982), respectively. These early films can still be described as art films, backed up by the kind of subsidized European modes of production, distribution, and exhibition that Neale described. The success of these films in that context has framed how their directors' subsequent films have been understood. Adding this feminist strand to the analysis allows us to see more clearly how the model of adaptation presented above can be inflected in different directions, and an analysis of the films themselves pushes further the discussion of the relationship of the art film with heritage cinema.

Mrs. Dalloway fits the *Swann in Love* model of a modernist adaptation. The novel was deemed very hard to film; it was described as "almost unfilmable" by Roger Ebert,[54] and the notion that cinema has difficulty with representing thought is repeated frequently by critics. The script is described as a labor of love, originating in Eileen Atkins's perception that her friend could play Mrs. Dalloway and Vanessa Redgrave's counter-suggestion that Atkins could and should write the script. Atkins's suitability is indicated by her research into the period and the fact that she had played Woolf in a one-woman theatrical production. In addition, the film had considerable production difficulties since inadequate financing meant that the production had to be halted during filming. Gorris herself commented that the film had a bigger budget than her earlier films but positions it firmly as a quality film and a European film in relation to Hollywood:

> By present-day American standards *Mrs. Dalloway* wasn't a very expensive film. It was only four and a half million dollars. And you know, if an American studio had made the film it probably would have been something like sixty million dollars. So, I think in Europe we manage to make quality films for much less money and I hope we continue to do so.[55]

Like Schlöndorff, Gorris has her own status as a feminist director of independent films and as an Oscar winner for *Antonia's Line* (1995). In part, her reputation as a woman artist reinforces and is deemed appropriate for an adaptation of a work by another woman artist, Woolf. But Gorris also saw the film as a product of her own artistic development. When asked whether *Antonia's Line* and *Mrs. Dalloway* were less angry about women's position than her earlier films, she responded, "I make the films that I want to make and the audience will see what they do. If they don't like it, well that's okay, they don't. If they do like it, great. But I think you should at least allow the artist the freedom of speech; the freedom to do what she or he wants to do."[56] Also like Schlöndorff, Gorris tried to distance herself from the novel and to play down the critical process of comparison. "It's important not to have too much admiration for the book," she told one interviewer. "The book is the book and the film has to be something else."[57]

This discussion of *Mrs. Dalloway* focuses on the elements in it that draw on the heritage genre and those that seem to connect the film to Gorris's earlier work. This will be useful in analyzing the critical response and the context in which the film found itself as a success or a failure. In terms of the heritage film, then, the film deploys the subject matter and aesthetic associated with the genre. The film is set on one day in 1923, the day on which Clarissa Dalloway holds a party, but it moves back to the 1890s to tell the story of the decisions Clarissa made as a girl that led her into marriage to Richard; making connections with this is the story of shell-shocked Septimus, who is haunted by a particular event in the First World War, which is also reprised in flashback. In this way, the film contrasts the past with the past as well as with our own present. Unlike *Time Regained*, the film works to smooth out narrative difficulties and to make connections between events and characters clear. The audience is led to an understanding of Clarissa and also is confirmed in its sympathy for the brutal treatment that Septimus receives at the hands of the doctor, sympathy that draws on late twentieth-century understandings of the Great War. As in many heritage films, the audience is offered both a nostalgic evocation of a gracious way of upper-middle-class life and confirmation of its own superior understanding of the social problems of the day.

Mrs. Dalloway also draws on the fascination with costume and sets that is a feature of heritage films, a genre that was much better established in 1998 than when *Swann in Love* was released in 1984. The story of Clarissa's girlhood deploys the characteristic iconography of the genre—the country house with its cluttered but comfortable rooms, the sunny, green lawns and formal terraces, and the lake with its rowing boats. The young women wear beautiful dresses (Clarissa's mainly in white), and the set pieces—formal dinner at the house, the nighttime rowing trip with the sound of singing softly drifting over the water, and the tea party on the lawn with which the film closes—are presented as episodes in a lost but perfect time. In the 1923 present, London venues—Big Ben, the green parks, and the squares and alleyways—are recreated with verisimilitude so that Clarissa seems indeed to take possession of the everyday life of the city. Her own home, though, is filmed in a more restrained mode; in particular, Clarissa's bedroom is, as she comments, an austere setting with "its sheets stretched and its bed narrow." In the 1923 scenes, flowers and dress provide sensuousness: the eau-de-nil coat and hat Clarissa wears to do her morning errands, for instance, and the texture of the beaded evening dress that she mends and holds against herself at several points during the day and wears for the party. But while in the 1890s sequence the visual pleasure of setting and costume tends to outweigh their narrative purpose, in the 1920s story they are delicately fixed into the story: Clarissa's extravagant hat permits Richard's loving commendation at Lady Bruton's lunch, revealing something of his feeling for his wife ("I love that hat," says the unromantic Richard in a revealing slip of sentiment); the baby on his uniformed nurse's lap in the park moves from being a charming extra touch to the unconscious cause of a chance meeting between Peter and Septimus's wife.

I will discuss the casting of Vanessa Redgrave later, but here we need to note that the ensemble cast features a whole range of British character actors in a manner characteristic of the heritage film. Different actors play the younger and older main characters—Clarissa, Peter, Sally, and Richard Dalloway—so inviting comparison of their looks, demeanor, and gesture; Michael Kitchen's rather seedy, middle-aged Peter is a contrast with the more winning forcefulness of his romantic younger self, while Natascha McElhone's Clarissa, though different physically, at points shares Redgrave's preoccupied, dreamy air. The doubleness of the adaptation is showcased in this comparison of younger and older selves (which draws attention to a similar comparison process that might be made to the book), but Robert Hardy is reassuringly recognizable as the brisk, brusque, and rather grand Sir William Bradshaw, while Rupert Graves is one of a number of actors with a history of parts in heritage films. Some of the cameo roles blur into the setting of the grand house (Phyllis Calvert as Aunt Helena), but others are sharp and self-contained. Margaret Tyzack precisely defines Lady Bruton as a woman whose girlish, flirtatious seeking of male power has grown practiced and rapacious with long use.

These heritage features overlap with rather than being separate from the elements in the film that suggest Gorris as the authorial presence. *Mrs. Dalloway*, like many heritage films, places a woman's decisions and feelings at its center. Gorris's *Question of Silence* controversially centered on an understanding between women who had never previously met that leads them to commit murder. Though *Mrs. Dalloway* is less overt, a thread of sympathetic understanding runs through the film in its presentation of Clarissa's relationship with women. This is most explicit in the relationship between young Sally and Clarissa, which is in many ways the most powerful in the film. The friendship between them is intimate and intense. Sally is bolder in her feminism ("marriage is a catastrophe for women") and her love for Clarissa ("we'll do everything together") but also understands something of Clarissa's doubts about being overwhelmed by Peter's love. The sexual feeling between Clarissa and Sally is unspoken but given physical expression in the way in which they touch each other, culminating in the sensuous dance and kiss interrupted by Peter; the length with which the shot after the kiss is held underlines Clarissa's excitement and puzzlement. She will shut down on the possibilities of this relationship more firmly but perhaps with more regret than the love affair with Peter, and the older Sally continues to understand and defend her friend's "charm, purity, generosity." This central relationship is underscored by the older Clarissa's encounters with women throughout the film. Unlike Lady Bruton, Clarissa puts no social barriers between herself and the women who serve her, responding enthusiastically to the woman in the flower shop and drawing her maid out of the house to share the fun of the plane writing slogans in the sky. And although, at the party, many of her comments are critical of the social roles played by the women who attend, the long scene in which she meditates on the unknown Septimus's death is marked by a look between her and an older women who is looking out from the window opposite; the two share a long gaze of understanding before the woman shuts the curtains and Clarissa's voice resumes.

This feminist discourse is intertwined with a more feminine discourse that reflects on both creativity and romance. Unlike the Proust films, there is no overt discourse of the writer here. Instead, Clarissa's creativity finds expression in the highly feminine way in which she makes social situations work through her personal investment in them. Her creative act is not just the party but also the connections made between everyday social actions and the inner life that suffuses them with meaning. This emphasis on the care with which personal life must be lived links to the presentation of Clarissa's rejection of romantic and indeed sexual love. The film draws attention to some of the consequences of this but is sympathetic both to her doubts about Peter and her fear of losing herself in desire. The older Clarissa draws on the character of Christine in *Question of Silence* who stops talking because she is not listened to. But *Mrs. Dalloway* also fits into the British tradition of restraint, which goes beyond the heritage film to a melodrama like *Brief Encounter* (Lean, 1945) in which the heroine's everyday life has hidden meanings and her voice-over shares with the audience the consequences of choosing her loving but unexciting marriage. Like Laura, Clarissa keeps her inner conversations to herself, and her final "here I am at last" to Peter at the end of the film is feminine, sociable, and performative but enigmatic.

The women of *Question of Silence* are held together by editing, particularly in the montage of exchanged looks between them before and during the murder of the shopkeeper. The editing in *Mrs. Dalloway* is less abrupt and challenging though there is a hint of this approach when Sir William brings news of Septimus's suicide into the party; Clarissa's subjective response is expressed through a series of brief close-ups of eyes and mouths, cut together as Clarissa's voice-over says, "Don't talk of death at my party." Generally, though, the cutting is more fluid, making narrative connections between past and present as the voice-over of Mrs. Dalloway takes us back into the past or the events in the past are cut into her present. Sometimes this editing is managed through dialogue and action. "What a plunge!" is repeated by the older and younger Clarissa as they joyously open a door and window respectively at the beginning of the film, while a shot of Mrs. Dalloway looking at herself in the mirror dissolves to a mirror shot of young Clarissa brushing her hair as she and

Sally get ready for bed. But part of the fluidity of the film is due to the fact that this intermingling of past and present is not just created through narrative connections but also through those of color, light, and feeling. So, we cut from the virginal whiteness of young Clarissa's nightdress to the soft whiteness of the curtains of the London bedroom, and then the image dissolves back into the vanilla white of the girl's costume as she moves into the camera. The color and sensuousness of the sweet peas in the flower shop dissolve into a close-up of pink and blue flowerheads floating in a bowl of water, a rather avant-garde table decoration created by young Sally. A shot of the rich colors of the evening dress the nostalgic Clarissa twirls round on its hanger dissolves in to a close-up of the silky, stretched fabric of the buttoned bodice of the younger girl as she luxuriously dances in Sally's arms. The female sensuality of this emphasis on color and texture is in contrast with Septimus's flashbacks that erupt into 1923 with a dramatic forcefulness, taking over the present rather than merging the two time periods.

Mrs. Dalloway therefore brings together the femininity of the heritage film and the feminism associated with the director. Again, for some critics the generic pull was too strong. It was "an enervated and discontinuous version of a standard Brit Lit costume drama."[58] And the London *Times* critic despaired at "the parade of dresses and vintage cars, the museum cabinet of social attitudes. This is not a Merchant-Ivory film. . . . But it often behaves like one."[59] The key to a more sympathetic approach was likely to lie with attitudes taken to Vanessa Redgrave who, it was frequently noted, bore a physical resemblance to Woolf. Redgrave could be associated with the heritage film's tendency to offer a showcase to the great actresses of British theater, and certainly, as Gorris herself suggested, the film depended on her performance. For critics concerned with Woolf's literary achievement, Redgrave's acting served to get over some of the problems of adaptation and was linked to the stream of consciousness of the novel. As a result, David Denby feels that *"Mrs. Dalloway* is at its most inventive, and most Woolfian, when Redgrave is front and center, behaving with elaborate social grace and thinking very different things to herself. . . . Redgrave makes the heroine all of a piece—timid, conventional, but alive to every breeze of consciousness."[60]

For Roger Ebert, too, Redgrave provided a way of rendering the novel's defining characteristic:

> Redgrave's performance steers us through. . . . Stream-of-consciousness stays entirely within the mind. Movies photograph only the outsides of things. The narration is a useful device but so are Redgrave's eyes, as she looks at the guests at her party. Once we have the clue, she doesn't really look at all like a safe, respectable, middle-aged hostess. More like a caged animal—trained, but not tamed.[61]

Vanessa Redgrave in Mrs. Dalloway *(1997). Vanessa Redgrave was likely chosen for this role because of her physical resemblance to Woolf and her status as one of the great actresses of British theater.* Source: *First Look Pics/Bayly/Pare/The Kobal Collection*

For such critics, it was acting rather than editing that rendered cinematically the modernist techniques Woolf was using, and the friendlier response that the film got in the United States can be attributed to this willingness to accept Redgrave's performance as the equivalent of Woolf's prose.

But Redgrave is also known as a feminist and a political activist whose views on Palestine, for instance, have been controversial. This linked her to a rather different Woolf, the author of *A Room of One's Own*, and gave Mrs. Dalloway's thoughts and actions a more political slant. Redgrave's persona and her acting could provide a bridge between the heritage aspects of the film and its feminist undertones. For Amy Taubin, this was critical: "What differentiates it [the film] from Merchant-Ivory costume claptrap," she argues, "is its feminism," which was exemplified in "Redgrave's extraordinary performance."[62]

Three female figures, Woolf, Gorris, and Redgrave, are brought together by *Mrs. Dalloway* and are used in different ways to create the criteria by which the film can be judged. In general, the feminist credentials of the director are noted but not treated as determining, and although the film had mixed reviews, it was successful in the U.S. art house market. Something rather different happens with an adaptation by another feminist director, Chantal Akerman. Akerman was offered the opportunity to

adapt *La Prisonnière* by the producer of *Time Regained*. The Belgian-born
Akerman, now based in France, saw the film as "a free adaptation, what
I call 'inspired by.' . . . You start by asking 'What do I remember of the
book?' Then what you get comes out of your own consciousness, so it's already different from the original."[63] Unlike Gorris and indeed Ruiz, Akerman translated the novel to a modern (though indeterminately dated)
Paris, in this way removing any danger of it crossing over the line into the
heritage genre. Instead, the adaptation is firmly associated with Akerman
herself and with cinema.

Akerman's earlier work was, as Annette Kuhn indicated, "important . . .
for the question of feminine writing in cinema."[64] In *Jeanne Dielman*, in
particular, she established a minimalist style that refused the continuity
editing and the shot/reverse shot mechanisms by which mainstream cinema engages the spectator. Instead, the use of medium shots, a static camera, and long takes amounted to a "refusal to set up privileged points-of-
view on the action."[65] It was a style that both distanced the spectator but
paradoxically created tension in the attentive viewer as small changes in
the character's pattern of action signified major turmoil. This work could
be positioned in various ways; Kuhn argues that *Jeanne Dielman* was appropriated for feminist cinema but "might in certain contexts be read as
an art-house movie or as a structuralist-minimalist film."[66] *La Captive* did
not change this approach. If Gorris moved to the mainstream with *Mrs.
Dalloway*, Akerman maintained her commitment to the avant-garde.

This meant that not only did Akerman refuse the "ornate *belle-epoche*
iconography" of the earlier Proust adaptations, but she also refused the
"baroque *mise-en-scene*" they drew on to stand in for his elaborate prose.[67]
Instead, *La Captive*'s style, in the manner of art cinema, carries the signature of the director as auteur. The story of Simon's obsession with Ariane,
his fruitless quest to find out what she is feeling, is taken from the source,
but the style of the film is Akerman's "trademark, minimalist style."[68] Although the film shows us Parisian streets and venues, the geography of
the film is determined by this rather than the realist detail associated with
mainstream cinema. How does Ariane disappear so quickly from the hotel when Simon is trailing her? Where are Sarah and Isabelle when Simon
questions them about their lesbian relationships? The spaces of the film
have no function but to render Stephen's obsession: the half-decorated
corridor in the flat that the characters move along and across; the deserted
streets and steep steps that echo with sounds of women's high heels; and
the backseat of the car with Simon and Ariane framed against the back
window through which the silent movement of traffic can be seen. In part,
we share Simon's viewpoint, but the camera serves to position him as
well. Like Simon, we see Ariane like the Sleeping Beauty in her cot, but
we also see him enter the frame to attempt an embrace. The still camera

and long takes frame characters in doorways and at windows but also' frame absence, the loss of the human from the image. When the camera does move, it does not necessarily follow the characters or help with the narrative line; when Simon and Ariane go to the park, the scene opens with a close-up of the grass as the camera moves with them but does not initially show them.

La Captive opens with Simon obsessively studying flickering home movie footage of Ariane and her friends at the beach. The film continually draws attention to the difficulties of the narrative in the classic manner of the art film, organizing space and time around the psychological obsessions of one character but leaving the audience with "really a very opaque movie."[69] Although reviewers refer to the film's adaptation status, it arouses much less controversy than was the case with *Swann in Love* or even *Time Regained*. Like *Mrs. Dalloway*, *La Captive* is placed in the critical context of feminist auteur and genre, but it is positioned in a rather different way. Its genre is the art film rather than the heritage movie, so its distribution and the critical response are more limited; indeed, the film found its most enthusiastic audiences on the festival circuit. Like *Mrs. Dalloway*, though, it was possible to read the film in three ways. For some, the feminist auteur was the key. Amy Taubin described it as a "contemporary surrealist masterpiece and Akerman's most fully realized feature since *Jeanne Dielman*"; in it she found not just the themes of the novel but Akerman's own preoccupations: "The most despairing depiction of her recurrent theme: the impossible desire to merge the self with the other—always in her films a stand-in for the long-lost mother."[70] Other critics explained *La Captive* as an art film, sometimes going back to the films that Bordwell had used to define the genre. Walker, unusual in giving an enthusiastic review in the popular press, framed his response in this way: *La Captive*, he wrote, "feels like an authentic art-house movie brought out of the 1960s deep freeze," comparing it to "those ambulatory 1960s' films of Antonioni or Agnes Varda."[71] The film's difficulty can then be linked less to the problems of filming Proust than to the handling of the genre; for one online critic *La Captive* felt like "an even more inert version of Antonioni's *L'Avventura* without the overriding mystery that made that film so compelling and enduring."[72]

As with *Mrs. Dalloway*, the film could be read in another way using a third figure as a way of explaining the interaction between authorship and genre. In this case it was not an actor but another director, Alfred Hitchcock. The theme of obsessive love was associated with Hitchcock as well as Proust, and Akerman herself in the interviews that publicized the film refers to *Vertigo* (1958) as one source.[73] The references were clear in the scenes when Simon follows Ariane to the museum and in the drive to the coast at the end as well as in the use of music. This tended to take

attention away from the source in Proust since *La Captive*'s stylistic references could be credited elsewhere. Hitchcock's reputation reinforced appreciation of *La Captive* as a highly cinematic film in which the director is
in control. But the reference also associates the film with both a more popular auteur than Michelangelo Antonioni and a more popular genre than
the art film, the thriller. Hitchcock could help make the balance right between Proust and Akerman, source and adaptation. Writing of the ending,
Hoberman notes that "the breakup—as dogged and excruciating as
everything else—takes its dialogue from Proust but feels like *Vertigo* once
more." The effect of balancing Proust and Hitchcock is to ensure the film
is assigned to its true author, and Hoberman concludes, "Akerman has
fashioned a great negative love story, a long stare into the abyss of the
night."[74] Even for those more doubtful about the literary source, the name
of Hitchcock ensures that the film works as a piece of cinema: "For all its
somber literary pedigree, Akerman playfully grounds her film in cinematic traditions by including resonant references to that other masterpiece of masochistic obsession, Alfred Hitchcock's *Vertigo*."[75]

ULYSSES AND THE BRITISH NEW WAVE

The critical response to *Mrs. Dalloway* and *La Captive* was mixed, but sympathetic critics were able to find resonances in both films by calling on the
status of the director and by mediating the film through a source other
than the original. In ending this chapter I want to discuss a film for which
this was not possible and suggest why this was so. Strick's *Ulysses* is generally now seen as a complete failure, though as we shall see critical response at the time was more mixed. Crucially, the film's reception was
dominated by questions of censorship. Once that was taken away, faithfulness was the dominant critical question—but could there be another
way of treating this impossible adaptation?

The critical response to *Ulysses* was framed by the arguments about reg-
ulation and censorship that Strick used to present himself as a champion
of artistic freedom. In the UK and elsewhere, the film became mired in
censorship problems, which meant that there was general press interest as
well as reviews when the film was finally shown. In relation to the film itself, though, the critical commentary covered the now familiar ground of
the critical discourse associated with a modernist adaptation. The difficulties of filming such an important and difficult novel, combined with its
challenge to the censors, generated publicity that emphasized Strick's
commitment to his much cherished project. The search for authenticity
with the filming in Dublin and the use of actors from the Abbey Theatre
was well rehearsed, and as the director, Strick presented his role as being

to serve the original author without interposing himself into the work. The British broadsheets felt that Strick "knows and sticks to his limits," providing a film that was "not overburdened with the director's imagination"[76] and praised the film for not "entering into competition with the great book."[77] For the tabloid the *Sun*, it was "not a great piece of film making but a great work of art given some loving justice."[78] There were, again, reflections on whether the audience who did not know the book would understand the film. John Coleman had tried and failed to reread the book: "What one can't judge," he commented, "is how coherent the film will be for those who have never embarked on the Joyce but to me it made refreshing sense."[79] *The People*, a populist Sunday paper, addressed its readers directly and warned that "if you haven't read the book—and how many people have at 30 shillings a time—you will find much of it confusing and some of it boring."[80]

Those who judged the film by its faithfulness to the book tended to conclude that the film had failed to render the achievement of Joyce as an author. Strick's attempts to illustrate Joyce's words were simply "inept" because "nothing of the psychomythical significance remains and very little of the Joyce voice and whilom Irish music."[81] "Some equivalent of Joyce's all-important tone of voice"[82] was lacking, and the reviewer for *Sight and Sound*, describing the film as "a vulgar reading of the novel," argued that there was a "a failure to see *Ulysses* as a novel in which the reader is constantly sensible of the author's presence. . . . Without Joyce . . . a void gapes at its very centre."[83] Such critics, if they found merit, tended to praise the rendering of Molly's final soliloquy, finding in Barbara Jefford's acting something of that element of performance that had been so important in critical acceptance of *Mrs. Dalloway*.

It was possible to see the adaptation as successful if its credentials as an art film were accepted. U.S. critic Bosley Crowther felt it was "as faithful and fine a screen translation of James Joyce's 'Ulysses' as anyone with taste, imagination and a practical knowledge of this medium could ask" and that "everything essential to the story . . . is packed [in]." Significantly, in discussing the Nighttown sequence, he makes a connection between art film discourse and the voice of the original author, commenting that this segment is "every bit as meaningful and brilliant as a similar passage in Federico Fellini's *8½*, and it is explicitly faithful to the spirit and the word of Mr. Joyce." Crowther also praised the film's "frank and honest quality" and felt that the film had been true to "Joyce's candid language, and his descriptions of the erotic fantasies."[84]

The advertising for *Ulysses* emphasized its truthfulness: "The most important novel of the 20th century now comes to the screen with all its frank, bold, searing insight into the heart and mind of man."[85] Although the censorship furor that surrounded it was exceptional, it was not unique. Other films of the late 1950s and early 1960s had gone this way before. They too were adaptations, though of new novels rather than modernist classics, and their challenge to British culture carved out a way of viewing that did not rely on comparison with their literary sources. The sensationalist way in which they were sold—*Room at the Top* (Clayton, 1959) was trailered as "a savage story of lust and ambition," while *Saturday Night and Sunday Morning* (Reisz, 1960) "makes *Room at the Top* look like a vicarage tea party"—attracted young audiences and those dissatisfied with the comedies and war films that were a key feature of British cinema in the fifties. Such films were identified as being part of the British new wave and so associated with the French and Italian films that Bordwell later drew on in his definition of art cinema. They pushed at the boundaries of what could be shown and said on British screens, making the X certificate acceptable for adult audiences. The critical discourse that surrounded them was exactly what *Ulysses* tried to invoke, praise for "sheer blatant honesty" and being "savagely frank and brutally truthful."[86]

It is possible to see some of the more interesting elements of Strick's film in relation to the conventions established by these earlier films. *Ulysses*'s black-and-white photography, its realist setting in the streets of contemporary Dublin, and its emphasis on everyday behavior and vernacular speech all speak of the British new wave's promise to show a different version of reality on the screen, a reality that was urban but not metropolitan London and that belonged to the working class. *Ulysses* consistently positions itself both inside and outside this reality, and its use of places beyond the streets of Dublin—the tower at the beginning, the cemetery, and the wide sweep of the beaches—fits the new wave's propensity for making a spectacle of the ordinary by observing it, in an aesthetically pleasing composition, from a distance. The Nighttown sequences have the surrealistic air of the fantasy sequences of *Billy Liar* (Schlesinger, 1963), while the emphasis on sexual behavior, sometimes presented comically but seen as central to an honest understanding of the human condition, had been previewed in the earlier films. Even Molly's monologue could be understood as the kind of representation of a mature, sexual woman that Simone Signoret had offered in *Room at the Top* or Rachel Roberts in *This Sporting Life* (Anderson, 1963). One could indeed argue that some of *Ulysses*'s problems occur when it fails to match the new wave model. T. P. McKenna's racy performance complemented Maurice Roëves's more dreamy air, but Milo O'Shea as Bloom dominated the film, and none of them could be viewed as a vivid and convincing young star in the manner of Laurence Harvey, Albert Finney, or Tom Courtenay.

This use of the new wave as a framework might explain the relatively sympathetic response of at least some of the British press, including the more populist papers. For them, notions of faithfulness were related not so much to the adaptation process but to the honesty with which the film handled sexual material. It is perhaps not surprising when a critic for an intellectual, progressive magazine praises the film for its "unusual interest in trying to be truthful about both sexual, and loving, material."[87] But the pervasiveness of this discourse is illustrated when a critic for a middle-brow paper comments that "above all it is an honest film which is probably why many people will find it shocking,"[88] while the frankly populist *The People* concluded that "for adults who don't mind a few shocks and want to brush up their culture, this is THE picture of the year."[89] In this kind of reviewing, for what is by any standards a difficult film in terms of narrative and language, we can see how the film might be differently positioned if it were read in terms of the preoccupations of 1960s (British) cinema rather than as an adaptation. For if Strick's *Ulysses* deserves our attention now, it is worth considering it not as an adaptation but rather as an oddity that throws light on British cinema of the 1960s.

NOTES

1. Deborah Cartmell, I. Q. Hunter, Heidi Kaye, and Imelda Whelehan, eds., *Classics in Film and Television* (London: Pluto Press, 2000).

2. David Bordwell, "The Art Cinema as a Model of Film Practice" (1979), reprinted in *The European Cinema Reader*, ed. Catherine Fowler (London: Routledge, 2002), 95.

3. David Bordwell, *Narration in the Fiction Film* (London: Methuen, 1985), 206.

4. Bordwell, *Narration in the Fiction Film*, 208.

5. Bordwell, "The Art Cinema as a Model of Film Practice," 99.

6. Bordwell, *Narration in the Fiction Film*, 207–8.

7. Bordwell, "The Art Cinema as a Model of Film Practice," 97.

8. Bordwell, *Narration in the Fiction Film*, 211.

9. Bordwell, *Narration in the Fiction Film*, 231.

10. Steve Neale, "Art Cinema as Institution," *Screen* 22, no. 1 (Spring 1981): 35.

11. Janet Harbord, *Film Cultures* (London: Sage, 2002), 52–54.

12. John Hill, *British Cinema in the 1980s* (Oxford: Clarendon Press, 1999), 78.

13. See Ginette Vincendeau, ed., *Film/Literature/Heritage* (London: British Film Institute Publications, 2001), for a range of articles on heritage cinema in the 1990s that also emphasises a European context.

14. Arthur Holmberg, "Proust Is Filmed at Last," *New York Times*, July 24, 1983.

15. *Evening Standard* headline, February, 24, 1984.

16. Phil Powrie, "Marketing History: *Swann in Love*," *Film Criticism* 12, no. 3 (Spring 1988): 33.

17. Holmberg, "Proust Is Filmed at Last."

18. David Robinson, "Magical Fragment of Remembrance," *Times* (London), April 6, 1984.

19. Holmberg, "Proust Is Filmed at Last."

20. Quoted in Powrie, "Marketing History," 37.

21. Powrie, "Marketing History," 37.

22. Derek Malcolm, "Coming Home to Proust," *Guardian*, April 5, 1984.

23. Schlöndorff, quoted in Holmberg, "Proust Is Filmed at Last."

24. David Denby, review of *Swann in Love*, *New York Magazine*, September 24, 1984.

25. Pauline Kael, review of *Swann in Love*, *New Yorker*, October 1, 1984, 112. Denby, review of *Swann in Love*, 94; Vincent Canby, "'Swann in Love': A Proustian Vignette from France," *New York Times*, September, 14, 1984.

26. Roger Shattuck, "Not Swann's Way," *New York Review of Books*, September 16, 1984, 40–43.

27. Denby, review of *Swann in Love*.

28. Claire Tomalin, "Proust Goes to the Movies," *Sunday Times* (London), March 25, 1984.

29. Jill Forbes, "Alas Poor Swann *Un Amour de Swann*," *Sight and Sound* 53, no. 3 (Summer 1984): 221.

30. Nigel Andrews, "Passion's Swann Song," *Financial Times*, April 6, 1984.

31. Peter Ackroyd, "Dressing Up," *Spectator*, April 14, 1984.

32. David Castell, "Faithful in Spirit," *Sunday Telegraph*, April 8, 1984.

33. Tom Hutchinson, "The Star in the Irons' Mask," *Mail on Sunday*, April 8, 1984.

34. William Russell, "Cheers for Proust without Tears," *Glasgow Herald*, April 28, 1984.

35. Richard Barkley, "When a Man Is Crazy with Desire," *Sunday Express*, April 8, 1984.

36. Janet Maslin, "From Sickbed to Boyhood and Back, Echoing Proust," *New York Times*, September 30, 1999.

37. Jonathan Rosenbaum, "The Sweet Cheat," *Chicago Reader*, www.chicagoreader.com/movies/archives/2000/0700/000721.html.

38. Keith Reader, "*Time Regained*—Review," *Sight and Sound* 10, no. 1 (January 2000): 61.

39. Rosenbaum, "The Sweet Cheat."

40. J. Hoberman, "The Searchers," *Village Voice*, June 14–20, 2000.

41. Tom Charity, "Memory Man," *Time Out*, January 5, 2000, original emphasis.

42. Rosenbaum, "The Sweet Cheat."

43. Adam Mars-Jones, "Le Temps Retrouve," *Financial Times*, January 6, 2000.

44. Michael O'Sullivan, "It's 'time' to get confused," *Washington Post*, December 15, 2000.

45. Philip French, "Time Regained," *Observer*, January 9, 2000.

46. Alexander Walker, "Marcel Marks Time," *Evening Standard*, January 6, 2000.

47. Rosenbaum, "The Sweet Cheat."

48. Gilbert Adair, "And It's Not Just for Proustians," *Independent on Sunday*, January 9, 2000.

49. Hoberman, "The Searchers."

50. Andrew O'Hagan, "Time Perfectly Managed," *Daily Telegraph*, January 7, 2000.

51. Reader, *"Time Regained*—Review," 61.

52. Rosenbaum, "The Sweet Cheat."

53. Jonathan Romney, "Masque of the Living Dead," *Sight and Sound* 10, no. 1 (January 2000): 31.

54. Roger Ebert, *"Mrs. Dalloway,"* March 6, 1998, rogerebert.suntimes.com/.

55. Augusta Palmer, "Seven Questions with Marleen Gorris," *IndieWIRE*, February 23, 1998, www.indiewire.com/people/int_Gorris_Marleen_980223.html.

56. Palmer, "Seven Questions."

57. Tom Lyons, "Who's Afraid of Virginia Woolf," *Eye Weekly*, February 26, 1998, www.eye.net/eye/issue/issue_02.26.98/film/dalloway.php.

58. Mathew Sweet, review of *Mrs. Dalloway*, *Independent on Sunday*, March 8, 1998.

59. Geoff Brown, review of *Mrs. Dalloway*, *Times* (London), March 5, 1998.

60. David Denby, "Grace Notes," *New York Magazine*, February 23, 1998.

61. Ebert, *"Mrs. Dalloway."*

62. Amy Taubin, "Between the Acts," *Village Voice*, February 24, 1998, 61.

63. Nick James, "Magnificent Obsession: Interview with Chantal Ackerman," *Sight and Sound* 11, no. 5 (May 2001): 21.

64. Annette Kuhn, *Women's Pictures: Feminism and Cinema* (London: Routledge and K. Paul, 1982), 174.

65. Kuhn, *Women's Pictures*, 174.

66. Kuhn, *Women's Pictures*, 195.

67. Ginette Vincendeau, *"The Captive,"* *Sight and Sound* 11, no. 5 (May 2001): 45.

68. Vincendeau, *"The Captive,"* 45.

69. Peter Bradshaw, *"La Captive,"* *Guardian*, April 27, 2001.

70. Amy Taubin, "Scavengers Uncover a Mother Lode," *Village Voice*, March 7–13, 2001.

71. Alexander Walker, "Love, Not Sex," *Evening Standard*, April 26, 2000.

72. Jeremy Heilman, *"La Captive,"* *MovieMartyr*, August, 5, 2002, www.moviemartyr.com/2000/lacaptive.htm.

73. See James, "Magnificent Obsession," for an example.

74. J. Hoberman, "Persistence of Memory," *Village Voice*, www.villagevoice.com/film/0111,hoberman,23036,20.html.

75. Ken Fox, review of *La Captive*, www.tvguide.com/movies/la-captive/review/135971 (emphasis in original).

76. Eric Shorter, "Sensitive *'Ulysses'* on Screen," *Daily Telegraph*, May 31, 1967.

77. Robert Robinson, "Stricksday," *Sunday Telegraph*, June 4, 1967.

78. Anne Pacey, *"'Ulysses'*: It's What She Says, Not What She Does," *Sun*, May 31, 1967.

79. John Coleman, "Bloomovie?" *New Statesman*, June 2, 1967.

80. Ernest Betts, "Great—If You Don't Shock Too Easily," *The People* (UK), June 4, 1967.

81. "Not the Best, Not the Worst," *Time*, March 31, 1967, 40.

82. Penelope Houston, "Words Fail Him," *Spectator*, June 9, 1967.

83. James Price, "Ulysses," *Sight and Sound* 36, no. 3 (Summer 1967): 144–45.

84. Bosley Crowther, "'Ulysses' Brings a Faithful View of Joyce's Dubliners: Movie Will Open Today for Three Days' Stay," *New York Times*, March 14, 1967.

85. Publicity material held in the British Film Institute library, London.

86. Reviews of *Room at the Top* cited in John Hill, *Sex, Class, and Realism: British Cinema 1956–1963* (London: British Film Institute Publications, 1986), 191.

87. Coleman, "Bloomovie?"

88. Ian Christie, review of *Ulysses, Daily Express*, May 31, 1967.

89. Betts, "Great—If You Don't Shock Too Easily" (emphasis in original).

3

Tennessee Williams on Film
Space, Melodrama, and Stardom

This chapter looks at the issues raised by the adaptation of plays for the screen through a study of some of the films made from Tennessee Williams's plays. In some ways, filming plays might seem more straightforward than filming novels. The time frame of a play and a film are comparable with most mainstream films and plays lasting between 90 minutes and 180 minutes; narrative time passing in a play can be aligned with that of cinema through the use of scenes in which dramatic action takes place uninterrupted by ellipses. There are generally fewer speaking characters in plays than in novels and fewer side stories and parallel plots. Both cinema and theater involve performance in a way in which the characterization in a novel does not, and both forms rely on an audience being brought together in a specialized space for the particular purpose of engagement with the form. As Gene D. Phillips puts it, both forms are "designed to be performed before an audience,"[1] though what is being performed clearly differs.

I have chosen to look at the relationship between theater and cinema through films based on Tennessee Williams's plays in part because they offer interesting examples of the issues involved but mainly because they have been judged as unusually successful. Williams willingly worked on the adaptations, and the films were also successful in terms of Hollywood and the industry, garnering large audiences at a time when cinema attendance was falling and gaining numerous Academy Awards. Phillips commented that Williams's plays "proved easily adaptable"; "his loosely constructed plots are easily modified; his central characters are boldly drawn figures experiencing an emotional crisis with which audiences can easily identify."[2] And it has been argued that Williams's adaptations in the 1950s (unlike those based on the work of his contemporaries Henry Miller and William Inge) "strongly influenced the development of the film industry itself."[3] Since their first release, the films have often been given a favorable response by those analyzing theater. There is a huge body of work on Williams, and although assessments about the films vary, the screen adaptations have been thought worthy of discussion and interesting in themselves. The films however have been less discussed in academic film theory. While they have provided material for specific studies on acting, for instance, as a group they have been overshadowed by interest in films of the same period by Nicholas Ray, Vincente Minnelli, and particularly, by Douglas Sirk's family melodramas.

Analysis of these film adaptations tends to emphasize the differences between the films and the original plays. This work has been shaped by issues of censorship. Williams was a controversial writer for the theater, and the 1950s adaptations of his plays for cinema often involved extensive negotiation with those administering the Production Code. Since cinema's self-regulation in the postwar period was stricter than theater's, it was inevitable that cuts and compromises would be made; examples include the oblique representation of the rape in *A Streetcar Named Desire* (Kazan, 1951), the removal of homosexuality as the hinge of the plot in *Cat on a Hot Tin Roof* (Brooks, 1958), and the deletion of venereal disease and abortion in *Sweet Bird of Youth* (Brooks, 1962).[4] Though some critics such as Phillips have been unusually sympathetic to the changes made, this focus on censorship has tended to present a version of adaptation in which the original text is once again transformed for the worse, this time because of the commercial interests of Hollywood and its lack of respect for the work of individuals such as Elia Kazan and Williams who struggled against it. This is reinforced by the tendency to associate the Williams adaptations with what is seen as the prevailing tendency to melodrama in 1950s Hollywood. "Overall," writes R. Barton Palmer in summary, "Williams' plays are melodramatized . . . provided with characters able to achieve, after a purgatorial journey of self-discovery, a happy ending."[5]

While acknowledging the impact of censorship, I want to begin from a different point. This chapter therefore starts by looking directly at the question of adaptation from theater to cinema by considering how the film theorist André Bazin presented the issues raised by film adaptations based on plays. It then explores two key issues—the handling of space and performance—in relation to adaptations of *A Streetcar Named Desire* and *The Rose Tattoo* (Mann, 1955). In the final section, I continue to discuss these issues in relation to *Cat on a Hot Tin Roof* but open up this analysis to an awareness of film genres and consider in particular the accusation of melodrama.

André Bazin was a highly influential figure in the development of film theory and criticism in the 1940s and 1950s, at the same time that Williams's work in theater and cinema was making him famous. Bazin's work has continued to inform critical debate about adaptations since then. James Naremore chose one of his essays, "Adaptation, or the Cinema as Digest," to open his influential *Film Adaptation* collection, praising its open-minded flexibility and suggesting, as Robert Stam later put it, that he "foreshadowed some of the later structuralist and post-structuralist currents which would indirectly undermine a fidelity discourse in relation to adaptation."[6] Here I will concentrate on Bazin's two essays on theater and cinema that offer an approach that appreciates the differences between the two media without, as Naremore and Stam appreciated, getting mired in questions of faithfulness.

Bazin offers a summary of how the difference between the two media is traditionally explained, an explanation that can still be found in much analysis today and that tends to create a hierarchy in which theater emerges as the more engaging and demanding medium. The differences are rooted in two defining concepts—physical presence and audience activity. In the theater, the audience is in the physical presence of the actors whose performances relate directly to the particular audience in front of them; in the cinema, the actors' performance is recorded and takes place is a different space from that of the audience. Both perform to an audience, but one involves a live performance by actors physically present, the other a mechanical recording of absent actors. This might seem to mean that the audience in the theater is the more readily absorbed by the medium, but it is argued that, unlike the film audience, the theater audience has to work to get engaged; it is not mechanically caught up as the film audience is in the close-ups and editing of mainstream cinema. The theater audience is envisaged as engaged in a social act that involves thought as well as feeling, while the cinema viewer is described as isolated, overemotional, and voyeuristic. In such a description, cinema's association with the mass media is clear, while theater's different relationship to its audience is deemed more likely to produce work of artistic value. And since this distinction is based on differences in media specificity, the processes of adaptation for the cinema once again seem set for failure.

Bazin does not dispute that there are differences that need to be acknowledged between theater and cinema but shifts the ground so that cinema is not inevitably the inferior form. This means changing a key element of difference, making it not the physical presence of the actor but the organization of space. The difference then is based not on something present in theater but absent from cinema but rather on the different approach to something they both share, the organization of space for an audience. Bazin suggests that theater marks out the stage as a "privileged spot," "an area materially enclosed, limited, circumscribed."[7] It is removed from everyday life and is unsuitable for the "slice of life" realism that is possible in cinema. Cinema's space, by contrast, "denies any frontiers to action," encouraging us to imagine limitless offscreen space rather than the wings to which actors retreat in theater.[8] For Bazin, therefore, the difficulty of filmed theater is centrally the difficulty of "transposing a text written for one dramaturgical system into another."[9] The dramatic force of the text and its performance is lost if cinema techniques are used to make us forget the boundaries of the stage. This is, he argues, a problem of décor, so that cinema, rather than opening up the stage, has to rein itself in so as to present "a space orientated towards an inner dimension only."[10] Neither cinema nor theater should be effaced in this process, but cinema must transform itself, "delve deeper into its own language," in order to effect a successful translation.[11]

Bazin argues that the organization of this defined space is written into the theatrical text and that the play "is unassailably protected by its text." This is not just a matter of retaining the words but recognizing that "the mode and style of production" are "already embodied in the text."[12] Because of this, a film that respects the play—and Bazin argues that adaptations of classics are bound to do so—has to follow "the direction it was supposed to go."[13] This means respecting the primacy that theater gives to words and the exploration of internal dilemmas of "the human soul."[14] Opening up a play (Bazin gives the example of a film of a Molière play set in a real forest) "in order to inject the power of 'cinema' into the theatre" actually skews the production "so that the dramatic primacy of the word is thrown off center by the additional dramatization that the camera gives to the setting."[15] This is the more painful because it is done in an attempt to compensate for cinema's "inferiority complex" as if "the 'superiority' of its technique" can lend "aesthetic superiority."[16]

In a typically paradoxical move, Bazin argues that rather than attempting to efface the differences between theater and cinema, filmed plays have to be faithful to the original and respect the different dramaturgical system that it was written for. As illustrations of the consequences of this approach, Bazin cites Laurence Olivier's *Henry V* (1945) and Jean Cocteau's *Les Parents Terribles* (1948). The former offers a realist revelation (rather than an effacement) of theatrical artifice, exposing to a cinema audience the devices and acting styles of Elizabethan staging. The latter renounces some of the more common cinematic editing strategies, in particular editing to clarify narrative events and the shot–reverse shot editing that engages the cinema audience with the subjectivities of the characters by alternating their point of view. Instead, Bazin argues that in *Les Parents Terribles* the editing returns to "the principle of audience-stage relations," taking on the "viewpoint of the spectator, the one denominator common to stage and screen."[17] The camera takes on the role, not of the narrator or a character, but rather of the watcher; the audience is nearer to the action than it is in the theater but is denied cinema's conventional use of editing to bridge the gap between the audience and the site of action.

It is possible to argue against Bazin's accounts of the potentialities of theater and film, to see them as another attempt at limiting the possibilities of each medium. But Bazin's essays, printed in the same year as the film of *Streetcar* was released, provide a way of looking at how a film adaptation can both exploit the resources of cinema and acknowledge its source in theater. Thinking about this form of screen adaptation as a transposition from one dramaturgical space to another encourages us to think about how framing and editing create space in cinema, how performers are positioned in that space, and how acting uses the rhetoric required for the stage to reach out to a cinema audience. In looking at Williams adaptations through Bazin's framework, I hope to follow Palmer's proposal that film/play adaptation can be studied "in a larger sense, as designating how one medium comes to relate to another."[18]

A STREETCAR NAMED DESIRE: ## "STAGING A PLAY BY MEANS OF CINEMA"

It seems appropriate to examine the 1951 adaptation of *A Streetcar Named Desire* in the light of Bazin's comments on filmed theater. The film was strongly associated with the original theater production. It featured three out of the four main stage actors and was described by Elia Kazan, who directed both play and film, as "a good record of the play . . . preserving it forever."[19] In numerous interviews, looking back on the process, Kazan described how he worked on the film script to open the play out by "work[ing] backwards into Blanche's past"[20] but decided that this approach would not work. The process of adaptation is then presented in deceptively simple terms: "I took the script of the play, and I just made the play. And that's all I did," he told *Movie* in 1971,[21] while elsewhere he recalled that the filming involved "a few moves, a few slow dollies but mainly I shot from eye level with no tricks."[22] A study of the organization of space and performance suggests something rather more sophisticated than this.

The film opens with shots of a train running into New Orleans and Blanche arriving at the station, which seems to indicate that the film will open out the play for cinema. But behind the credits we have already seen what appear to be sketches of the main set, and when Blanche finds the two-story building the artificiality of the set itself confirms that the film is

set not so much in New Orleans as on stage. Although it was made on location and the set is full of domestic detail, it is not filmed to give the texture and situatedness of a real place. Exterior shots consistently give us
the two levels of the set as if viewed in the theater. Internally, the Kowalski apartment retains the organization of the theatrical set making, as de
Beauregard points out, "a diegetic space [that] looks like a 'cul de sac'"[23]
with three main areas: upstage, beyond the curtains, and the bathroom
"connotes a star's boudoir"; in the middle is the space "where she can
freely perform her role as an upper-class lady," while the downstage area
is an area she contests with the men.[24] For Kazan, the setting was expressive and malleable rather than realistic with its own solidity; he famously
made the rooms smaller, as the "shelter" Blanche seeks turns into a
"threatening dead-end."[25]

Although the film does show some streets of the quarter, these too are
heavily stylized. Compared with the streets of gangster films and thrillers
on which cars race and gunfights break out, these streets are cramped and
restricted. The arrival of the car in the front yard of the building confirms
the artificiality of the set and the limitations it places on the vehicle's
movements. The street scenes are used not so much for realism as to mark
the passage of the scenes of the play. And although some scenes are taken
out of the confines of the main set they too tend to retain the restrictions
of the stage. Blanche's date with Mitch is seen rather than just reported
on, but the couple quickly moves out of the main restaurant, away from
the dancing and the crowds, to sit on their own in the restricted space of
an outside landing. As with the main set, there is no sense here of a real
"outside." Darkness and mist confine our view to the space occupied by
the actors, the water reflects light back on to them, and we have no knowledge of or indeed interest in the offscreen space beyond the landing. The
presentation of the set and its restrictions could be compared to the way
in which the film of *Henry V* put the play into quotation marks, marking
the edges of theatrical space. It marks out the limits of the staging and
works within them.

A Streetcar Named Desire also deploys editing strategies that emphasize
its origins in theater. The film's editing strategies are not those of classical
Hollywood, and in particular they construct a position for the spectator
that is different from that created by the classic shot–reverse shot structure. Analysis of the opening sequence and of two early exchanges between Stanley and Stella and then Stanley and Blanche illustrates this. The
film's opening shots are accompanied by music appropriate for a thriller
as a blonde woman in a light dress is picked out by the camera. She is held
in a medium shot until the exchange with the sailor that includes a close-
up of him and her in a shot–reverse shot exchange. This is all conventional, but the next shot signals something different. The shot of the street-

car moving to its stop at first seems to be from Blanche's point of view since it is preceded by a close-up of her looking offscreen; however, as the shot is held, she herself enters the frame and boards the streetcar. In a thriller or horror film, this shot would be ascribed to the viewpoint of a hidden watcher to be revealed by the narrative; in this film, it is the viewpoint of the audience.

This subtle reworking of cinema's editing conventions can be seen throughout the film, although the pattern of editing is different for Stella and for Blanche. The first scene for analysis occurs between Stanley and Stella after he has brought in Blanche's trunk, which stands in the middle of the front room. Stella tries to persuade Stanley to be nice to Blanche; Stanley queries the sale of Belle Reve and their rights under the "Napoleonic Code" and pulls apparently expensive clothes out of the trunk, while Stella tries to tidy up around him. The two actors continually move, but there is no looking/reverse cutting between them; the dominant shot is a two-shot in which the two are either parallel with each other or in a diagonal line with one closer to the camera. In a scene of four and a half minutes, there are only five cuts, and reframing occurs not through cutting but as the camera follows an actor (normally the one who is speaking) into a different space, establishing a different relationship with the other actor and with objects in the apartment (the trunk, the sink, and the refrigerator). The effect of this is twofold. First, the spectator is not cut into the space of the action by being invited by editing to share the viewpoint of either character. Instead, we observe the action from outside in a manner that preserves the distance of the theater audience while lending it the closeness of cinema. Through the use of the moving camera, we are inside the proscenium arch, as if on the stage, but we are not implicated with the viewpoint of either character. The second effect is to give a physical rhythm to our understanding of the relationship between these two characters. They are conducting an argument, but their movements and the framing indicate a complete harmony between them. As if in a dance, they move together and away, weaving an elaborate pattern around each other. Stella has spoken to Blanche about how she "can't stand it" when Stanley is away; here we see the relationship between them given physical form, through space and movement, but are not invited to share it.

After Stella leaves, Blanche enters fresh from bathing, and the subsequent scene between her and Stanley also revolves around the trunk and the sale of Belle Reve. In this scene, too, there is an emphasis on two-shots, on changing the framing through movement rather than cutting as, for example, when the camera follows Blanche as she attempts to retrieve the love letters. However, the scene is also marked by the use of a wider range of editing strategies, including the exchange of looks between the characters through reverse cutting so the audience takes on the viewpoint of first

Marlon Brando and Vivien Leigh in A Streetcar Named Desire *(1951). The editing in the love-letter scene confirms that the film is "staging a play by means of cinema." Source: Warner Bros/The Kobal Collection*

Stanley and then Blanche as they look at each other. The scene starts with a shot of Blanche at the curtain followed by shots of her view of Stanley, and there are a number of points when we get shot–reverse shot close-ups exchanged between the two, for instance, when Stanley stops Blanche's flirtatious use of perfume. This editing strategy, therefore, while still maintaining the distance associated with the spectator's viewpoint, at various points draws on cinema's more voyeuristic devices to implicate the spectator in the relationship between these two characters. However, most of these close-ups strongly emphasize also the back or profile of the character who is looking so that, to amend Bazin's comment on Cocteau's framing, "the purpose of the shot is to show not that [they are] looking, not even [their] gaze, it is to *see [them] actually looking*."[26] In this way, while overall the spatial distance of theater is maintained, it is interwoven with the cutting characteristic of Hollywood cinema. Far from simply recording the play by recreating the proscenium arch, this editing, which indicates the different relationships between the characters and binds the audience into watching them watching, confirms that the film is "staging a play by means of cinema."[27]

So far I have emphasized patterns of movement and looking in this analysis of the organization of space through editing in the 1951 *Streetcar*. But speech is also an issue in filmed theater. Sarah Kozloff's valuable book *Overhearing Film Dialogue* reminds us that the common assertion, which Kazan himself upheld,[28] that film emphasizes image and theater dialogue is unhelpful. The point is more that, as Bazin argued, theater and film dialogue is written for different spaces and different audience positions. The editing patterns of cinema tend to suit the exchange of dialogue, and the long speeches that are a dramatic focal point in much theater can cause problems in the translation to cinema precisely because they are "inherited from theatrical practice."[29] Emphasizing the theatricality of such speech would seem to follow Bazin's logic, but Kazan takes a rather different route of maintaining the wholeness of the speeches but refusing the full visual dramatization that cutting and lighting might give. So, the speech in which Blanche tells Mitch about the suicide of her husband is visually downplayed. It starts with a medium close-up with Mitch in profile watching Blanche, who looks ahead with soft light on her face. The shot is held for over a minute with one brief two-shot intercut for a change of angle. Blanche, then, rises on the phrase describing her husband as "crying like a baby" but turns her back to the camera as she continues so that the audience is refused access to her face. She finally faces the camera in a restrained medium shot to describe the dance and the suicide, and the speech concludes with a shot of them both in long shot on a diagonal that Mitch breaks as he moves to embrace her. The language and length of the speech indicates its theatrical origins, but there is little use of the dramatic powers of close-up and lighting to reinforce its rhetoric.

Finally, in this discussion, there is the question of Marlon Brando. Much has been written about Brando's performance style and the highly influential promotion of the "Method" for male stars in Hollywood. Film theorists, in particular, have commented on the way in which the camera positions Brando as the subject of its gaze, suggesting that here the film adopts the highly conventionalized way in which female stars are presented to the audience. Kristen Hatch, for instance, argues that this reverses "the primary structure around which classic Hollywood cinema is constructed: women function as the object of the gaze, men as the bearers of the look" and that this reversal makes "Brando a feminine object of gaze."[30] To argue that the "rendering of his body as an erotic object" through this shot "threatened to strip Brando of his masculinity"[31] seems an extreme step and in any case is not borne out by the rather more subtle way in which the space for looking at him is constructed. We have seen how the audience's view of Brando is frequently covered by Blanche's look (or in the staircase scene Stella's look), providing a female (albeit transgressive) cover for the camera's gaze. The statement that the film "takes every opportunity to display him bare-chested"[32] is also something of an exaggeration since, in accord with Hollywood's conventions, the change of T-shirt takes place in the background; similarly, in the shower scene a shadow is strategically placed across the bare chest, and much of the scene involves what is, for this film, a tight close-up of Brando's head.

Steven Cohan, in a less deterministic and more culturally informed approach, has analyzed Brando's Stanley in terms of his performance of a complex masculinity with indications of bisexuality and homoeroticism. He argues, "Brando's celebrated naturalness signified the theatricality of his acting, not as technical expertise, but as the ground on which he performed 'maleness' and wore it on his body as masquerade."[33] Cohan's emphasis on theatricality underlines that, like the set and staging, Brando's performance involved representing a theatrical experience for cinema in a way that drew attention to its origins. In this context, it worth noting that the power of Brando's erotic force is carried as much by movement and proximity as by "the gaze." The first shot of him in the apartment is framed via Blanche's look, but he then moves through the rooms to pass close to her twice; similarly, her brief look at him changing his T-shirt is followed by his movement toward her, which brings him into the same shot as her and clearly makes her uneasy. It is this proximity that causes her to touch him on the arm when alarmed by the cat's screeches. A similar pattern of looks and proximity marks the exchange between them that precedes the rape, though, in this scene, Blanche's looks are marked by fear rather than desire; when Stanley challenges her to leave, he remarks, falsely, "You've got plenty of room to get by me." It is the confined space associated with the stage that draws attention to the "real bodies [and] actual movements"[34] of the actors and heightens the impact of Brando's physical presence. The theatricality of Brando's performance in the film is highlighted by the fact of adaptation. As we shall see, the "Method" had to be streamlined in order to fully enter into cinema's lexicon.

The success of the 1951 film in restaging the play for cinema can be brought into focus by a comparison with the television version by John Erman in 1984. This version seemed to be as much a reproduction of the film as of the original play, and in that sense, as June Schlueter points out, it has been seen as rather unnecessary.[35] The justification was the removal of the censorship restrictions so that this version was advertised as being able to deal with what could not be put on screen in 1951. Pamela Anne Hanks indeed notes that the rape is presented more explicitly and becomes "a brutal act of aggression in which Stanley's misogynist nature is fully and finally exposed."[36] She and Schlueter comment on Ann-Margret's interpretation of Blanche as a stronger woman than usually played who is aware of her own sexuality.

For our purposes, though, the 1984 version offers sufficient variation in its use of setting and editing to allow us to see a shift away from the staging of the play to a more conventionally cinematic version, a version that is opened out more. The film starts with Blanche on the streetcar looking at streets that are more realistic than those of the earlier film. The main set, the Kowalski apartment, though it clearly resembles that of the earlier version, has a greater air of solidity and is shown more fully from a wider variety of angles. The recourse to cinema's power to show a world wider than the stage is most clearly seen however in the scene in which Blanche tells Mitch about her husband's death. As in the 1951 film, this scene is moved away from the apartment but is stretched across a number of settings: a romantic bridge leading to dark paths in the wood; a crowded restaurant; and a horse-pulled open carriage moving along a wooded road. While Vivien Leigh performed her major speech on the film's equivalent of a stage, the carriage rides along as Ann-Margret speaks, and cinematic dramatization is provided by the light changes generated by the movement of the carriage under the trees. Similarly, at the end, the film moves again out of the confined set as Blanche is driven away so that the final shot moves up to the spire of the church as a bell chimes over the streets beyond the quarter. In both cases, the film opens out the play and aims for a cinematic use of space beyond the set to express Blanche's plight.

So far as the editing is concerned, the 1984 version recognizably takes on the 1951 organization of space in the apartment, but there are different emphases in editing. The scene between Stanley and Stella, for instance, now has over twenty-five cuts in a scene of similar length to the 1951 version. The reverse cutting between them tends to reinforce a sense of them being on opposite sides and lays less emphasis on fluid space around them. The first exchange between Blanche and Stanley is more comparable to the original in its mix of shots, but in accordance with the greater stress on Blanche's use of her sexuality, there is a stronger emphasis on the exchange of looks between them. This use of the cinematic gaze is reinforced by the fact that there are more clear shots of Stanley that are not framed on one side by the watching Blanche, and therefore there is more focus directly on him and less on the characters' act of looking. However, proximity is less played on. The scene starts with an exchange of looks, but Stanley does not then pass Blanche in the same, close way, and as he changes his T-shirt there is a table between him and the watching Blanche. Only toward the end of the scene does touch figure when Blanche's raised hand nearly touches his stomach, rather than his arm, in an act that hovers on the deliberate. This is a more overt gesture but one that is less carefully positioned in the overall staging of the exchange.

I am not suggesting that Bazin's notion of representing the stage boundaries and recreating a sense of proximity and danger in performance is the only way of adapting plays for cinema. But I think it does explain more precisely how the 1951 adaptation "remakes the play as a singular cinematic achievement."[37] Filming the play in this way both transformed the presentation of the male star and, by reminding the audience of the spaces of the theater, transformed the play into cinema.

ACTING AND PERFORMANCE IN *THE ROSE TATTOO*

The traditional arguments that emphasize physical presence and its lack as the central difference between theater and cinema have their consequences for how acting is understood differently in the two media. This is powerfully linked to the different relationships that the two media are deemed to have with the external world, taking us back to Bazin's differentiation between theater as a confined space while film presents itself as limitless in what it can show. For Bazin, "'realist theater'" was impossible: "The mere fact that it is exposed to view on the stage removes it from everyday existence."[38] The most natural gesture then must be transformed into acting by the fact of being on stage, and the stage marks the limits within which the characters created by performance exist. The work of creating a character is assumed to be the work of the actor, but it is informed by the relationship with the audience in the theater that might change each performance. Good acting is recognizable and acknowledged in the applause at the end.

Cinema in this contrasting binary is shaped by its commitment to a realistic representation of the world, which means that acting that draws attention to its act of creation is problematic. In cinema, it is assumed that "good acting is 'true to life,'"[39] with gestures and speech that are not far removed from everyday behavior. Acting is hidden by this apparent naturalness so a film actor is deemed to be most successful when offering a variant of his or her own personality. Good acting in cinema then is "expressive of the actor's authentic, 'organic' self" so that the character and performer blend together.[40] Different too is the relationship with the audience; "On screen," as one acting handbook puts it, "you never play to the audience—you don't even play to the camera. The camera observes you." The actor is therefore advised to "cut out any sense of playing to a watcher or listener."[41]

This assessment of the essential differences between acting in theater and film carries over into judgments about how the actor's body and voice should be used in cinema. The body and voice are often deemed less essential to the overall effect, and it is possible to think of actors as props whose performances are generated by mise-en-scène, camerawork, and editing. Gesture, some argue, has to be restrained because the size of the screen magnifies it and will make it look overgrandiose. The face becomes the major site of acting since it can be seen in intimate close-up, and expression must be understated and consistent with the tone of voice. The voice itself need not be projected into the space of the theater but modulated into the microphone to be mechanically replayed in the cinema. Dialogue should be naturalized as if it were overheard conversations between characters, and spoken material is often introduced that is redundant to the narrative but reinforces the sense of a recognizable social exchange. Such is the gap between the two approaches that to describe acting as "theatrical" is one of the most derogatory remarks a critic can make about a film actor's performance. The author of another acting manual comments, "The reason why good actors are not good on screen is that they have their vocal levels wrong. Time and time again, I see a good performance . . . ruined by speaking too loudly, and the performance coming across as 'too theatrical.'"[42]

And yet for actors and audiences the differences between the two modes might not be as great as these ontological explanations suggest and at the very least need to be placed in context. Cynthia Baron has argued, from her study of the 1930s and 1940s cinema, that "professionals working in Hollywood after the coming of sound no longer saw acting on the stage as fundamentally different from acting on screen."[43] The size of the screen, the repetition of an action, and the different use of the voice were technical matters needing attention, but the basic responsibility for building up a character remained the same. The movement of actors between stage and studio in the fifties and the impact of the "Method" on both media indicate a continuum to be worked with rather than a line to be crossed. In addition, genre, as Kozloff suggests, provides different contexts for the expressive devices of acting. The heroes of 1930s gangster films used flamboyant gesture and language in a more overtly dramatic way than did the controlled and taciturn film noir private eyes; melodramas emphasized talk as much as action and combined highly rhetorical language with gestures that have to be understood as significant rather than natural. And for cinema audiences, acting, far from being invisible, is often a source of pleasure and a matter for judgment.

Since an emphasis on acting is so bound up with theater's difference from cinema, I want to examine more fully what it means for acting to be the central feature in a film adaptation by looking at the performance of Anna Magnani in *The Rose Tattoo*. This was the third film to be based on a Williams play, and although now much less well-known than *A Streetcar Named Desire* and *Cat on a Hot Tin Roof*, its success on release was confirmed by its eight Oscar nominations, which indicated that it had gained industry respect. Like *Streetcar*, the film of *The Rose Tattoo* was directed by the director of the original play in New York, in this case Daniel Mann who had previously directed the film *Come Back, Little Sheba* (1952) from a William Inge play. The cinematographer, James Wong Howe, won an Oscar for his black-and-white work on this film.

The Rose Tattoo* was sold as "the boldest story of love you've ever been permitted to see," following *Streetcar* in a further indication of how Williams's plays could be used in cinema to attract an audience pushing on the limits of the Production Code. But the film could also be seen as part of a movement toward the art film, which seemed to be developing in the midfifties. The success of certain Italian neorealist films in the United States (including *Rome Open City* [Rossellini, 1945], featuring Anna Magnani, and *The Bicycle Thief* [De Sica, 1948], which had managed a profitable run in U.S. cinemas without the Production Code Administration's [PCA] approval) seemed to indicate that there was an audience that might respond to similar local material. One commentator in 1952 predicted to the business community that "'art houses' . . . represent the most encouraging trend in the movies,"[44] while critic Robert Brustein, looking back in 1959, could write that "the heyday of Hollywood glamour is drawing to a close."[45] Brustein included *The Rose Tattoo* among a group of films that he argued turned against Hollywood's emphasis on size and glamour and were marked by controversial subject matter and a "modesty of . . . presentational devices" including black-and-white photography, standard screen formats, and the use of "actual locales rather than artificial studio lots."[46] They were often made by practitioners honed in New York theater, like Williams, Kazan, and Mann, and embodied "whatever their actual merits, a conscious artiness at which producers would formerly have shivered."[47] In this case, the "artiness" included not just a version of the neorealism of the art film but also an overt style of acting that drew attention to the film's theatrical roots; both features were reinforced by the presence of the Italian Magnani in a loquacious role full of emotional energy and opportunities for bravura acting. The film, like the play, is set in a small emigrant community outside New Orleans, and Magnani takes on the central role originally written by Williams for her to play in the theater but that she refused because of doubts about being able to sustain such a demanding English-speaking role on stage. She plays Serafina, who is widowed early in the film and devotes her life to the memory of her (unfaithful) husband until, while she battles to maintain the innocence of her fifteen-year-old daughter, her own sexuality is given a new object with the appearance of a fellow Sicilian, Alvaro, played by Burt Lancaster.

Unlike *Streetcar*, *The Rose Tattoo* does not use setting to emphasize the film's origins on the stage. The film is opened out in a more conventional way, and the flexibility of cinema is drawn on to show places and events only referred to in the play—the crash that kills Serafina's husband, the school dance at which her daughter Rosa meets Jack, and the casino where Serafina finally gets proof that her husband had a mistress. The confined space of Serafina's house in which most of the action occurs is organized like a stage set with a number of rooms opening onto the space of the main action, but it is surrounded by real trees and roads, and real chickens feed in the gardens. The house and the other settings were filmed on location with Howe seeking to bring "an authentically realistic look" rather than confirm its status as a filmed play.[48]

The film showcases Magnani's performance by providing the space in which her acting can be observed. Long takes and medium shots offer the viewer a position from which a performance can be viewed without the modified shot–reverse shot invitation to identification. The film positions the spectator outside the action and invites not so much consideration of the psychological motivations of the character but rather appreciation of the gestures, expressions, and vocal registers that signify feeling. What we participate in is the unfolding of a performance that is in many ways excessive, uncontained by the film's narrative. The performance uses more words and gestures than are needed to convey Serafina's character, repeating phrases and gestures as if relishing their power; it refers to timeless, archaic feelings beyond the provincial setting and the cramped rooms; the meaning of the words used is less important than the dramatic emphasis with which they are spoken; the range of expressed emotions and their swift movement from comedy to anger to grief is disconcerting; and the performance overwhelms other stories in the film, in particular that of Rosa's burgeoning sexual feeling. Serafina's nationality provides some naturalizing cover for this performative emphasis; she cherishes her Sicilian identity and struggles to pass it on to Rosa, who is being wooed by a young male representative of modern American democracy. But while ethnicity provides some explanations for Serafina's passion, the pleasures offered by the film largely hinge on an appreciation of Magnani's performance.[49]

Looked at more closely, the performance can be broken down into four modes that demonstrate the interaction of the cinematic conventions and modes of performance in *The Rose Tattoo*. The first mode dominates the opening of the film in which Serafina is discovered among a group of women in a shop. This is the film's expository mode, positioning Serafina in her community. Magnani's gestures and tone fit with those of the other women and fit the narrative purpose of the scene by marking Serafina as the heroine of the film but establishing her relationships with her husband, the shopkeeper, the other women, and the priest. The editing and camerawork is functional and unobtrusive and the timing brisk, moving Serafina out of the shop, through a conversation on the street with the priest (which gives us the clue that she is pregnant), and onto the porch of her home. At this stage in the film, Magnani's performance is in the re-strained style of cinema acting, functional in establishing character and ef-fective in its emphasis on moving through plot and setting. The film's strategy of opening up the theatrical setting is underpinned by this style of acting.

The second mode of performance is used in scenes in the house in which Serafina is alone, with Rosa, or with Rosa and Jack. These scenes are dominated both visually and verbally by Serafina and give the audi-ence access to the range of Magnani's acting. They have a narrative func-tion since they lay down Serafina's rules for her daughter. They also have a psychological function in that they provide material for the audience to understand why Serafina behaves as she does. But their main purpose is to provide a setting in which Magnani can use the varied skills of her act-ing to express Serafina's grief and her maternal protectiveness. These scenes are handled in different ways, but the focus is always on Serafina/Magnani. For instance, after Serafina has found out rumors of her hus-band's faithlessness from two of her sewing clients, Jack and Rosa return home to find her sitting at her sewing machine in the dark. The scene that follows is dominated by Serafina's silence and Magnani's face. Most fram-ings use a medium shot that frames all three characters with Jack and Rosa looking at Serafina. There is also a two-shot of Jack and Rosa look-ing at Serafina and a medium shot of Serafina alone, looking forward into space. In these shots, Serafina is looked at but does not look, and her white face against the shadowy background is emphasized by the organ-ization of shots and the lighting. By contrast, the comic scene that follows takes place in the main room of the house and makes use of the setting's theatrical qualities. Serafina makes Jack kneel before a statue of the Virgin to swear to respect Rosa's innocence; Serafina has sent Rosa, outside but she repeatedly reappears at the door and pushes her head through the window in protest at her mother's action. Largely filmed in a long shot that includes all three characters, the composition still puts Serafina at the center, turning from Jack to Rosa and back again, and does not, for in-stance, use close-ups to give us access to Jack's feelings as he makes the vow. This mode of performance then shows Serafina's interaction with her family through a variety of moods and showcases Magnani's skills in playing such a range of sentiments. The audience, though, is still posi-tioned as observers of the performance, and the editing isolates Serafina by generally refusing her a viewpoint.

The third mode of the performance has resource to the more Italian ne-orealist elements of the film, generated by Magnani's reputation as a Eu-ropean star in the United States and the appeal to realism signified by the black-and-white photography, the use of location sets, and the themes of poverty and immigration. This mode of the performance is not itself realist. Instead, the realist settings of the crowded church bazaar and the decorative interior of the empty church provide the background for a performance that is almost operatic in the way in which the emotions of the central performer are set against the commentary of the chorus. Serafina is at the point when her grief is first being tested by rumors of her husband's infidelity, and she goes to seek further information from the priest. At first she moves against the weight of the crowds who, intent on fun, ignore her; then she meets Alvaro for the first time, and a small group of women become aware of her distress; moving into the church and alone with the priest, she remembers the dramatic pathos of her wedding when she fainted at the first sight of her desirable husband; and finally, back outside the church she has to be literally pulled away from a violent physical and verbal attack on the priest who has refused to tell the secrets of her dead husband's confession.

The focus of this sequence is again on Serafina, but here the tone is more consistent and the acting overtly pitched at a more intense level. The camerawork continues to make Serafina the central focus, keeping her face almost continuously in view but ensuring, through the dominant use of medium and long shots, that the movement of her body can also be seen. In the scenes outside, Serafina's black shawl and dark hair stand out against the white church and the strong light. Inside the church, the black shawl and the dark robes of the priest set off her tearstained face and the movements of her uncovered arms and hands. Overall, the sequence intensifies the emotional register of Magnani's performance; at the beginning in the crowd, Serafina is subdued and silent, but by the end, as she attacks the priest and is rescued by Alvaro, she is voluble and declamatory, mocking the shocked women surrounding her with loud laughter and banging her fists against the closed door of the church. Within the sequence, though, Magnani also varies the tone, starting the scene in the church on a quiet note and building up to her proud claims about her marriage. Language and gestures come together to create exaltation and despair. Her body is frail and continually seems on the verge of giving way until reanimated by pride in her grief. She glances upward as she says, "I gave my husband much glory," as if indeed claiming heavenly glory on the basis of sexual pleasure. She repeats the gesture and reinforces it by pointing upward, first with a finger then with a closed fist, as her speech disintegrates into repeating first "glory, glory, glory" and then "I don't believe he gave me whores." This sequence uses Magnani's acting to give a spiritual dimension to Serafina's loss, while at the same time she presents the audience with an extravagant rendering of physical and emotional disintegration.

The fourth mode occurs when Magnani has to share the audience's attention with her male costar, Burt Lancaster. This sparring between potential lovers who have yet to sort out the terms of their relationship is the staple of screwball comedies. Here, it is played at full throttle, and the differences between the two are exemplified in their different acting styles. Lancaster goes for a broad comedy and uses physical clumsiness, a broad smile, and exaggerated comic gestures to demonstrate Alvaro's sincerity and good-heartedness. This throws Magnani's performance into a different context. On the one hand, she can continue to deploy the melodramatic expressiveness that has marked the performance so far as, for instance, when she responds with physical and emotional distress to the sight of Alvaro's tattoo or when she laughs, full-throatedly, at his antics. On the other hand, Magnani can now become the straight partner to Lancaster's excess. Just as Serafina tries to calm down Alvaro's boisterous wooing, so Magnani provides a quieter counterpoint to Lancaster's performance. This allows Magnani to display some of the more restrained style conventionally associated with film acting and sets off a deft comic manner more in line with romantic comedies of the 1930s and 1940s. The lightly ironic, sexual innuendo with which Magnani delivers her final line as a poised Serafina welcomes Alvaro into her home—"Now we can continue our conversation"—appropriately summarizes the change in the character and a shift in the acting register.

In addition, the scenes with Lancaster are the points at which the editing begins to present an equal exchange between the two rather than the focus on the central heroine that marks the previous two modes. This is indicated when they enter the house together after the sequence at the church. Serafina returns to the seat by the sewing machine, which she had occupied in the scene with Jack and Rosa discussed above. This time, however, she does not dominate the shot with her silent stare; the camera is positioned to the side of her so that she has to turn to look at Alvaro, who is in the foreground. This more equal composition is used throughout the remaining scenes between the two and is accompanied by greater use of shot–reverse shot conventions that allow the audience not only to see Serafina but also to see what she sees. Her view of Alvaro's upper body in the light from the window is a shock not just to Serafina but also to the audience since this is virtually the first time her viewpoint has coincided with that of the audience in looking at another character/performer. The editing and camerawork is used to emphasize the growing sexual interest Serafina has in this potential lover and to allow the audience a view of the male star. In this fourth mode, then, the focus on Serafina shifts. This does not however detract from the focus on Magnani; instead, it further demonstrates her range and her control as an actress.

This focus on Magnani's performance as the main source of pleasure in the film is underpinned by the narrative organization that puts the audience into the position of knowing more than Serafina. Right from the start, the audience knows that Serafina's husband has betrayed her and that therefore her grief is excessive. Applying a knowledge of fifties psychology (gained from other movies), which Serafina entirely lacks, it knows that her attempts to protect her daughter are both fruitless and unwise. It knows also, from its understanding of genre conventions, that the bootless Alvaro has to become Serafina's lover and the film will end happily. There is therefore no narrative suspense, and if the audience is to enjoy the film it has to do so via an overt appreciation of the central performance. This runs the risk of alienating those who find the acting excessive, but Magnani's Academy Award for best actress indicates that the film had successfully showcased a theatrical role and turned it into a particular kind of screen performance.

The contrast between Magnani's performance and that of Marisa Pavan as Rosa provides an interesting coda and a link into debates about melodrama that will be taken further in the next section. Film theory has associated melodrama with the repression of emotion, particularly of female desire; as Kozloff puts it, melodramas "which seem so verbally over-explicit—actually hinge around the *not said, the words that cannot be spoken.*"[50] Repression is hardly a feature of Serafina's character or Magnani's performance in *The Rose Tattoo*. Serafina's sexual impulse toward Alvaro is expressed through look and gesture, while her desire for her husband is the explicit mainspring of many of her speeches. Rosa, however, is in a different position. Her dialogue is limited and repetitive, taking place in exchanges with her mother and Jack in which her wishes are largely thwarted. The romantic scenes with Jack are short and shot in a flat style in which the main purpose seems to be to move the narrative on; the exchange on the school stairs signifies the beginnings of the romance, the scene on the yacht the first argument. Crucially, Rosa's desire for sex with Jack cannot be spoken and is transmuted into Rosa's sudden demand that Jack marry her. Honoring his promise to Serafina and worried about being observed, he resists Rosa's attempted embrace, and she dives off into the water after declaring, "I'm not satisfied with dreams." This repression is translated into a contradiction between the mise-en-scène for Rosa and the actress's performance. Rosa is consistently positioned in the light and dressed in white with all the connotations of virginity so implied; she wears girlish high collars, bib fronts, and broderie anglaise that are matched by Jack's white sailor suit, in this context, to Serafina's surprise, also a sign of innocence. But the acting style places the emphasis on intense sexual and romantic longing that gets fixed into an hysterical, repetitive demand for marriage; during these scenes, Pavan's face is transformed into a white mask, her gaze is intent, and her gestures indicate repressed violence. The film accommodates Rosa's story by having her run off hand in hand with Jack to marry with Serafina's blessing, but the sheer force of the acting indicates that the imposed happy ending cannot accommodate Rosa's needs.

CAT ON A HOT TIN ROOF:
THE MELODRAMA AND THE ADULT FILM

The success of Williams's work in cinema was particularly important since Hollywood was experiencing upheavals that appeared to challenge its previously unparalleled position as the main source of mass entertainment. Throughout the fifties, Hollywood felt itself to be under threat thanks to declining audiences, largely blamed on the increasing availability of television, the loosening of studio control over exhibition following the Paramount case, and the challenge to the centralized censorship of the PCA that had sustained the notion of film as family entertainment. Williams's work in the cinema seemed to offer something that Hollywood needed, controversial themes allied with a proven track record and theatrical respectability. In the adaptations of the late fifties, this was allied with the color and wide-screen formats with which Hollywood hoped to defeat television. Adaptations of Williams's plays in the late fifties and early sixties were made in the context of other films that combined spectacular visual style and sensational stories of family secrets. These glossy melodramas used music, color, and the wide screen to dramatize stories of romance and conflict among the American wealthy.

The trailer for *Cat on a Hot Tin Roof* drew on the prestige of theater by emphasizing its source as the work of "the most talked-about dramatist of our day," the Pulitzer-winning Tennessee Williams. "MGM," it proclaimed, "gives new dramatic stature to the screen." The credits confirmed that the drama was "as presented on stage," and in this public deference to the author and the theater the film followed earlier Williams adaptations. But the trailer also demonstrated the technical allure of MGM in the 1950s in its use of Metrocolor and a wide-screen format. Set in the home of a rich Southern family, the story examined the troubled marriage of the younger son, Brick, and Maggie, within the context of his relationship with his father and his dead friend, Skipper. The secrets at the heart of the family were made the more obscure by the need to abide by the PCA ruling that homosexuality could not be mentioned on screen.[51]

This was an adaptation that respected the theatrical organization of space and time despite some opening out of the restrictions on location. Brick's drunken accident that opens the film takes place in an empty athletics stadium, the diverse family group gathers at a small airfield to welcome Big Daddy home, and Brick's attempted flight ends with the car stuck in real mud. The house too has the feel of a location, with the décor and rooms being presented in a more realist way than were those in *Streetcar*. Nevertheless, the action takes place within the time span of a single day, and the house is used like a theatrical set with the action largely restricted to three areas—an upstairs bedroom, the ground floor on which action can flow between the garden and the main rooms, and the basement. Unlike *Streetcar*, in which the barriers between the separate spaces are weak and continually breached, the bedroom and the basement belong to particular characters. Although the dialogue emphasizes the lack of privacy in the house, the bedroom belongs to Brick and Maggie while the basement is claimed by Big Daddy and is the scene of his reconciliation with Brick. In addition, the separation of these areas is reinforced by the way the action broadly moves down the house, away from the bedroom through the ground floor into the basement, following, in a rather literal way, the working through of the themes of the story.

Stairs and balconies join the main spaces of the action and link them through the movement of the characters and the sounds that carry from room to room—the children singing, the piano playing, and voices raised in arguments. At points, the décor of these liminal spaces feeds into the action. The bedroom balcony is the space for overhearing: Mae is caught eavesdropping there, and Brick and Maggie stand there looking out, separated by the image of Big Daddy whom they can hear declaring, "I'm not going to die" in the room behind them. The main staircase with its red carpet is both a vantage point and a site for awkward confrontations. Here, Big Daddy withholds his crutch from the fallen Brick, demanding to know why he drinks; Maggie sees Mae and Gooper harassing the doctor to tell Big Mama the truth; and the black servant, deferentially passing Brick, tells of his father's retreat to the basement. At the end of the film, Brick finally triumphs over Mae and Gooper on these stairs and, moving upward, calls for Maggie to join him.

Within these spaces, the camerawork largely serves the function of preserving the proscenium arch by using camera position and editing to observe, often in long or medium shot, the actions of one or more characters. Like *The Rose Tattoo* and unlike *A Streetcar Named Desire*, it seeks a stable position from which to view the characters, and the handling of action and dialogue still seems to be determined by "the architecture of the auditorium."[52] Medium shots consistently frame the characters in a group with the occasional use of medium close-ups to mark significant lines of dialogue or to clarify the narrative. Again, this restraint means that cinema's conventional shot–reverse shot editing is used relatively rarely. This is particularly marked in the exchanges between Maggie and Brick. In their bedroom scenes, the camera is relatively stable, giving the audience either a still shot of the two characters in a balanced framing or following their movements from a distance. There are very few close-ups and very limited use of shot–reverse shot editing from the character's point of view, though sometimes such editing is used to balance the audience's view of the couple as it is, for example, when Brick and Maggie discuss Big Daddy's illness with the bed between them. Even when looks are exchanged from a character's viewpoint, they tend to be from a distance, using long or medium shots rather than close-ups. One example of this occurs on Maggie's line in response to Brick's question about how she is to have a child "by a man who cannot stand you." Her pause and the words "that, boy of mine" are spoken in a medium shot of her facing the camera with Brick's back seen from the waist up; the cut (as she says, "is a problem I'll just have to work out") reverses the angle but gives us a more distanced view, no longer associated with Brick's viewpoint, of her back and then of her turning and rising from the sofa to move across the room. In this way, the editing seeks to maintain a viewpoint that is distanced from both characters.

This has an impact on how we are invited to experience the relationship between the married couple since the refusal to use the shot–reverse shot conventions of looking/desiring means that it is not until the end of the second bedroom encounter that we get a shot of Brick looking at Maggie that is comparable to the exchanges in *A Streetcar Named Desire* between Stanley and Blanche. Brick's refusal to look at Maggie is motivated by the plot, but it is perhaps surprising that Maggie's desire for Brick is denied this visual expression. The effect is twofold. First, their mutual desire has to find other expression, in Maggie's dialogue and in a rather clumsy shot of Brick holding and smelling her nightdress. Second, although the camerawork and editing serve to emphasize the theatrical origins of what we are seeing, they do so by holding back from the devices of cinema to give the audience a theatrical view rather than reworking them, as Kazan had done in *Streetcar*, for a different kind of space.

The exceptions to this use of the camera occur when an unusual camera angle or a close-up serves to emphasize a thematic or symbolic point. A close-up of a glass confirms to Gooper that Brick is still drinking heavily; the exchange between Brick and his father on the stairs is marked by high and low camera angles that emphasize Brick's position on the floor and Big Daddy's dominance; an extreme low angle shot, initially from Gooper's viewpoint but maintained when he moves away, underlines that Big Daddy is ready for the showdown. Big Daddy, indeed, tends to be filmed from below, emphasizing his bulk and his dominance within the family.

So, *Cat on a Hot Tin Roof* offers an example of a naturalized theatrical adaptation. The adaptation's origins are clearly acknowledged, and the space is generally used to present the best view of the whole drama to the audience, with cutting or camera angles used to make a narrative or thematic point. But the use of space and camerawork neither transforms the drama through the devices of cinema nor restages the play in recognition of a different medium. The use of expressive camera angles or close-ups signals that at certain points a different route might have been taken as the film appears to move toward the melodramatic visual style of other 1950s melodramas. The narrative in *Cat on a Hot Tin Roof* is indeed organized around a series of intense exchanges about family and sexual relations, and its denouement provides the moments of accusation and revelation that are necessary in melodrama for order to be restored. Despite or perhaps because of the clear indications of Maggie's sexual desire, it gradually becomes clear that it is the repressed relationship between Brick and his father that has to be acknowledged for resolution to be reached. Maggie seeks to return to the sexual relationship she had with her husband, but in order to achieve this Brick has to establish a new relationship with his father. The story that starts in the couple's bedroom is moved on when on the ground floor Maggie tells both father and son what she did with Skipper; it is only resolved in the basement by Big Daddy acknowledging that he needed and was supported by the love of his own father, a poor tramp. Father and son return to the ground floor, with Big Daddy refusing morphine because he now wants "to feel everything"; together, they sort out the presumptions of Gooper and particularly Mae as the claimants to Big Daddy's power and ensure that Maggie is brought back under male control.

Film theorists have argued that the family melodramas of Sirk, Ray, and Minnelli laid open the contradictions of bourgeois family life, and *Cat on a Hot Tin Roof* has been associated to some extent with that genre-based critique. Thomas Schatz and Jackie Byars discuss the film as a "southern dynastic melodrama,"[53] and Kenneth MacKinnon argues that the film's ending offers a "highly wishful and 'incredible' closure,"[54] which is comparable to the "happy endings" of films such as *Written on the Wind* (Sirk, 1956) and *Home from the Hill* (Minnelli, 1960), conventional endings that cannot resolve the contradictions in gender and family relations the films have expressed. *Cat on a Hot Tin Roof*, however, lacks the excessive and resonant mise-en-scène that it is argued works against the narrative in these family melodramas. The cutting and editing works with the narrative to offer a distanced, theatrical view—not an engaged, contradictory one—and lighting and color provide a bland, realist background rather than the "highly elaborated, complex mode of signification,"[55] which Elsaesser described as a key feature of the family melodrama in the 1940s and 1950s. Those symbolic references that are used lack dynamism. The debris in the basement, for instance, clearly refers us to the lost hopes and dreams of Big Daddy and Brick, but it appears on cue as required by the plot. Compare that with the threatening décor of Wade Hunnicutt's den in *Home from the Hill*, which from the start indicates both Wade's over-bearing presence and the monolithic assertion of masculinity that will destroy him. The one moment of melodramatic resonance in *Cat on a Hot Tin Roof* occurs outside the main narrative when Big Daddy emerges from the basement for a brief exchange with the black servants who are repairing the lanterns damaged in the storm. He hugs a huge dog, acknowledges the good wishes of the servants, who address him cheerfully as "Cap'n," and reassures them the rain "has done some good." For a moment the whole basis of the family's wealth and corruption opens up and then shuts down again.

Instead, much of the décor serves another purpose, offering the pleasures of affluent consumption that Barbara Klinger associates with the adult film. This 1950s genre presented "a heightened and bold expression of heterosexual conflict" but could also offer "a display of capital, invoking the acquisitive dispositions of the [female] audience."[56] Rather than engaging the spectator's absorbed "gaze," this display requires a more distant "glance" of appraisal from the spectator. The tone is perfectly set by the credits of *Cat on a Hot Tin Roof*, which are more appropriate to the "battle of the sexes" comedies popular in the late fifties and early sixties. To the accompaniment of modern jazz, they feature, against a red background, a cartoon sketch of a woman half lying on a bed with an elaborate, curving bedstead behind her; they give a light, comical take on the very bed that Big Mama will tap on to indicate that she knows the source of Brick and Maggie's problems. This sets up an approach that treats this home of the nouveau riche family as a setting for the display of modern furniture and decoration that aspires to a stylish version of quasi–period elegance. Everything matches: the bedroom has a gold and white theme dominated by the art nouveau, brass bedstead; and the lilac walls of the lounge coordinate with the sofa and long curtains. From this aspect, Maggie's materialism is not a matter for criticism, and it is appropriate that this adaptation of *Cat on a Hot Tin Roof* ends on a light note with a long shot, through the bedstead, of Brick jokily throwing a cushion on to the marital bed.

This generic twist with its emphasis on the upwardly mobile desires of the audience is also strongly reflected in the way in which the film uses dress to present Paul Newman and Elizabeth Taylor as a star version of a successful, modern couple. The stylish simplicity of their clothing matches them as clearly as the plot drives them apart. Newman's muted blue silk pajamas, the bathrobe in a subtly different tone of blue, and his dazzlingly austere white shirt and khaki cord jeans are paralleled by Taylor's outfits, initially a cream blouse and tight beige skirt, cinched with a tan belt, and then a white, "Grecian" dress with classical drapes from the bare shoulders and a graceful skirt. The simplicity of their dress underpins a stylish approach readily accessible to fans in the audience. But of course in the case of Taylor and Newman, it also served to reinforce the glamour and beauty that marked their star image.

This shift to the adult film can also be seen in the presentation of performance. As in *Streetcar* and *The Rose Tattoo*, acting is an important element in the film's claim for "dramatic stature." The critics praised the acting in this adaptation, and both Newman and Taylor were nominated for Academy Awards. It is Newman's performance that is critical, though, putting him in the line of angst-ridden masculine heroes that began with Brando in *Streetcar*. Like Brando, Montgomery Clift, and James Dean, he deploys the "naturalistic rhetoric and the same feeling of power and nobility hidden beneath a vulnerable, inarticulate surface" that Naremore ascribes to Brando's performance in *On the Waterfront*.[57] This method-influenced acting style is pared down and refined in Newman's performance as Brick. His role is a reactive one, and his acting is marked by stillness. Brick is always watching, and Newman keeps his face immobile, his eyes expressionless; he is repeatedly framed outside the main sphere of action, sometimes watching it, sometimes with his back to it as gazes into the middle distance. Andrew Higson associates this kind of highly controlled style with the repressions of 1950s film melodramas, marked as it is by the "tension created between periods of minimal, apparently expression-less and emotion-less acting . . . and sudden explosive bursts of facial, gestural and postural movement." The body, he suggests, is not just "restrained but visibly *strained* . . . the outbursts function as the return of the repressed, the out of control."[58] Newman offers a variant of this approach in which control and, arguably, repression win out; Newman's watchful stillness, even while playing an out-of-control drunk, dominates the film. Influentially, he had naturalized and streamlined the "Method" to make it fit cinema rather than refer back to the acting style coming from the original source in theater.

The success of Newman's performance is also due to the way in which the audience is positioned to look at him as a pinup as well as an actor. As we have seen, the editing of the film does not invite the audience to identify with the relationship between the two characters but positions us as onlookers. This puts the actors' bodies on display in shots unmotivated by character; they are detached, by this editing, from their roles in the drama but inserted into "the strong emphasis on sexual display,"[59] which is a feature of the 1950s adult film. There are points when the role of the actor and those of the star clash; in particular, the limp that symbolically maims Brick has the effect of restricting Newman's ability to move with the litheness of a male film star. But generally with Newman this mode of looking is integrated with his acting style in that it relies on his stillness and control. His characteristic pose, looking broodingly out toward the audience, offers the spectator an image that fits the pinup. Medium close-ups present him facing the audience, holding his face and upper body in view. The neutral, eye-level position of the camera has the effect of emphasizing Newman's most famous asset as a star—the blue eyes that are flattered by the blue of his robe and pajamas. Since Brick's outsider status in the family is written into the story, this pinup pose can be maintained even when Brick is only observing the action while the dialogue goes on elsewhere. And the cover for the audience's looking is provided by the film's use of acting as a key attraction.

Even in this adult film, the male body is treated carefully, and the one shot of Newman's bare torso is in a brief medium shot, though it is characteristically directly presented for the audience rather than via Maggie's look. This contrasts with the more overt treatment of Taylor's body, and her position as a pinup as well as an actress is established from the beginning. A child throws ice cream onto her legs and so Maggie's first conversation with Brick is conducted as Taylor changes into a pair of new stockings. Several low shots, at the beginning of the scene, give the audience a clear view of her legs, the suspenders, and the sheerness of the stockings as she shakes them out. This unmediated looking is repeated later in the scene when Maggie asks Brick to check her seams; Brick is lying behind her, refusing to look, but the audience is given a view, from the front, of Taylor's body and legs from the waist down, positioning her as a sex symbol who is open to the camera's gaze. Although the second bedroom scene is also marked by Maggie undressing to her slip, there is nothing this overt in the rest of the film, but by setting up this image early on, the film has established how we should look at Taylor. The emphasis on sexual display threatens to undermine Taylor's status as an actress but is clearly entwined with the emphasis on clothing and dress discussed earlier, and the combination of sexuality and consumption confirms her star status.

Cat on a Hot Tin Roof (along with *Sweet Bird of Youth* also starring Paul Newman) helped to streamline melodrama into the late fifties and early sixties adult film. While the patriarchal dominance of Big Daddy was a familiar trope of melodrama, the potentially adult, potentially equal relationship between the young couple fitted into a different mode, which could move toward comedy as well as romance. Despite the emphasis on the reputation of Williams's play, the film works because of the glamour and slickness of the stars and setting.[60] Like the other adaptation formats, this translation from theater to screen is haunted by the specter of the genre that might devour it, in this case melodrama. The glossiness of *Cat on a Hot Tin Roof* and the ending that restores the couple to marital sexuality makes it particularly prone to this critique. Peter Lev, in his reference work on U.S. cinema in the 1950s, acknowledges the importance of melodrama in the period. He, nevertheless, ends his comments on *Cat on a Hot Tin Roof* with a critique of the happy ending: "It is still a melodrama however; it describes sympathetic people . . . who find the way to a positive conclusion."[61] Palmer, too, while acknowledging the importance of Williams adaptations in changing Hollywood's representations of sexuality and masculinity, suggests that in the end *Cat on a Hot Tin Roof* was "melodramatized in a typical Hollywood fashion" and became a "standard, early 1960s adult film, with its initial implications of sexual irregularity and dysfunction dispelled by a plot that restored a solidly bourgeois normality."[62] It is arguable though that what the film needed was actually to delve more deeply into its own language and to remember that in adapting plays the "role of cinema was . . . to intensify."[63] A more cinematic use of melodrama in the organization of space and mise-en-scène and a bolder use of color, camerawork, and editing might have been a less cautious way of "staging a play by means of cinema."[64]

Taking Bazin's work as a starting point offers a way of analyzing how these adaptations work as they do and what they represent in a study of adaptations. Bazin, while refusing the discourse of faithfulness, does not shy away from asserting that there are medium-specific differences between theater and cinema, associated with the use of space, which have consequent effects on how an actor's voice is heard and the body seen. The shift from stage to screen can often still be seen in the way in which theatrical conventions associated with staging and performance persist in film adaptations as if the stage setting remains a ghostly presence. Such conventions work against the organization of cinematic space, which, through conventions of editing and framing, seeks to position the spectator inside the mise-en-scène and therefore into a different relationship with the actor's voice and body. The films based on Williams's plays offer a paradigm of how the different organization of space in cinema and theater can be worked through in adaptations that use the original theatrical experience as a reference and that overtly present performance as a source of pleasure. *A Streetcar Named Desire* stands out as a film in which a play is re-presented as a theatrical event by using rather than suppressing cinema's resources of camerawork and editing. *The Rose Tattoo* presents a theatrically referenced role as cinema, offering the kind of Oscar-winning, culturally valued performance that cinema associates with theater; nevertheless, in its use of different registers of acting, supported by changes in lighting and camerawork, it foregrounds the very differences between cinema and theater that adaptations often seek to efface. *Cat on a Hot Tin Roof* maintains the dramatic spaces of theater but tries to blend them into a more realistic setting; it gives the audience a distanced view associated with the auditorium and deprives them of the more dynamic relationship with the action that cinematic use of space offers. Ironically, the film's legacy lies with Taylor and, in particular, Newman, who provide performances that, insofar as they can work against the theatrical staging, underline cinema's different relationship with the voice and look of its central figures.

NOTES

1. Gene D. Phillips, *The Films of Tennessee Williams* (London: Associated Universities Press, 1980), 20.

2. Phillips, *The Films of Tennessee Williams*, 18.

3. R. Barton Palmer, "Tennessee Williams and the Evolution of the Adult Film," in *Cambridge Companion to Tennessee Williams*, ed. Matthew C. Roudané (Cambridge: Cambridge University Press, 1997), 205.

4. See Leonard J. Leff, "And Transfer to Cemetery: The 'Streetcars Named Desire,'" *Film Quarterly* 55, no. 3 (Spring 2002), for a discussion of censorship of the 1951 film in the context of the release of a "restored" video version in 1993; see Leonard J. Leff and Jerold L. Simmons, *The Dame in the Kimono: Hollywood Censorship and the Production Code from the 1920s to the 1960s* (New York: Grove Weidenfeld, 1990), for a more general account.

5. Palmer, "Tennessee Williams and the Evolution of the Adult Film," 230.

6. Robert Stam, *Literature through Film: Realism Magic and the Art of Adaptation* (Oxford: Blackwell, 2005), 257.

7. André Bazin, "Theater and Cinema—Part Two," in *What Is Cinema?* trans. Hugh Gray (Berkeley: University of California Press, 1971), 104.

8. Bazin, "Theater and Cinema—Part Two," 105.

9. Bazin, "Theater and Cinema—Part Two," 106.

10. Bazin, "Theater and Cinema—Part Two," 111.

11. Bazin, "Theater and Cinema—Part Two," 117.

12. André Bazin, "Theater and Cinema—Part One," in *What Is Cinema?* trans. Hugh Gray (Berkeley: University of California Press, 1971), 84.

13. Bazin, "Theater and Cinema—Part One," 85.

14. Bazin, "Theater and Cinema—Part Two," 106.

15. Bazin, "Theater and Cinema—Part One," 86.

16. Bazin, "Theater and Cinema—Part One," 87.

17. Bazin, "Theater and Cinema—Part One," 93.

18. Palmer, "Tennessee Williams and the Evolution of the Adult Film," 206.

19. Quoted in Jeff Young, ed., *Kazan on Kazan* (London: Faber and Faber, 1999), 80.

20. Quoted in Michel Ciment, *Kazan on Kazan* (New York: Viking Press, 1974), 66.

21. Quoted in Stuart Byron and Martin L. Rubin, "Elia Kazan interview," *Movie* 19 (Winter 1971–1972): 5.

22. Quoted in Young, *Kazan on Kazan*, 86.

23. Raphaelle Costa de Beauregard, "*A Streetcar Named Desire* (1947/1952) as a Freaks Show," in *A Streetcar Named Desire: Tennessee Williams—Elia Kazan*, ed. Dominique Sipière (Nantes, France: Editions du Temps, 2003), 114.

24. de Beauregard, "*A Streetcar Named Desire* (1947/1952)," 112.

25. de Beauregard, "*A Streetcar Named Desire* (1947/1952)," 114.

26. Bazin, "Theater and Cinema—Part One," 93 (emphasis in original).

27. Bazin, "Theater and Cinema—Part One," 93.

28. William Baer, *Elia Kazan: Interviews* (Jackson: University Press of Mississippi, 2000), 49.

29. Sarah Kozloff, *Overhearing Film Dialogue* (Berkeley: University of California Press, 2000), 70.

30. Kristen Hatch, "Movies and the New Faces of Masculinity," in *American Cinema of the 1950s: Themes and Variations*, ed. Murray Pomerance (Oxford: Berg, 2005), 56–57.

31. Hatch, "Movies and the New Faces of Masculinity," 58.

32. Hatch, "Movies and the New Faces of Masculinity," 58.

33. Steven Cohan, *Masked Men: Masculinity and the Movies in the Fifties* (Bloomington: Indiana University Press, 1997), 244.

34. Timothy Corrigan, *Film and Literature* (Upper Saddle River, N.J.: Prentice-Hall, 1999), 47.

35. June Schlueter, "Imitating an Icon: John Erman's Remake of Tennessee Williams' *A Streetcar Named Desire*," *Modern Drama* 28, no. 1 (Spring 1985).

36. Pamela Anne Hanks, "Must We Acknowledge What We Mean? The Viewer's Role in Filmed Versions of *A Streetcar Named Desire*," *Journal of Popular Film and Television* 14, no. 3 (Fall 1986): 121.

37. Corrigan, *Film and Literature*, 48.

38. Bazin, "Theater and Cinema—Part One," 89.

39. James Naremore, *Acting in the Cinema* (Berkeley: University of California Press, 1990), 2.

40. Naremore, *Acting in the Cinema*, 2.

41. Mel Churcher, *Acting for Film: Truth 24 Times a Second* (London: Virgin Books, 2003), 8–9.

42. Patrick Tucker, *Secrets of Screen Acting* (London: Routledge, 2003), 69.

43. Cynthia Baron, "Crafting Film Performances: Acting in the Hollywood Studio Era," in *Screen Acting*, ed. Alan Lovell and Peter Krämer (London: Routledge, 1999), 35–36.

44. Stanley Frank, "Sure-Seaters Discover an Audience (1952)," in *Moviegoing in America*, ed. Gregory A. Waller (Oxford: Blackwell, 2002), 255.

45. Robert Brustein, "The New Hollywood: Myth and Anti-myth," *Film Quarterly* 12, no. 3 (Spring 1959): 23.

46. Brustein, "The New Hollywood," 27.

47. Brustein, "The New Hollywood," 23.

48. Phillips, *The Films of Tennessee Williams*, 111.

49. I am indebted to George Kouvaros, "Improvisation and the Operatic Cassavetes' *A Woman under the Influence*," in *Falling for You: Essays on Cinema and Performance*, ed. Lesley Stern and George Kouvaros (Sydney: Power Publications, 1999), for a discussion of performance that influenced this analysis.

50. Kozloff, *Overhearing Film Dialogue*, 242 (original emphasis).

51. See Chon Noriega, "'Something's missing here!': Homosexuality and Film Reviews during the Production Code Era," *Cinema Journal* 30, no. 1 (Autumn 1990), for a discussion of the treatment of homosexuality.

52. Bazin, "Theater and Cinema—Part Two," 106.

53. Jackie Byars, *All that Hollywood Allows: Re-reading Gender in 1950s Melodrama* (London: Routledge, 1991), 232.

54. Kenneth MacKinnon, "The Family in Hollywood Melodrama: Actual or Ideal?" *Journal of Gender Studies* 13, no. 1 (March 2004): 32.

55. Thomas Elsaesser, "Tales of Sound and Fury: Observations on the Family Melodrama" (1972), reprinted in *Home Is Where the Heart Is*, ed. Christine Gledhill (London: British Film Institute Publications, 1987), 52.

56. Barbara Klinger, *Melodrama and Meaning: History, Culture, and the Films of Douglas Sirk* (Bloomington: Indiana University Press, 1994), 61.

57. Naremore, *Acting in the Cinema*, 208.

58. Andrew Higson, "Film Acting and Independent Cinema," *Screen* 27, nos. 3–4 (May–August 1986): 128.

59. Klinger, *Melodrama and Meaning*, 56.

60. For a contemporary assessment, see Albert Johnson, "*Cat on a Hot Tin Roof,*" *Film Quarterly* 12, no. 2 (Winter 1958).

61. Peter Lev, *Transforming the Screen*, 1950-1959 (New York: Charles Scribner's Sons, 2003), 238.

62. Palmer, "Tennessee Williams and the Evolution of the Adult Film," 279.

63. Bazin, "Theater and Cinema—Part One," 90.

64. Bazin, "Theater and Cinema—Part One," 93.

4

Feminism, Authorship, and Genre

Adaptations of the Novels of Edna Ferber and Pearl S. Buck

This chapter will look at adaptations of highly successful, middle-brow novels written by two well-known female authors in the late 1920s and 1930s, Edna Ferber and Pearl S. Buck. These adaptations offer interesting case studies in a number of ways. They are examples of novels with a mass appeal that extended into the middle classes; they are positioned between the difficulties of high art and the dubious appeal of pulp fiction, a categorization confirmed by the endorsement of books like *The Good Earth* and *Saratoga Trunk* by the influential Book-of-the-Month Club. While emphasizing the importance of a compelling story, they also aspire to something more. Both authors were Pulitzer prize winners for literature early in their careers: Ferber for *So Big* in 1925 and Buck for *The Good Earth* in 1932. Ferber claimed for her own novels that "in their very core there lay something more solid, more deeply dimensional, than mere entertainment. They had power they had theme they had protest [*sic*]."[1] Buck was awarded the 1938 Nobel Prize in Literature in recognition of her early novels set in China. Critics contested these claims for seriousness, and Buck's Nobel Prize shocked the U.S. literary establishment. Nevertheless, the books could be seen as literature as well as best sellers, a combination that proved useful in their adaptation.

The authors were also female and feminist, demonstrating through their own lives that women could have successful careers and engage with the public world; they used their novels to portray, often controversially, nonwhite, non-American cultures. Edna Ferber came from a Jewish German-Hungarian immigrant family and started her career as a journalist. *Cimarron* was published in 1929, and Ferber had a lengthy career until her death in 1968, writing plays with Gerald Kaufman and books with a strong regional flavor that were regularly adapted for cinema. Her female characters were often strong minded and independent, and she took a particular interest in working women. Pearl S. Buck was the daughter of and later wife to U.S. missionaries to China and spent almost all her first forty years in China. Her return to the United States in the early 1930s was marked by a break with the missionary establishment including divorce from her husband and remarriage to her publisher; her daughter was born with mental disabilities and brought up in a residential home, which Buck financed. Her presentation of China has been criticized for being racist and patronizing, but it has also been argued that her "realistic portrayal of the Chinese characters in her phenomenally successful novels gradually improved the American image of the Chinese."[2] She became not only a prolific writer but also an internationally known figure in the development of U.S. foreign relations with Asia. So, both Ferber and Buck were women who were often in the public eye, another useful attribute for a film industry interested in what was popular with its female audiences. Adaptations of their books offered the possibility of a prestige product with a particular appeal for women.

These adaptations share some of the characteristics of the classic adaptations discussed in chapter 1. As with classic adaptations, the relationship with the original is part of the selling point, and indeed, when the adaptation is made quickly, more of the audience is likely to have read the book recently. The original is therefore referred to prominently in publicity, and the credits give ownership to the novel's author. However, these novels lack the layers of reworking that trail classic adaptations, and readers might more accurately remember characters and narrative incidents from the books since the film conventions for rendering key plot elements or characterizations have had less chance to get embedded. This can encourage a greater emphasis on faithfulness at least to the main narrative elements and characters; as Paul Muni, star of *The Good Earth* (Franklin, 1937), put it in publicity for the film, "You can't deal lightly with a masterpiece that millions of readers have read and acclaimed."[3] In addition, like classic adaptations, these middle-brow blockbusters often deploy landscape, costume, and décor as a strong source of pleasure. But while classic adaptations might be considered to have established their own generic frameworks, in these adaptations, the use of landscape, costume, and décor is strongly linked to cinematic genres, and the films work to fit the novels into well-established patterns of iconography and narrative. How the adaptations fit cinema's genres is part of the subject of this chapter.

This chapter looks at the first adaptations of early novels by Ferber and Buck—*Cimarron* (Ruggles, 1931) and *The Good Earth*. *Cimarron* is a family saga and a western novel in which Sabra Cravat accompanies her husband, the flamboyant Yancey, to the new territory of Oklahoma. Yancey becomes a leading figure in the new town of Osage but cannot settle. Sabra is concerned about a female rival, Dixie, but Yancey is lured away from his family and job for other frontier adventures. Sabra at first is mainly positioned as a wife and mother but eventually outdoes her husband as a newspaper editor and proprietor and in her political career. The book features detailed descriptions of the U.S. landscape as it changes with historical development, and it brings the story of Osage almost up to the present with the boom generated by the discovery of oil. *The Good Earth* is the story of Wang Lung, detailing his rise from a simple farmer to a rich and successful man in the community. At the same time, the book traces his personal history through his first marriage to O-Lan, previously a child-slave in the House of Hwang, who becomes the mother of his five children; his second marriage to the prostitute Lotus; and his failure to persuade his sons to take over the land. In these ways, both books link the family to social change, and both seek to present a detailed picture of life outside the reader's experience—on the U.S. frontier or in the rural landscape of China. Neither really relies on suspense—the future is known both in historical terms and often in relation to the characters—and the narrative is organized through a series of key moments in which the strands of the story—past and future—are caught up together. Both novels have a distinctive narrative voice; in the case of *Cimarron*, Ferber often adopts a critical and even sardonic view of her characters while Buck uses quasibiblical rhythms and repetitions to reference her story's wider meanings. While both novels take a strong interest in the role of women in patriarchal systems, they are also concerned with issues of nationhood, race, and ethnicity. Because of the importance of authorship in the discourse that surrounds these films, this discussion will refer more directly to the original novels and their authors, but the main focus is still on the films themselves. In looking at the adaptations of these books, I will look at their status as prestige productions, the way in which they organize time and present history, their engagement with film genres of different kinds, and the role of the central heroine in each film.

Both *Cimarron* and *The Good Earth* are good examples of the way in which the status of a film adaptation works as a marketing opportunity. *Cimarron* was adapted quickly, and the film was advertised as a prestigious picture using cinema's new sound recording technologies.[4] It was promoted through civic premieres and shown in separate screenings in more expensive cinemas; in Washington, the secretaries of war and of the interior attended a special screening, and state functionaries attended the premiere in Oklahoma despite the fact that the book had caused some controversy in the state. As the author, Ferber was promoted alongside stars Richard Dix and Irene Dunne; the film was sold as "Edna Ferber's

Romantic Adventurous Epic of a New Empire," and the program featured a picture of Ferber signing her contract with the studio.[5] Film magazines drew on the author as a selling point; as *Film Weekly* put it, the film was "a powerful tale of dramatic love, given to us just as Edna Ferber . . . gave it to us."[6] Hollywood's love of statistics in publicity for its big films is here used as evidence not only of the scale of the studio endeavor but also of the emphasis on accuracy. The discourse of faithfulness has a double dimension since it is a matter of being faithful not just to the book but also to the historical record the book described. The publicity for *Cimarron* reported on five months of preparation before filming really began as "three camera units scoured Oklahoma for background and atmosphere."[7] The opening land rush scene apparently used five thousand extras and forty-seven cameras while the costume and makeup departments are praised for their skills.[8] The authenticity of the photographs and props is endorsed in the publicity by the fact that after filming they were given to the Oklahoma Historical Society. Ferber as a highly successful author is integrated into all the other talents that go to make a film, and faithfulness to the book becomes one element that positions the adaptation as innovative and prestigious, an early sound film that will stand alongside "immortal moments of the screen" from the silent era.[9]

The Good Earth, too, was the subject of a major publicity campaign with press material and programs and a guide that suggested how discussion groups of "older students, women's clubs, and community forums" might use the film.[10] In this, the author of the novel was compared to her own heroine and described as a "slow-moving, strongly-built woman with a silent reserve."[11] The trailers for the film showed the pages of the book and promised "line by line, just as you read it so you will see it." In all the material, emphasis is placed on the extent to which the studio was prepared to go to provide settings that accurately represented Chinese society and culture. In particular, a Chinese landscape was created in California by terracing and irrigating five hundred acres of land; building villages, marketplaces, and towns; and using thousands of props brought back from China. The art director, Cedric Gibbons, commented that "authenticity . . . [was] observed to the finest detail" and felt that "aside from their dramatic quality . . . these sets have a distinct educational value."[12] The acting talent of Paul Muni (Wang Lung) and Luise Rainer (O-Lan), who both won Oscars for previous performances just after the film's release, is a major feature of the publicity with particular attention being paid to the way in which Muni spent weeks with the Chinese communities of the Pacific Coast in meticulous preparation for his role as Wang Lung. Like *Cimarron*, the publicity seeks to claim a place in film history for the film as "the boldest thing that Irving Thalberg ever did"[13] and "the latest evidence of the new and more far-reaching artistry of the screen."[14] In such comments, we can see how the success and prestige of the novels is deemed to be complemented by the studios' careful emphasis on authenticity and the positioning of the films as educational as well as spectacular and enjoyable.

HISTORY AND THE ORGANIZATION
OF TIME IN THE FAMILY SAGA

Although the time span of both *Cimarron* and *The Good Earth* is less than one person's life, both films draw on the family saga in which a number of generations live through a particular period of national history. They both therefore have to deal with time passing and the interaction of personal milestones with public events in history. In *Cimarron*, the novel's narrative of past events is given a historical dimension that both controls the narrative organization and underpins its themes. The film's first intertitle promises a progressive history of epic proportions: "A nation rising to greatness through the work of men and women . . . new country opening . . . raw land blossoming . . . crude towns growing into cities . . . territories becoming rich states." The first action is the land rush that marked the opening of the Oklahoma territory for settlement. It is a spectacular event, and the vivid use of sound and camerawork, drawing on newsreel techniques of immersing the filmmaking in the event, offers the audience the experience of observing history in the making. Critics complained then and since that the film could hardly live up to such an opening,[15] but that is perhaps the point. The land rush, followed by Yancey's account of it to Sabra's languid Southern family, presents the heroic and romantic myth that the narrative then unpeels as it reveals how the new land was settled with all the old prejudices and assumptions unshaken by the stirring start.

Once the Cravats have reached and decided to stay in Osage, the passing of time is marked by intertitles giving the date, an indication of an important event, and a shot of the town main street, always taken from the same angle. So, 1890 marks "one year past," and 1893, 1898 ("Spanish-American War"), and 1907 ("Oil") are marked until the film concludes with the virtually contemporary 1929. This repeated shot does more than provide a background to the date since it acts as an invitation to the audience to note not just the passage of time but also how it is passing. The shot is recognizable as the main street, but the state of the road, the buildings, the means of transport, and the sounds change. These shots are often followed by shots of pages of the newspaper that Yancey and Sabra produce with its mixture of local and national headlines; stability and change are combined and brought to our notice through these devices. Yancey and Sabra both have an effect on history and are caught up by it.

But history is not just a matter of the great events and spectacular changes marked by these shots. It also involves the small details that the film records. The 1890 episode is concerned with Yancey's gun battle with The Kid, a notorious bank robber whom Yancey kills despite his own sympathy for The Kid's position as a rancher booted off the land. The gunfight takes place in the main street among the hay bales and shop goods that support the developing economy, and Yancey finds shelter in the trenches that have been dug out for the town's drains. In 1893, pavements are being laid in the main street though their quality attracts comments from Osage's ladies. Domestic detail is similarly historicized so that Ferber's intended satire of domestic consumption is here translated into an attention to detail that makes Sabra's concern to have fashionable dresses, wallpapered walls, and refined lunches as much a part of history as the discovery of oil and the declaration of war. The film acknowledges women's consumption as part of the driving force of development; Sol Levy's rise from a peddler with a pack on his back to the owner of a prosperous department store is as significant in the history of the West as the move from horse to car or the discovery of oil.

If *Cimarron* marks out time and change with historical precision, *The Good Earth* references timelessness. This was a way of rendering the "formal, quasi-biblical rhetoric" of the novel that had "helped to lift the plot towards a sense of universality."[16] It is achieved by the use of montage sequences and dissolves, indicating repetition and continuity, which are broken by specific events that involve change. This pattern is present from the start. The film opens with an intertitle that gives no date for the action but emphasizes the same interest in national identity as *Cimarron* but with less sense of change and movement: "The life of a great nation is expressed in the life of its humblest people. In this simple story of a Chinese farmer may be found something of the soul of China." The opening shot of dawn breaking over the hills gives way to a series of shots dissolving into one another, which show people going about the everyday tasks of getting water, herding geese, collecting their tools, and walking or riding on carts to the fields. The camera frames a particular house, and a title appears: "It was Wang Lung's marriage day." This dissolves into a shot of the landscape seen through a window from inside the house, and the camera pans slowly down to Wang Lung lying on the bed; he eventually names the day for himself by whispering, "This is the day." In this way, a day is singled out as significant for the film but only in the context of all the other days that begin in the same way and flow into each other. As the film moves on, the passing of time is marked by the organic growth of the peach tree outside the house, and even the scenes of revolution and war are unidentified by the kind of historical marking of time that *Cimarron* adopts.

The opening scene is the first of a number that organize time through editing and montages, varying the use of dissolves and cuts depending on the relationship between the particular event being shown and the rhythms of the seasons and the years. So, after the wedding celebrations, a montage of shots held together by dissolves shows Wang Lung and O-Lan working at first separately and then together on the land until O-Lan tells him of her pregnancy by saying, "I am with child"; Wang Lung stops the work by halting time, saying "Not for today," and goes to tell his father, marking this moment as unique and taking it out of the normal flow of their farming life. However, the use of dissolves within a montage can return what might seem to be a unique event into the flow of time; a series of dissolves showing the effect of the drought underlines that, while this famine will have particular consequences for the family, it is a natural event that will reoccur in this rural life. The separation of shots in the montage by cuts rather than dissolves has a rather different effect. The frantic scene of the harvesting of the wheat as the storm threatens cuts between long shots of the landscape of dark sky above waving wheat and close-ups of heavy heads of corn, hands scything, and the sheaves being blown away. This montage indicates a natural occurrence, but it also signifies a unique event as O-Lan gives birth to their first son immediately after she has helped rescue this harvest from the storm.

This emphasis on time as part of the natural order, rather than a series of historical markers, gives the narrative its sense that events are being fulfilled through fate. "Well then it's time," says Wang Lung as he comes forward to sign a lucrative contract for selling his wheat. "He is on the land again with his sons," says O-Lan of Wang Lung after the battle to drive off the locusts, "and this day is his." The ending of the film refers back to the opening. "It's a wedding again," says Wang Lung's father, now elderly and rather confused. It is his grandson's wedding day, and the boy, like his father at the beginning, is bashful and excited. O-Lan's death during the celebration of the marriage means it is fitted into a pattern of birth and death that is sustained, as I shall discuss more fully later, by her association with the land.

For part of the film, however, time is measured not through the natural rhythms of the land and nature but rather by the cause-and-effect editing that more usually sustains the narrative in Hollywood films. This rather different mode is associated with the story of Wang Lung's rise to riches, but the specific narrative line is prefigured by his uncle's suggestion that he is now rich enough to have a second wife. In this manner, the convention of the woman as an enigma is set up (Will he marry again? Who will she be? How will this affect O-Lan?) and is reinforced by his aunt's comment on Wang Lung's changed behavior: "When a farmer buys silk robes and washes his whole body every day, there's a woman, that's sure."

Lotus is first seen when Wang Lung, in the company of his uncle, watches her dance in a tea house. The narrative line now follows not the pattern of the farmers' seasons but rather the consequences of an individual obsession. Wang Lung buys the Great House of Hwang to impress Lotus and moves the family off the land so that she can be accommodated. The presence of a second wife in the family causes trouble and breaks up the family: his father attacks her as a "bad woman" and no longer recognizes Wang Lung; O-Lan is mournful and silent; and the younger son is himself seduced by Lotus and has to leave home. It is only when Wang Lung learns the truth about Lotus that he can move out of this narrative-driven history and be restored to the timelessness of the good earth.

CIMARRON, THE WESTERN, AND THE WOMAN'S FILM

Critics have argued that the emphasis on the enduring presence of the land was one of the reasons for *The Good Earth*'s success during the Depression, putting it alongside (though not in terms of quality) Steinbeck's *The Grapes of Wrath*. Colleen Lye takes the film as evidence for this, arguing that the film, by changing the ending of the book to allow the family to be reunited on the land, placed the "emphasis on rural displacement and homecoming [that] reflects the compelling fantasy of returning to the land."[17] Lye suggests that "as a space of freedom . . . Wang Lung's land bears a great deal more resemblance to the mythic American Frontier than to any Chinese countryside,"[18] linking the work to the more familiar tropes of the western.

But of the two films, *Cimarron* is much more clearly identifiable through setting, iconography, and narrative incident with the western. It emphasizes the lived experience of the historical moment, but the film is also deeply concerned with the foundation myth of U.S. expansion, the pursuit of national claims of ownership into the "empty" spaces of the West. As a western, it explores America's history in relation to the shifting boundaries between civilization and the wilderness and presents characters who represent the construction of the nation. In 1931, *Cimarron* was drawing on the conventions established by the successful cycle of silent epic westerns led by *The Covered Wagon* (Cruze, 1923) and *The Iron Horse* (Ford, 1924). These large-scale A films were, as David Lusted has described, aimed not just at western fans but also at the "widest inclusive audience centrally targeted at the female and urban market."[19] They placed human stories of the humble and dispossessed against an epic landscape, telling stories of settlement and of attempts to claim and farm the West. Women had a clear role as the stable center of the pioneering family and were strongly associated with the "religious dimension" of the myth, generated by "scenes of stoicism, sacrifice and loss."[20] *The Covered Wagon* in particular used the popular image of the Prairie Madonna, the "passive but hardy women [who] were figured as the 'precious cargo' to be brought West" in a mission of civilization.[21] As "a saga of America that focused on the *women's experience* of nation-building," Ferber's novel must, as Peter Stanfield indicates, "have suggested to the producers that a film adaptation would appeal to a diverse audience."[22] But the film also had to place the story and characters from a recent best seller into the framework of an established cinema genre.

In her novel, Ferber gave an account of the settlement of Osage and its transformation into a major, modern city in which she tried to get behind the romance and myths of the West. She commented that the book contained "chapters of satire, and, I am afraid, bitterness, but I doubt that more than half a dozen people ever knew this."[23] Much of her satire was aimed at the popular figure of the Prairie Madonna, though Ferber also mocks Sabra's more modern aspirations to fashionable dress, décor, and fancy cookery. More generally, Ferber, from a German Jewish background herself, presents "a revisionist picture of a multi-racial and ethnic West" in which a Jew and a young black boy actively help the pioneering family, and Yancey and Sabra's son, Cim, marries a woman from the Osage tribe.[24] The book presents in detail the political and cultural position of the Osage tribe that Yancey champions and relishes the mixed heritage of the various characters. The family line continues with young Yancey, the product of the interracial marriage, with what the novel describes as his "bewilderingly handsome mixture of a dozen types and forbears—Indian, Spanish, French, Southern, Southwest."[25]

The cinematic settlement of the West often involves, as in *The Iron Horse*, "constructing one nation . . . by wiping out, or at least suppressing difference,"[26] but the film of *Cimarron* seeks to maintain the novel's representation of the West as a place where different ethnic groups should be able to settle and mix. The film shares Ferber's critique of the treatment of these groups by the white majority whether they be the rough cowboys or the snobbish women. Although the film devotes less time than the book to the Native Americans (and indeed it is arguable that the detail here actually unbalances the final third of the book), they are an intrinsic part of the settlement process. They participate in the land rush and are welcomed by Yancey to the extemporary church service alongside all the other denominations; with the discovery of oil on their reservation, they too join in the excesses of Oklahoma's other millionaires. The film maintains Yancey's critique of the U.S. treatment of the Osage people, and the initially prejudiced Sabra reprints one of his scandalous editorials demanding full "Indian citizenship" to mark his vindication in 1929. In her home life, too, Sabra learns to accept Yancey's embrace of Native American culture. Her

opposition to her son's marriage is overcome when, at the dinner celebrating her election as a member of Congress, she welcomes Ruby, Cim's
wife, dressed in the costume of the Osage tribe, and introduces her two
grandchildren to the visitors from Washington.

Although the Native Americans are influential in the plot and the history, they carry less emotional weight than two other figures—Isaiah, the
black servant from Sabra's home who smuggles himself onto the wagon
and so joins the pioneer family, and the Jewish Levy, who is one of Sabra's
most consistent supporters. The film refuses Sabra any of the religious imagery associated with the Madonna of the Prairie; instead, the religious
symbolism is associated with these two outsiders. Both characters are
stereotyped in terms of speech, gesture, and roles in accord with Hollywood's treatment of ethnic difference in this period; Levy is a shopkeeper,
and Isaiah has the comic, childish faithfulness of the black slave. However, both are given close relationships with the white characters, Levy
through his relationship with Sabra and Isaiah through his care for the
two children in the family. These characters are thus humanized, but they
also at key points are invested with a religious significance that carries an
overt symbolism unusual in the film. For Levy, this occurs, as in the novel,
when he is terrorized by Osage's cowboys, who lasso him, force him to
drink whiskey, and shoot at him. Yancey comes to his rescue, underlining
that his western skills in repartee and shooting are still of value at this
stage in the story. Levy's significance is confirmed during this episode
through his association with Christian symbols—the donkey that carries
his goods and his position as he falls against the scale, with his arms
spread as on the crucifix. It is possible to see this as an attempt to Chris-
tianize a Jewish character, but in the context of Levy's role in the film and
his understated humor about his ancestry (he points out to the superior
Mrs. Wyatt that his family goes back to Moses rather than to a mere sig-
natory of the Declaration of Independence), it acts more effectively as a reminder of the origins of Christianity in Judaism.

The treatment of Isaiah is both different from the novel and less specific
in its religious reference.[27] Isaiah is fatally shot in the gunfight between
Yancey and The Kid. His fall is unnoticed by the participants but picked
out by the camera, which takes the time to hold him in long shot as he col-
lapses slowly onto the barrels. After the fight, the camera again returns to
Isaiah's level so that we see Yancey's boots going past as Isaiah makes a
final plea for help. Finally, his dead body is brought into the Cravat house
by Levy and then held by Yancey, as Sabra and her son look on in silence;
as in a silent film, the shot is held in a tableau of family grief that was
highlighted in the official program as one of film's key moments that
would enter into Hollywood history. Again, it is possible to read this as a
sentimental ending for a stereotyped figure, but the accidental brutality of

his death in a white men's fight and the passing by of Yancey as the boy dies does seem to make an unusual comment on the way in which the Southern habits of slavery, implicit in Isaiah's devotion, have been picked up and used by the pioneer family.

This emphasis on the diversity of the Western settlement and the symbolic resonance given to the Jew and the slave is part of the process whereby *Cimarron* "confronts America's myths rather than memorializing them."[28] But this process is most directly addressed in the treatment of the hero. Richard Dix as Yancey was publicized as a "two-gun poet in buckskin, dreamer, crusader, fighter, who helped make history in a day."[29] But Ferber does not allow the romantic appeal of Yancey as the western hero to disguise his irresponsible and dangerous restlessness, and the film's narrative follows this. Yancey dominates by his personality but is incapable of making an America based on his ideals; how far that comes about depends on the willingness of the more pragmatic Sabra to champion his views. At first, Yancey performs the classic tasks of the western hero whose self-confidence and ambitions feed into his search for truth and defense of the underdog. He uses his gun and his oratory to promote justice and commits the newspaper to attack corruption and social snobbery. He triumphs in a number of key situations early in the film, in gunfights with the villains, at the prayer meeting, and in the law court. Yancey also has the vices of the cowboy; he won't work in the office, he wants to keep moving into uncivilized territory, he seeks out opportunities for adventure, and he does not want to be tied down. This inability of the hero to accept the civilization of which he is the front rider is a familiar trope in the western, but *Cimarron* presents these "patriarchal absences" not as a tragedy or a loss but rather as a vacuum at the heart of the myth.[30] Yancey vanishes from large parts of the second half of the film to pursue U.S. expansion elsewhere in the west and in the Spanish-American War. He reappears as a barely recognizable drifter to perform one more heroic act and to be embraced by Sabra as "my boy." In a final twist, as he is released from the complicated life of the living man, he steps forward into myth in the form of a statue dedicated to the spirit of the pioneers. The western hero has been gradually hollowed out so that it becomes possible to hail him only when he can be fixed into a position that he never fully fulfilled.

The undermining of the hero is a major risk in a western, a film genre that from its silent days provided a space in which white masculinity was the subject of celebration and nostalgia. This is not to say that women are absent from westerns (though they largely are from some), since the very dependence of the western on concepts of masculinity means that it relies (even if only implicitly) on the balancing power of femininity. Women's roles are limited and mark out the boundaries of the civilization that is being established on the frontier; the mother of the pioneer family functions in opposition to the bargirls and whores who also follow the trail. For some critics, the ideal Western community, found in the films of John Ford, involves "an accommodation of masculinity to feminine views."[31] For others, though, the western is centrally concerned with masculine identity and its resistance to feminine concerns. Jane Tompkins's argument is particularly interesting in relation to *Cimarron* since she proposes that the western was developed in opposition to and as a means of fending off the different worldview being proposed in women's nineteenth-century fiction. "The Western *answers* the domestic novel," she writes. "It is the antithesis of the cult of domesticity that dominated American Victorian culture."[32] What such fiction values—church, home, reform, abstinence, and monogamy—is what the male hero is fleeing. The western then can be seen as working against the very traditions of women's fiction that Ferber is also working with and indeed often satirizing.

We can see what this might involve by looking at *Cimarron* as woman's film. Although the woman's film was less recognizable than the western in terms of iconography and setting, Tanio Ballio records it as an important genre at this point: "Introduced as a production trend in the teens, the woman's film was enriched by the talkies and during the thirties it flourished."[33] Maria La Place suggested that it was "distinguished by its female protagonist, female point of view and its narrative which most often revolves around the traditional realms of women's experience: the familial, the domestic, the romantic."[34] The world is seen from the woman's viewpoint, and the active heroine is confronted with "emotional, social and psychological problems that are specifically connected to the fact that she is a woman."[35] Her problems are made concrete in plots that depend on the woman actively choosing between mutually exclusive options that are often represented by two or more men or by different versions of her female self. While the endings of such films often endorse the conventionally feminine option of becoming a wife and mother, the process of the narrative frequently involves the opportunity to engage in actions outside the feminine norm, leading Jeanne Basinger to argue that such films allow for "a covert form of liberation."[36] As La Place showed in her analysis of *Now, Voyager* (Rapper, 1942), décor, clothing, and fashion are used not just as a reflection of women's engagement with consumption but also to express some of the dilemmas faced by the heroine and as a visible sign of the choices she makes.

Basinger's study of the woman's film spans 1930–1960 but does not include *Cimarron*. She argues that any genre "can be feminized when the issues become those associated with women's daily life,"[37] though she suggests that the western's position as "a solidly established genre" with a "real historical context" perhaps makes this more difficult.[38] Nevertheless, if we read *Cimarron* as a woman's film, the vacuum at its center disappears, for the diminution of the hero is paralleled by Sabra's development into an independent and autonomous heroine. A number of factors are important here. Right from the beginning, it is Sabra's choices that are stressed, and as the film goes on, her choices—to stay in Osage, to take on the running of the paper, and to be reconciled with her children—drive the narrative. Although the film does not always take her side (in her prejudice against the Indians, for instance, or her spoiling of her daughter), the audience is invited to understand what drives her and how she learns to work with change. The domestic setting, uncharacteristic of the western, fits the generic patterns of the women's film particularly in the sketch of Sabra's problematic relationship with her children. The emphasis on consumption, in particular, gains from being seen from this perspective. Sabra's desire to be fashionable now becomes not an irrelevance nor a mark of civilization's excesses (as Ferber herself might have intended) but rather a sign of legitimate self-esteem and expression. Sabra's success in having the first balloon sleeves in Osage deploys a metaphor of female consumption that predicts her later success as a businesswoman and leader. The immature girl who used dress and décor to assert her superiority becomes the immaculately dressed congresswoman, and the legitimacy of dress and fashion as such a signifier is reinforced at the celebratory dinner when Sabra's elegant hat and costume, acknowledged by Mrs. Wyatt, underline that her political success has also fulfilled her as a woman. This use of dress is also an indication of how the women's film operates so often within a framework of class. While the western is concerned with the fate of those outside society, the woman's film is often concerned with the class gradations within society that block off a woman's choices and with the modes of behavior required to breach them. Sabra's development, from the Southern girl rebelling against her family into a woman who takes pleasure in her work and her political activity, is comparable in its trajectory to later women's films such as *Imitation of Life* (Stahl, 1934), *Now, Voyager*, or the first part of *Mildred Pierce* (Curtiz, 1945).

The pulling together of the two genres, very different in status and definition, undoubtedly causes problems for the film. Kim Newman's summary is clear that the problems lie in its origins as an adaptation: "With its novelettish emphasis on the stoic forbearance of Dunne when faced with the fecklessness of Dix, the film is perhaps best considered as a woman's picture out West rather than a true Western."[39] That feminine adjective "novelettish" hardly does justice to Ferber's book and ignores the very real achievement of the film in putting Sabra's rise at the heart of the historical process. Newman's determination to keep the true western away from the feminine is symptomatic, but such a tendency ignores the finest moments in the film when the two genres work together. The first night at Osage, for instance, is the more vivid because we first see it through Sabra's frightened eyes; Yancey's visit to the bar is framed by the family's arrival in their wagon down the wild Main Street; and the sequence closes with Sabra pulling up the window blind to look out over the "Hall of Chance." Even more strikingly, Sabra accompanies Yancey in their first stroll down the street to confront the rougher elements of the town. Here, the interest the woman's film takes in fashion combines with the dandyism of the western; Sabra in black lace, heels, and a parasol walks alongside Yancey in his long coat, white Stetson, and spurred boots. Yancey's offence when his enemy puts a bullet through the crown of his signature hat is paralleled by Sabra's indignation at the affront to their dignity. The gang is seen off by a combination of Yancey's skills with his guns and Sabra's with her tongue. Yancey's shamefaced chagrin at being defended by his wife in this way provides an early indication that Sabra's rise will have to be at the expense of his masculinity, but in this scene the pleasures of the traditional western are reinforced by Sabra's unusual prominence.

THE GOOD EARTH AND THE "PRESTIGE MELODRAMA"

The success of Buck's novel was largely attributed to two factors, the realism in its rendering of Chinese life and its appeal to the common humanity of readers to whom that life had previously been unknown. Buck claimed to her publisher that "her interest has always centred on the normal life of human beings"[40] and specifically set herself to portray the ordinary life of a poor farmer in contrast to more intellectual and urban Chinese figures favored by Chinese writers and the "foreign and orientalized image of China and Chinese that populated American culture."[41] The novel contained dramatic scenes of famine and revolution, but it followed realist conventions in giving a detailed account of the everyday tasks of living and working on the land; it aimed at communicating "a fully rounded feeling of rural existence."[42] The book could therefore present something unfamiliar to its readers but also reassure them of the underlying connections between ordinary people. As the Book-of-the-Month Club News commented, "The people in this rather thrilling story are not 'queer' or 'exotic,' they are as natural as their soil. They are so intensely human that after the first chapter we are more interested in their humanity than in the novelties of belief and habit."[43] In transforming the book into "the solid seriousness of prestige melodramas,"[44] the film pays attention to both these aspects. Establishing a particular kind of Chineseness through an emphasis on different customs and behavior is important in maintaining the adaptation's realism, while the emphasis on underlying humanity is part of its claim to seriousness. Both of these drives are linked to gender and genre.

We have seen how publicity for the film emphasized the effort put into bringing genuine buildings, farming equipment, and decorative artifacts from China. The authenticity claimed for the décor is paralleled by the film's emphasis on customs and traditions that are markedly different from those of western viewers and carry a similar claim to realism. The film starts with Wang Lung's wedding and so introduces the main characters within the context of the rituals of a familiar yet very different event. The groom's bathing, the collection of the bride, the cooking of the wedding dinner, the celebratory joshing by family and friends are all laid out. This attention to detail continues throughout the film with an emphasis on local customs in, for instance, the red eggs distributed at the birth of the first son, the prayers to the gods at the local shrine, and the fireworks and celebratory songs at New Year. Traditional superstitions are acknowledged such as the belief that bad luck will follow boastful speeches or that the giving of a slipper indicates a woman's interest in a man. And traditional customs such as arranged marriages and the possibility of taking a second wife provide plot devices.

All this was deemed highly convincing, with *Film Daily* praising it as "China seen through Chinese eyes."[45] The emphasis on authenticity did not extend to the use of Chinese or Chinese Americans in the main speaking roles, as Buck had apparently desired, although publicity emphasized the use of hundreds of Chinese actors in small parts and as extras. Instead, European actors took the three main roles of Wang Lung (Paul Muni), O-Lan (Luise Rainer), and Lotus (Tilly Losch), while U.S. character actors played Wang's father and uncle.[46] The language used by the main characters does not follow the conventions of realism by being direct and demotic; much of the dialogue drew on the book, and the effect is to reference its difference from U.S. speech. Characters speak with an elaborate syntax and a formal tone; phrases like "It is well you were here" or "It shall be done" indicate that a different language is being spoken. The uncle and his wife, in particular, use what appear to be traditional sayings or proverbs. In its use of language, the film tries to establish its Chineseness through an attention to difference as well as to realism; the folk sayings refer to common ideas about how all rural people speak, but the difference is also emphasized. This is reinforced by the manner of speaking that Muni and Rainer adopt so that their European accents (particularly in Rainer's case) are inflected by a light, rather breathy tone and a rising inflection that comes to stand for a Chinese way of speaking.

The film does not therefore seek to convince us of its transparency in filming the real world as if it were a documentary; instead, drawing on the book's reputation as an authentic account, it spectacularly constructs a world that it presents to the audience as the real China. Publicity material indeed commented that that the studio had abandoned filming background footage in China because, ironically, the difference between it and the more accurate studio material would undermine the realism.[47] But the film's use of realism does not play down but rather draws attention to the film's construction, as can clearly be seen in the way in which farming is dealt with. Documentary realism would tend to emphasize the mundane repetition of labor, but *The Good Earth* uses self-conscious special effects to show Wang Lung's farming. This is true of the montage sequences discussed above that show sowing, hoeing, and irrigation. It is even more true of the spectacular scenes in which the harvest is collected in the teeth of the storm or a plague of locusts is fought off. The painterly effects as the wind ripples the fields of wheat or the locusts are seen as dark clouds in the sky are matched by the editing of image and sound to create a strong emotional impact.

The film's strategy of seeking to be realistic by drawing attention to the care with which it constructs difference can clearly be seen in the characterization of Wang Lung and in Muni's performance. Wang Lung is the central character, and the world of the film is largely seen through his eyes. It is his entry into the social world, into the House of Hwang, the grain merchants, and the tea house, which we share. His rise in the world is accompanied by changes in dress and behavior that illustrate the class structure, and although he values tradition and custom he also, by the end of the film, has allied with his eldest son in valuing more modern techniques of farming. Wang Lung therefore represents a particular social type in the Chinese society being presented, a type that has strong associations with U.S. values of hard work and independence but that is also differently positioned within Chinese rural life. In addition, Wang Lung is a strongly individuated character. He expresses his emotions freely, going against the stereotype of the inscrutable Chinese. He is shown as having a sense of humor and jokes with his friends; he expresses tenderness and anger with his children; he gives into temptation over Lotus; and falls into pride over his own achievements. Though presented as typically Chinese, Wang Lung is a rounded character with the foibles and faults of a real person.

It is important therefore that Paul Muni played Wang; in the publicity, Muni claimed, "I have never played myself. . . . I don't wish to play two parts that are alike."[48] He was respected as an actor and at this stage strongly linked to the biopic; *The Good Earth* was sandwiched between an Oscar-winning performance as Louis Pasteur and a much admired Émile Zola. His portrayal of the Chinese farmer has much in common with his other performances in its emphasis on an individual life and on the work of acting. His appearance is transformed through elaborate makeup giving him distinctive cheekbones and a high, bare forehead matched by a long Chinese-style "queue." In the publicity, Muni emphasized that his research had shown that the Chinese expressed their emotions strongly, and he therefore uses broad gestures and emphatic reactions to create the character. Along with the distinctive voice, he adopts a flat-footed, rolling walk and a short chuckle that turns into a full belly laugh. His eyes move continually, watching for the reactions of other characters. All this emphasizes that the realistic character of Wang has to be created by the skills of the actor and, so, associates Muni with the film's more realist ambitions of representing the distinctive features of Chinese rural life.

The character of O-Lan and Rainer's performance carry rather different values. For literary critics, the rewriting of the character for the film has been the most controversial aspect of the adaptation and provokes the familiar criticism of Hollywood's commitment to melodrama. In the book, she had been "the first strong ordinary woman in Chinese literature,"[49] the novel's "most memorable character," and "the story's moral center, a figure of courage, perseverance and instinctive commonsense."[50] She had however been subservient to Wang Lung, whereas in the film, James L. Hoban argues, various changes made in her role along with the decision to end the film with her death rather than following her husband's life afterward mean that "she becomes significant . . . to the point of standing alongside Wang in importance."[51] Conn is among those who maintain that this treatment has detrimental effects. It threatens to "suffuse" the book's "naturalism and sexual candor in a haze of Hollywood sentimentality. . . . O-lan is transformed into a glamorous creature"; the relationship between her and Wang Lung is reshaped into "a Westernized boy-meets-girl drama" in which Wang treats her "with an egalitarian respect almost completely at odds with the traditional patriarchal assumptions" that Buck was drawing on in her account of marriage in China (and experienced indeed in her own first marriage).[52] All of this, he argues, threatens to detract from the film's strength, which lay in the realist emphasis that created "powerful, authentic images of Chinese rural life."[53]

As so often in this kind of criticism, it is assumed that the accusation of sentimentality and romance is sufficient to block off further exploration, but it is worth considering the representation of O-Lan further in the light of the generic framework the film is working with. It is not an accident that the changes Conn and others criticize are associated with O-Lan, since what the film does is to balance the realist character created by the male star with the timeless symbolism associated with female stars. Just as the framework of the woman's film supported the characterization of Sabra Cravat, so a different version of melodrama supports the representation of O-Lan. In 1937, the year *The Good Earth* came out, *Stella Dallas* (Vidor, 1937) provided the quintessential version of the maternal melodrama, featuring Barbara Stanwyck as the working-class mother, sacrificing herself in order to ensure the well-being of her daughter. "Maternal melodramas are," according to Mary Ann Doane, "scenarios of separation, of separation and return, or of threatened separation";[54] they present a scenario in which the imperfect mother lets her child go in order for them to achieve the social success that she cannot provide. Christian Viviani argues that during the period of the Depression and the New Deal this valorization of maternal sacrifice had a particular resonance "in a period when America really needed to mobilise good will and dedication without promise of immediate recompense."[55] But the scenario made for a highly emotional recognition of the difficulty of female choice. In other forms of melodrama, the woman who chooses (as in *Cimarron*) against her own desires might be otherwise rewarded (with a job, a child, or a different kind of husband); in the maternal melodrama, her reward is her own negation as she is subsumed into an ideal version of self-sacrificing motherhood. Submission to social norms is transformed into a positive act but one that clearly punishes the woman.

The Good Earth does not follow the story line of the classic maternal melodrama, but the same emotional identification with self-sacrifice underpins the characterization of O-Lan. The film stresses her unstinting work in supporting Wang Lung on the farm and in her household duties, which include caring for her "retarded" daughter and her aged father-in-law. But beyond that the narrative involves a series of threats of separation or loss that equate with those of the maternal melodrama. O-Lan does not sacrifice herself for her child but rather for her husband, even though she knows that his rise in status will take him further away from her since she believes herself to be unworthy of his love as he grows more successful. This motif of female sacrifice underpins key narrative moments: O-Lan drives herself to exhaustion, working to bring in the threatened harvest just before the birth of the first child; she suggests that the second wife be brought into the home so that the family is not broken up by Wang Lung's obsession; she gives up her pearls at her husband's demand when she knows he wants them for Lotus; and she accepts that her second son must leave home when she learns that he is attracted to Lotus. Her death, although not overtly caused by these sacrifices, is nevertheless linked to her selflessness; she even asks for forgiveness when a contrite Wang Lung refuses to accept that she must die. While Wang Lung's actions work to create a character who is rooted in the film's Chinese context, O-Lan's sacrifices take on meaning within what the film promotes as the universally feminine roles of wife and mother.

The glamorization that O-Lan undergoes does not result in the conventional spectacle accorded to a female star. Her appearance is in fact contrasted with that of Lotus, whose exotic beauty is emphasized in her first appearance as a dancer; the editing here offers the fragmented, fetishistic emphasis on the face and hands associated with Hollywood's treatment of sexual women. The body of the more homely O-Lan is hidden by thick, padded clothing, and her face is often averted. The glamorization of her face is effected largely by the use of light and accompanies particular moments of exaltation associated with womanhood—the night of her marriage, the birth of her son, her request to be able to keep the pearls, and most fully at the moment of her death after she has given her blessing to her daughter-in-law, the next woman in the family. The face is lit as if from within and is accompanied by eyes raised upward and a mouth often open in fear or astonishment; at such moments, she becomes a female symbol, a visible sign of moral strength and sacrifice.

Because of this, O-Lan's characterization does not require the realist detail that creates Wang Lung. It is literally a monotonous characterization in which O-Lan is consistently presented as the moral center, the one who makes the major judgments and takes action as the huge forces of nature and war press on the family. Despite the emphasis on her silence and submissiveness in much of the accompanying publicity, it is O-Lan who kills the ox and accepts stolen food when the family are starving, who refuses to sell the land during the famine but insists on going South, who apparently kills the newborn child whom the family cannot support, and who refuses to have slaves in the house even when Wang Lung's status might demand it. This strength is associated not with masculinity but rather with a specifically feminine understanding of what is needed. Wang Lung farms the earth, but O-Lan represents the spiritual link to it that underpins the film's symbolic structure. Her actions are to be understood in the context of fate that links her to larger forces of nature. The film symbolically links timelessness, femaleness, and the earth through the figure of O-Lan. "The land will be there after me," she tells Wang Lung on her deathbed, and the peach stone she planted on the night of her marriage becomes the flowering tree that Wang Lung stands by after her death as he says, "O-Lan, you are the earth." The heavily symbolic moment closes the film with an overt reference to Buck's best seller but one that calls on the heavily gendered codes of melodrama to create identification and emotion. This treatment of O-Lan might be criticized as sentimental, as Conn suggests, but it needs to be put in the context of the gendered structures of feeling that Hollywood melodrama consistently drew on to render the impossible demands of femininity.

Just as the publicity about Muni's acting fitted the realism with which he is associated in the film, so the publicity for Rainer reinforces the association of emotional sacrifice and natural order that underpins her character. In her interviews, much is made of the character's submissiveness and silence; Rainer comments on how O-Lan "expresses herself with almost no verbal expression"[56] and talks about using her eyes to express emotions that are unspoken but that "every woman has."[57] Rainer's acting skills, like those of Muni, are praised, but the emphasis is not on the research involved or on the craft of acting but rather on her capacity to

feel the character's emotions, illustrated by stories of how her performance made even the technical staff on the shoot cry.

Halfway through the film, there is a shot from inside the covered
wagon that brings the family home from the south; a reverse shot gives us
the halo effect of the wagon's cover around O-Lan's head, making her
briefly into the Prairie Madonna whom Ferber mocked. It is a reminder
that *The Good Earth*, even in its emphasis on "Chineseness," is drawing on
a mix of generic conventions that provided a repertoire for these adaptations. *Cimarron* as well as *The Good Earth* can be seen as a prestige melodrama. Both films use the associations of the middle-brow novel to in-
crease their own prestige and represent that association by a realist
emphasis on the detail of frontier life in the past or in a foreign country. In
both films, the claim to accuracy and authenticity is related not just to the
original novel but also to the society portrayed in each novel; Hollywood's emphasis on spectacular realism in its presentation of "Osage" or
"China" is endorsed by its association with the original source. Both films
give a central role to the heroine, *Cimarron* using the conventions of the
woman's film to do this while also maintaining its status as a western,
whereas *The Good Earth* reworks the heroine's role so that she becomes an
idealized, self-sacrificing partner and in doing so makes the story more of
a melodrama. In *Cimarron*, the woman's position works against the
generic themes of the western; she is positioned in history and in the public sphere, while the man is restricted to a mythic position. In *The Good
Earth* the woman's position works with the generic conventions; the man
is in history, the woman becomes mythic.

ESTABLISHING THE COUPLE

We have seen that *The Good Earth* has been criticized for transforming its
story into "a Westernized boy-meets-girl drama." It is indeed the case
that, as Virginia Wexman argues, the construction of a compatible and
complementary couple by the end of the film is one of the most basic conventions of the Hollywood film; it is also one of the most criticized in
terms of adaptations. But it cannot be assumed that all such narratives
work in the same way or that the creation of the couple is necessarily a
simple task.[58] The successful genre novels by women writers like Ferber
and Buck might seem to be a good source for such stories, but as *Cimarron* and *The Good Earth* show, these family-based sagas actually prove
more difficult to bring into line than might have been thought. Both end
with a final understanding between the couple, but it is only achieved
through death when Yancey and O-Lan are valorized. In ending this chapter, I want to look further at the use of the romantic couple in Hollywood

adaptations through a brief commentary on some of the other commercially successful film adaptations of Ferber's novels. Ferber's work offers an interesting test case in this respect since, as we have seen with *Cimarron*, although the novels deal with romantic relationships, their central figure is generally an independent, working woman who is positioned within a discourse of national or regional identity. Romance and marriage are important to the books, but other stories intervene and even take precedence. The handling of these stories demonstrates not only the importance of the couple in these adaptations but also the variations in handling what were not straightforward romances.[59]

Both *Cimarron* and *Show Boat* offer the opportunity to look at the differences between adaptations of the same novel. The 1960 *Cimarron* (Mann), filmed in wide screen and color, made a number of changes that both put the couple more firmly at the center of the film and diminish Sabra's role outside it. Although the emphasis on historical change is still present, it is less clearly foregrounded through the intertitles and setting, and Sabra achieves her standing in the community via her ownership of the paper. Her participation in the women's club is seen as a social distraction rather than an attempt to address some of the social problems of the town and one source of her later political success. She does not enter public life and make her own career in Washington, so the celebration at the end is very much of Yancey's spirit rather than Sabra's own achievement. In the final scene, she learns that Yancey has been killed in the First World War, and so the gap between Yancey as a drifter and his status as a mythic hero is less striking.

In the 1931 *Cimarron*, Yancey and Sabra had represented different positions within myth and history. In 1960, the emphasis is on their personal life and, in particular, on Yancey's psychological motivation in relation to his wife and in terms of other characters. Yancey's relationship with Dixie is filled out; it is made clear that he has had a relationship with her in the past, and he is given the opportunity to defend himself to her and, unknown to Sabra, rejects her offer of a continuing relationship. More crucially, Yancey's relationship with The Kid is given a psychological rationale, providing a version of the relationship between a father and an angry adolescent son that was a popular topic in 1950s melodramas. At the first meeting, the relationship between them is joshing and affectionate, and The Kid tells his companions that he always wanted to be like Yancey. Later, Yancey explains The Kid's troubled background to Sabra, his loss of his father and home when he was a boy ("What do you suppose that would do to you?"), and blames himself for not doing more. The final showdown takes place when the gang has taken refuge in the Osage school. The Kid saves the life of one of the children and is shot not by Yancey but by one of his own gang. Dying, he tells Yancey, "I told you not to have faith in me"; Yancey touches his head gently with his hand just as he had touched the head of his own son on the night of his birth. "I felt responsible," he later tells Sabra.

All this gives background to Yancey that is not given to Sabra. Her practicality and her desire for social esteem are set against not just Yancey's idealism but also, rather oddly, his greater sense of commitment. At the beginning of the film, Sabra had been committed to her husband; "I have to go where my husband goes," she tells her mother. But, as she changes her position, Sabra's anxiety about the family's security begins to take the form of nagging, and Yancey's failure to commit himself to the family becomes her failure to appreciate not only his idealism but also his love for her. At points, as, for instance, during the argument about whether they might leave Osage for the next land rush, Glenn Ford plays the role humorously as a henpecked husband, agreeing in a bemused way, "We're not going. I guess that's the end of it." But at more serious moments, Yancey expresses his own sense of guilt and failure in a way that seems to turn the problem back to her. "You and I see things differently," he tells her. "Maybe you picked the wrong man." "Am I the wrong woman?" she replies, but he responds by accepting his responsibility with, "I can't please you." This has implications for their final breakup, which occurs after Yancey has been offered and effectively turned down governorship of the state. On their trip to Washington, we see Yancey's decision from the inside; he wants to make it up to Sabra but in the end cannot go along with the corruption that would accompany accepting the post. But we see Sabra from the outside—her rather febrile excitement at the luxury on offer in Washington and her desire to use social success to make her son behave as she wants. Reflecting on her own success, in a later scene, she points out that it has been built on both her son and her husband running away, and the final scene shows her alone with the telegram telling her about Yancey's death. In making these changes, this version of *Cimarron* moves in the direction of the family melodrama by making the couple more central and making Sabra more emotional. But it maintains the western's interest in masculinity and attempts to offer an insight into Yancey's character by treating him as a flawed man as well as a western hero. Ironically, having diminished Sabra's public success and increased Yancey's psychological motivations, the film still "has a great void at the centre"[60] and cannot manage even the symbolic moment of the couple's reunion through death provided by the earlier version.

In contrast with the western, the musical as a genre supports the creation of the couple, and indeed Thomas Schatz describes it as a genre of integration in which society is prefigured and celebrated in the coming together of the couple. In *Show Boat*, Ferber's heroine, Magnolia Ravenal, met and married Gaylord as an infatuated young woman but established herself as a successful singer when abandoned by her gambler husband. The book ends with her as an old woman reasserting herself as the owner of the *Cotton Blossom*, the boat on which she had been raised, while her daughter, Kim, continues her career as a successful actress. The 1927 musical had already streamlined the novel to provide for the reunion of Magnolia and Gaylord through their love for their daughter Kim. Both sound film versions follow this, but the way in which they approach the reconciliation shows again that the 1930s version was more at ease with the notion of a successful woman. In James Whale's 1936 *Show Boat*, Gaylord abandons his wife and daughter in Chicago after building up gambling debts. Magnolia, played by Irene Dunne, who had starred in *Cimarron*, turns to singing to earn a living and after a shaky start becomes a well-loved and successful performer. She retires as Kim begins to establish her own career. During rehearsals, Gaylord, unrecognized, gets a job as the doorman to observe his daughter. At the triumphant finale, a white-haired and dignified Magnolia recognizes Gaylord, but he tries to leave again; he is attracted back by the power of music as Magnolia, invited by Kim, starts to sing. He joins in offscreen and is brought back in by Magnolia, who introduces him to the audience not as her husband but as her first leading man, and the two are reunited in their duet of "You Are Love." Here the couple reestablish their initial relationship in a show business context that underlines the success of both mother and daughter.

The 1951 film, however, works to eliminate the successful women and to bring Gaylord back as an essential element of family life. In this version, Gaylord abandons his wife before he knows she is pregnant with Kim, and after one successful performance, Magnolia rejects the possibility of becoming a big star in New York and returns to her father and mother on the *Cotton Blossom*, where she has the baby. The film then shows Gaylord being told some years later about the birth of his daughter. Returning immediately to the show boat, Gaylord first sees his daughter, playing with her dolls; she explains that they are named after her mother and her absent father. He plays with her, singing "Make Believe," the song he sang with Magnolia at their first meeting. Magnolia approaches and Kim introduces her to Gaylord as "my mummy." Magnolia is at first hesitant, but the two embrace and slowly move onto the boat, watched by her father and mother, as Joe and the chorus sing "Ol' Man River." In this way, the initiative for the reunion is passed to the father, and his lovingly playful approach to his unknown daughter is a further example of the "changing perception of the role of fathers within the family," which Chopra-Gant identifies in U.S. films of the immediate postwar period.[61] Certainly it is striking not only that two successful female careers are wiped out in this version but also that Magnolia never sings once she has returned to the family. The couple is reestablished, but the lack of a romantic duet to express their love means that Magnolia's feelings find no expression.

Giant (Stevens, 1956) is now probably best known for the performance of James Dean, but its generic status as a family saga is underpinned by a narrative structure based on the relationship between the Texan rancher Jordan Benedict played by Rock Hudson and his Eastern/Southern wife, Leslie, played by Elizabeth Taylor. Here, as in the other Ferber novels, the romantic relationship is established early. Jordan, visiting Washington on business, returns to Texas with Leslie as his bride, and the film, like the novel, pits her more refined sensibilities and liberal views against the brashness of Texas and the traditions that Jordan follows on the ranch. As in the other films, this is represented by the way in which Leslie redecorates the ranch, and her dress and glamour underline her difference from the other Texan women. The relationship between the couple brought together at the beginning is specifically tested at key points. In the middle of the film, Leslie goes back to her home in Virginia with her two small children. She has suggested that they need time apart immediately after a scene in which Jordan has tried to force their son to ride a horse, a sign of his intention that Jordy, whatever his own talents and desires, is to be forced to take over the ranch from his father. There is a danger that Leslie will stay in her parents' more civilized home, but the couple is reestablished when Jordan arrives unexpectedly in the middle of a family wedding. As the bride and groom exchange their vows, Leslie becomes aware of him and finally turns to embrace him. They will go back to Texas though she warns him, "I'm no different now than when I left."

Her warning looks forward to the ending. Like the other films discussed, *Giant* ends with the couple coming together again, achieved in this case by Jordan moving toward Leslie's more liberal position. This time the couple has been at odds over Jordy's marriage to a Mexican girl, Juana, a marriage that has produced a mixed-race grandchild for Leslie and Jordan. In the final sequences, though, Jordan experiences the prejudice that Juana and her child suffer and gets into a fight over the right of a Mexican family to be served in a diner. In the final scene, Jordan and Leslie watch their two grandchildren, one blond, the other dark, standing side by side. Jordan declares that he's been a failure and that nothing has turned out as he planned. Leslie finally affirms that she now belongs in Texas and, referring back to the fight, tells him that he is now her hero. Like the other films, then, the marital relationship comes under scrutiny, but unlike *Cimarron*, the establishment of a couple in this film is secured by a softening of the hero's patriarchal stance, which allows the differences to be maintained in balance; Jordan's final comment—"If I live to be ninety, I'll never be able to figure you out"—underlines Leslie's femininity, while Leslie has both approved Jordan's change of heart and reaffirmed his masculinity.

June Hendler suggests that the "western and family melodrama converge in *Giant*,"[62] but although the film's credit sequences of cattle in the vast landscape seem to presage a western, the emphasis on personal relationships, the working through of generational problems, and the presence of Hudson, Taylor, and Dean as stars skews the film toward family melodrama. In fact, rather than a full-blooded melodrama, the story's focus on the couple's parting and coming together draws on conventions of the romance in which both parties reach accommodation through change. Jordan and Leslie are seen to work toward a marriage based on companionship and understanding in which both have to change. This is carried through in a highly gendered way when the film dwells on their role of parents. When the twins are babies, Leslie consistently takes the girl and Jordan the boy, but in adolescence Jordan resists the boy's plans for the future and Leslie resists the girl's. The parallelism of this is asserted in a scene with strong resonances with sex comedies of the late 1950s in which the humor lies in the fundamental similarity yet gendered difference between the couple. Lying in twin beds and primed separately by their offspring, the marital couple try to persuade each other to let one child go while resolutely maintaining their own plans for the other. In the ending, discussed above, Jordan's inability to figure Leslie out is asserted humorously; sexual difference has resolved itself into the stuff of comedy, and social integration between the two (sexes, families, and regions) is achieved.

Both *Giant* and the 1960 *Cimarron* allow for their heroines to express sexual attraction. As we have seen, more explicit sexual behavior had become a selling point for cinema during the 1950s, and within marriage both Sabra and Leslie offer sexual love as a way of overriding differences. However, it is the 1945 adaptation of *Saratoga Trunk* that offers the most explicit representation of an erotic attraction between the couple. There are a number of reasons for this. First of all, the film does not begin with marriage, and therefore the final achievement of the couple is not established until the end; the film draws upon the conventions of the romance, and the woman is uncluttered by other roles of mother, worker, or pillar of the community. Second, the film draws on some of the visual conventions of films noir with its use of shadows and contrasts of light and shade, particularly in the New Orleans sequences. Third, as in all the Ferber adaptations, the dress and décor carry meaning, but here rather than redecoration and fashion endorsing the woman's civilizing mission, the setting in languorous New Orleans and the emphasis on fashion, décor, food, and furniture are deliberately put into play as part of the heroine's mission of seduction. Finally, Ingrid Bergman, playing Clio, brings to the role the freedom Hollywood was more likely to give European actresses and the sensuality exploited also by Hitchcock in the contemporaneous *Spellbound* (1945) and *Notorious* (1946).

Saratoga Trunk tells the story of Clio, the illegitimate daughter of the son of one of New Orleans' aristocratic families and his long-standing mistress. Clio returns to New Orleans after her mother has died in exile in Paris determined to extract revenge and money from her father's family, who had broken up the relationship between her parents. She succeeds with the help of Gary Cooper's Texan Clint, a gambler living on his wits, with whom she falls in love. Determined to marry a millionaire, she breaks into high society at Saratoga Springs. Held back by her love for Clint, she cannot finally commit herself to the men she attracts, and the film concludes with her giving herself to Clint, who has fortunately himself become a millionaire by busting up a cartel on the newly arriving railroads. Apparently subdued by love, she tells him, "I let you wear the pants," and the film concludes with a huge close-up of the pair finally established as a couple. Publicity material described *Saratoga Trunk* as "a glittering period romance" in which "famous Ferber characters come to life."[63] It put the film in the tradition of *Cimarron* and *Show Boat*, in which the "American scene forcefully comes to life in the novels of Edna Ferber." Like many of the other Ferber adaptations, it was extremely successful at the box office.

Chopra-Gant argues that Clio's behavior is marked by delinquency that can be attributed to the lack of the authority of a father. As the romance structure requires, the hero and heroine represent different positions that have to be brought together. The work to establish the couple at the end involves a reordering of the binaries that they represent—Europe/America, femininity/masculinity, and East/West. Clio is at home in New Orleans, itself a town marked by sensuality and a mix of races, languages, food, and music; there, she threatens to "both de-Americanize and feminize Clint" by changing his dress and manners.[64] It is only in Saratoga where Clint gets a chance to behave like a western hero that Clio begins to change. Her declaration of love at the end also involves giving up her ability to control the relationship. The generic pressures of the romance to provide the couple at the end are here unfettered by those of the woman's film or the various versions of melodrama; the shift to the conventions of the western and Gary Cooper's persona as a western star strongly support Clio's submission to Clint's patriarchal authority in a way that neither *Cimarron* (1931) nor *Giant* allow. However, this underestimates what has happened earlier in the film and, in particular, the power with which Clio is established as desiring as well as desired. Chopra-Gant rightly draws attention to the extraordinary first meeting of Clio and Clint, when Clio exerts the female gaze that cinema was supposed to deny and looks him up and down in a deliberate act of appraisal and admiration. Such moments stand out from the narrative and give Clio an independent and outsider status that is reinforced by Ingrid Bergman's self-willed and sexual star persona.

Despite the recent championing of Buck and Ferber by cultural and literary critics, the adaptations discussed here are not generally understood through the discourses of authorship that were discussed in chapter 2. Nevertheless, these adaptations draw on a notion of popular authorship that can be transmuted into cinema more readily than literary or modernist classics because they have already proved their selling power to middle-brow audiences. The popularity of the source novels is both respectable and gendered, and the studio publicity emphasizes their educational aspects. They deal with big themes of nationality, ethnicity, and social change within the context of the family; the passing of time and the movement of history underpin the individual stories. In this way, they provide the stuff from which large-scale, prestige films of whatever genre could be made. But their strong-willed heroines also offered the cinema characters who could carry a story, and the Hollywood publicity machine attempted to position their equally strong-willed authors as the cocreators of prestige works of cinema. But while faithfulness to the ambition of the novels and to their central role for women was important, it is also clear that other factors shaped the adaptations. These included the social factors that in the 1930s made O-Lan into a selfless, idealized wife and in the 1950s positioned Sabra and Magnolia firmly into the home. At the same time, the heroine had to be adapted into the well-established cinematic conventions of the western, the musical, the woman's film, and the maternal melodrama while the emphasis on a family saga in the books was transmuted into cinema's emphasis on the creation of a couple. Many of the films here mix genres, overlaying stories, settings, and characterizations. While this is not unusual in mainstream filmmaking, in these adaptations it seems to indicate the attempt to interweave the ambitions and intentions that Hollywood was buying in the novel with the generic expectations of popular cinema. Sometimes this had mixed consequences in terms of reception as well as achievement. The 1931 *Cimarron* seemed to reflect a strong emphasis on faithfulness to the original, and its success in winning an Oscar for best picture might be ascribed to its historical sweep and its themes of expansion and modernity. This success was however mitigated by disappointment at the box office, a failure that has also been ascribed to its association with Ferber's authorship: "Given her gender, urban or ethnic allegiances, she was perceived as having no intuitive connection to the frontier legacy" that the western genre embraced.[65] This clash between authorship and genre can also be seen in *Giant*; the use of romantic comedy to siphon off the pressures placed on the heroine by the patriarchal order contrasts with film melodrama's summoning up of emotion to override the contradictions of the woman's position. But this clash between authorship and genre was by no means the rule. A transmutation can occur that keeps the woman central but makes her character work with the genre; the intensification of O-Lan's selflessness into the image of the sacrificial woman, Magnolia's public performance of independence in the1936 *Show Boat*, and Clio's assertion of her right to look as well as her enjoyment of being looked at are all significant instances of authorship, gender, and genre coming together to make popular cinema.

NOTES

1. Edna Ferber, quoted by Donna Campbell, in "'Written with a Hard and Ruthless Purpose': Rose Wilder Hare, Edna Ferber, and Middlebrow Regional Fiction," in *Middlebrow Moderns: Popular American Women Writers of the 1920s*, ed. Lisa Botshon and Meredith Goldsmith (Boston: Northeastern University Press, 2003), 42.

2. Kang Liao, *Pearl S. Buck: A Cultural Bridge across the Pacific* (Westport, Conn.: Greenwood Press, 1997), 80.

3. Quoted in *"The Good Earth," Picturegoer Weekly*, July 17, 1937 (Billy Rose Collection, New York Public Library of the Performing Arts).

4. See Heidi Kenaga, "Edna Ferber's *Cimarron*, Cultural Authority, and 1920s Western Historical Narratives," in *Middlebrow Moderns: Popular American Women Writers of the 1920s*, ed. Lisa Botshon and Meredith Goldsmith (Boston: Northeastern University Press, 2003), for a discussion of RKO's reasons for picking up the option on the novel. I am indebted to Kenaga for her acute account of *Cimarron*'s handling of historical themes.

5. *Program for Official Washington Opening*, RKO Theater, January 23, 1931.

6. "Edna Ferber's Epic of Empire," *Film Weekly*, January 27, 1931 (Billy Rose Collection, New York Public Library of the Performing Arts).

7. "The Making of 'Cimarron' Matter of Time-Patience-Genius" [*sic*], *Washington Program*, 1931 (Billy Rose Collection, New York Public Library of the Performing Arts).

8. "Cimarron," *International Photographer*, AFI catalog, December 1930, 28.

9. Picture caption, *Washington Program*, 1931 (Billy Rose Collection, New York Public Library of the Performing Arts).

10. Title page, *Group Discussion Guide* 2, no. 1 (January 1937) (Billy Rose Collection, New York Public Library of the Performing Arts).

11. "Author of the Novel," *Group Discussion Guide*, part 3, 20 (Billy Rose Collection, New York Public Library of the Performing Arts).

12. "How the Film Was Made," MGM U.S. program for *The Good Earth*, undated (Billy Rose Collection, New York Public Library of the Performing Arts).

13. "How 'The Good Earth' Was Made," *The Magazine Programme*, Palace Theatre, London, April 5, 1937 (Billy Rose Collection, New York Public Library of the Performing Arts).

14. "China Rises out of Hollywood," *Picturegoer's Famous Films Supplement* 18 (December 1937): 2 (Billy Rose Collection, New York Public Library of the Performing Arts).

15. Jim Hitt, *The American West from Fiction (1823–1976) into Film (1909–1986)* (Jefferson, N.C.: McFarland, 1990), 203.

16. Peter Conn, *Pearl S. Buck: A Cultural Biography* (Cambridge: Cambridge University Press, 1996), 131.

17. Colleen Lye, *America's Asia: Racial Form and American Literature 1893–1945* (Princeton, N.J.: Princeton University Press, 2005), 233.

18. Lye, *America's Asia*, 212.

19. David Lusted, *The Western* (London: British Film Institute Publications, 2003), 126.

20. Lusted, *The Western*, 131.

21. Kenaga, "Edna Ferber's *Cimarron*," 173.

22. Peter Stanfield, *Hollywood, Westerns, and the 1930s* (Exeter, UK: University of Exeter Press, 2001), 32.

23. Quoted in Campbell, "'Written with a Hard and Ruthless Purpose,'" 30.

24. J. E. Smyth, "*Cimarron*: The New Western History in 1931," *Film and History* 33, no. 1 (January 2003): 10.

25. Edna Ferber, *Cimarron* (Cutchogue, N.Y.: Buccaneer Books, 1958), 280.

26. Lynne Kirby, *Parallel Tracks: The Railroad and Silent Cinema* (Durham, N.C.: Duke University Press, 1997), 205.

27. In the book, Isaiah grows to manhood and fathers a child by an Osage woman; all three are rumored to have been killed by the tribe.

28. Smyth, "*Cimarron*: The New Western History," 14.

29. Publicity material, *Film Weekly*, January 27, 1931 (Billy Rose Collection, New York Public Library of the Performing Arts).

30. Stanfield, *Hollywood, Westerns, and the 1930s*, 35.

31. Gaylyn Studlar and Matthew Bernstein, "Introduction," in *John Ford Made Westerns: Filming the Legend in the Sound Era*, ed. Gaylyn Studlar and Matthew Bernstein (Bloomington: Indiana University Press, 2001), 11.

32. Jane Tompkins, *West of Everything: The Inner Life of Westerns* (Oxford: Oxford University Press, 1992), 39.

33. Tanio Ballio, *Grand Design: Hollywood as a Modern Business Exercise, 1930–1939* (New York: Scribner, 1993), 235.

34. Maria La Place, "Producing and Consuming the Woman's Film: Discursive Struggle in *Now, Voyager*," in *Home Is Where the Heart Is*, ed. Christine Gledhill (London: British Film Institute Publications, 1987), 139. *Now, Voyager* was a speedy adaptation of a best seller by another female author, Olive Higgins Prouty.

35. Jeanne Basinger, *A Woman's View: How Hollywood Spoke to Women, 1930–1960* (London: Chatto & Windus, 1993), 506.

36. Basinger, *A Woman's View*, 506.

37. Basinger, *A Woman's View*, 464.

38. Basinger, *A Woman's View*, 468.

39. Kim Newman, "*Cimarron*," in *The BFI Companion to the Western*, ed. Ed Buscombe (London: Andre Deutsch, 1988), 255.

40. Buck, cited by Karen J. Leong, in *The China Mystique* (Berkeley: University of California Press, 2005), 24.

41. Leong, *The China Mystique*, 27.

42. Conn, *Pearl S. Buck: A Cultural Biography*, 131.

43. Book-of-the-Month Club News, cited in Liao, *Pearl S. Buck: A Cultural Bridge*, 67.

44. John Belton, *American Cinema/American Culture* (New York: McGraw Hill, 1994), 73. See James L. Hoban, "Scripting *The Good Earth*: Versions of the Novel for the Screen," in *The Several Worlds of Pearl S. Buck*, ed. Elizabeth J. Lipscomb, Frances E. Webb, and Peter Conn (Westport, Conn.: Greenwood Press, 1994), for an account of the script development for the film.

45. *Film Daily*, cited in Leong, *The China Mystique*, 28.

46. There could have been miscegenation issues had the actors made a white/Asian pairing, though Susan Courtney notes that in this period the PCA was generally concerned with white/black romances. See Courtney's *Hollywood Fantasies of Miscegenation* (Princeton, N.J.: Princeton University Press, 2005).

47. "How 'The Good Earth' Was Made."

48. Paul Muni, in interview feature, *Picturegoer Weekly*, July 17, 1937 (Billy Rose Collection, New York Public Library of the Performing Arts). See also "The Muni Method" and "Drama behind the Drama," in *Picturegoer's Famous Films Supplement*.

49. Liao, *Pearl S. Buck: A Cultural Bridge*, 4.

50. Conn, *Pearl S. Buck: A Cultural Biography*, 124.

51. Hoban, "Scripting *The Good Earth*," 131.

52. Conn, *Pearl S. Buck: A Cultural Biography*, 192.

53. Conn, *Pearl S. Buck: A Cultural Biography*, 193.

54. Mary Ann Doane, *The Desire to Desire: The Woman's Film of the 1940s* (Bloomington: Indiana University Press, 1987), 72.

55. Christian Viviani, "Who Is without Sin? The Maternal Melodrama in American Film, 1930–39," in *Home Is Where the Heart Is*, ed. Christine Gledhill (London: British Film Institute Publications, 1987), 96.

56. Luise Rainer, in "Analysis of the Photoplay Dialogue," *Group Discussion Guide*, part 4, 27 (Billy Rose Collection, New York Public Library of the Performing Arts).

57. Luise Rainer, in interview feature, *Picturegoer's Famous Film Supplement*, December 18, 1937, 2 (Billy Rose Collection, New York Public Library of the Performing Arts).

58. Virginia Wright Wexman, *Creating the Couple: Love, Marriage, and Hollywood Performance* (Princeton, N.J.: Princeton University Press, 1993).

59. Buck's novels also continued to be adapted, though they are now less well known.

60. Philip French, *Westerns* (Manchester, UK: Carcenet Press, 2005), 83.

61. Mike Chopra-Gant, *Hollywood Genres and Postwar America: Masculinity, Family, and Nation in Popular Movies and Film Noir* (London: I. B. Tauris, 2006), 81.

62. June Hendler, *Best Sellers and their Film Adaptations in Postwar America* (New York: Peter Lang, 2001), 121. Hendler's discussion is particularly valuable in relation to the way racial issues are presented in the film and book of *Giant*.

63. "American Scene Recreated in 'Saratoga Trunk,'" *Look America's Family Magazine Discussion Guide*, n.d., "published as a public service of Warner Bros." (Billy Rose Collection, New York Public Library of the Performing Arts). Like the other publicity materials cited in this chapter, the guide gives a wealth of statistics about the film.

64. Chopra-Gant, Hollywood Genres, 43.

65. Kenaga, "Edna Ferber's *Cimarron*," 279.

5

Revising the Western

Movement and Description in The Last of the Mohicans *and* Brokeback Mountain

This chapter continues the discussion of the western genre in relation to two more adaptations but does so for rather different purposes, one of which might be deemed ideological and the other formal. In the first place, the two films under discussion have been involved in debates about representation and identity, which have been important to theoretical work on the western but which have also helped to create what has been called the revisionist western, a western that takes into account different ways of thinking about gender and ethnicity and that has questioned some of the modes of characterization conventionally associated with the genre. In the case of *The Last of the Mohicans* (Mann, 1992), the adaptation claimed to work against its source in dealing with the representation of Native Americans; in the case of *Brokeback Mountain*, the film seeks a close relationship with its source in presenting what was hailed as a mainstream breakthrough in the representation of gay sexuality. In both cases, the question of faithfulness to the source is raised again and repays further discussion.

In addition, in both films, the setting offers specific pleasures and indeed is one of the things that makes them identifiable as westerns. This raises the second area for exploration in this chapter—the use of landscape. This is a key area for discussion of adaptation because it raises what has been seen as one of the central differences between cinema and literature—a film's reliance on images and a novel's on words. The treatment of setting appears to be a clear example of this difference in that novels use a particular form of words—"description"—to tell readers about the landscape and inform them of its importance, while films show the

landscape with a specificity and solidity appropriate for cinema's reputation as "the 'phenomenological art' par excellence."[1] Without claiming
that these two examples can possibly cover the relationship between
western films and their sources, I hope that this discussion will again
demonstrate that films do not all work in the same way and show how
differently a film's setting can relate to "description" and the impact this
has on narrative action and characterization.

Although many westerns were based on popular novels and stories,
this fact is now largely disregarded. The two films that are the subject of
this chapter—Michael Mann's 1992 version of *The Last of the Mohicans* and
Ang Lee's 2005 *Brokeback Mountain*—are unusual as westerns in the status
given to the fact of adaptation. Both are commercially successful Hollywood films, though neither is a straightforward mainstream product.
Mann, a writer, director, and producer, came to *The Last of the Mohicans*
from television, though *Manhunter* (1986), his early adaptation of Thomas
Harris's *Red Dragon*, had had success. He was a genre/commercial director in charge of a remake of a classic novel, and the film cast the British
Daniel Day-Lewis in the central role, turning him into a blockbuster star.
Ang Lee, by contrast, was known for the variety of his films, nearly all of
which have been adaptations, including the classic adaptation, *Sense and
Sensibility*, the Chinese crossover success, *Crouching Tiger, Hidden Dragon*
(2000), and the comic book *Hulk* (2003). Neither director was associated
with westerns. Although both films are adaptations, their sources are very
different. *The Last of the Mohicans* is based on a classic American novel by
James Fenimore Cooper published in 1826, which has been subject to
many forms of adaptation, while *Brokeback Mountain* is (so far) the only
version of the short story of the same name, first published in 1997 by E.
Annie Proulx. The relationship between the films and these sources is also
very different, as this chapter will explore. As we shall see, *The Last of the
Mohicans* (1992) has become the center of a critical debate, which demanded that the film should have been more unfaithful to its source while
the faithfulness of *Brokeback Mountain*, continually asserted in its marketing, allowed it to challenge the conventions of the western and Hollywood's homophobia.

Once a Hollywood staple, the western has fallen on hard times. Its
complex and rich intertwining of a frontier setting, male action, and
themes of national identity and history no longer sustains a viable genre,
and the framework for analyzing it through the oppositions of civilization and wilderness, the garden and the desert, has been challenged. Its
lack of resonance in contemporary discourses makes Jack Nachbar argue
that "during the last quarter century we have become disillusioned by
the racism, sexism, imperialism, and environmental naiveté all too often
present in Westerns."[2] The western's status as "the paradigmatic Ameri-

can narrative" is ignored or resisted, and audiences cannot be relied on to understand or work with the western's generic features.[3] Insofar as it continues to exist as a genre, a new western has to identify clearly its difference from the old and is, in this way, already involved in an overt process of adaptation.

Critical work on the western has also reassessed the genre. Ed Buscombe and Roberta Pearson point to the influence of "'new' Western historians ... substituting a narrative of genocide and environmental destruction for the more traditional one of the triumphal progress of white American civilization."[4] The task of settlement, always problematic in the western, is now loaded with cultural baggage that is very hard to ignore. The terms "savagery" and "wilderness" have particular connotations in relation to the culture of Native Americans, and critics can no longer describe the West unproblematically as "space, unpeopled space."[5] The nature of the frontier has changed, and "recasting" it as "a border between the powerful and the dispossessed, men and women, whites and people of colour has unearthed new meanings for the form."[6] In such work, the concept of the frontier as an imaginary line moving westward is replaced by the notion of a contested space, "'middle ground' on which empires, European colonies and Indian republics intersected, mixed and co-existed."[7]

Further controversy has been caused by a focus on masculinity in the western and the argument that the genre is "deeply haunted by the problem of becoming a man."[8] Jane Tompkins has been the most controversial proponent of this approach, polemically arguing that the western "isn't about the encounter between civilisation and the frontier. It's about men's fear of losing their mastery, and hence their identity, both of which the Western tirelessly invents."[9] Tompkins suggests that the silent, self-contained, ever-enduring hero who is "harsh and pure like the desert" is the product of "a massive suppression of inner life."[10] In addition, westerns pass this onto their audiences; they "teach men that they must take pain and give it, without flinching."[11] Other scholars have resisted the tendency to focus the complexity of the western into a monolithic trope of masculinity, and Tompkins has been criticized for pushing "a brilliant argument to a polemical extreme."[12] However, Martin Pumphrey's argument that "the ideal of masculinity offered by Westerns in their heroes is fundamentally contradictory" has been more widely accepted; "the hero's masculine toughness must be partially feminised," he suggests, if he is not to fall into the role of villain.[13]

Work on masculinity can be positioned into a broader context in which the study of identity and representation has combined with new approaches to the history of the West to shift critical emphases. Attention to the representation of masculinity has been accompanied by greater attention paid to the role of women, Native Americans, and other races in the

genre. In addition, the separation of the (male) western from other (female) genres is now less emphasized with, for instance, both Douglas Pye
and David Lusted drawing links between the western and the romance
and proposing that the work westerns did on masculinity could be best
understood as melodrama "dramatising the psychic and emotional con-
flicts within and between men."[14]

It is these changes that have led to the appearance of what has been
called the revisionist western. In some ways, this concept underestimates
the continual revisions and changes that permitted the western to flour-
ish for so long as a genre and seems to overlook the fact that, at least since
the late 1940s, some westerns have attempted to present their Indian characters more favorably.[15] Nevertheless, the term revisionist western is a
useful one to describe films that are made for an audience that lacks the
detailed familiarity with conventions that could previously be assumed
and that attempt to make a deliberate and knowing comment on some of
those very conventions. As Dowell suggests, "The new Westerns are
oddly disconnected from the old, even though (perhaps precisely because) they rely so heavily and simplistically on a dusty notion of what
constitutes a 'classic' Western."[16] Such films have to not only underline
their own status, often by referring self-consciously to the history of the
genre, but also draw on a "'new,' essentially *popularised* history of the
American west" that pays particular attention to a different "treatment
and image of the Indian."[17] The Oscar successes of *Dances with Wolves*
(Costner, 1990) and *Unforgiven* (Eastwood, 1992) indicated that the revisionist western could gain respectability as well as audiences, and in different ways, both *The Last of the Mohicans* (1992) and *Brokeback Mountain*
continued down that path.

COOPER'S LANDSCAPE AND THE WESTERN

Cooper's Leatherstocking novels, published between 1823 and 1841, have
been widely discussed as precursors of the western. The reasons for this
provide us with an indication of some of the generic features of the traditional western as well as being important for a discussion of the 1992 *The
Last of the Mohicans*. First, Cooper was "the first American writer to use the
frontier as a continuing theme."[18] His concept of it as "a constantly moving imaginary line between wilderness and civilization" allowed the frontier to cover the eastern setting of *The Last of the Mohicans* as well as the
more familiar western setting of *The Prairie* a year later.[19] What was important was that the land was so "wild, magnificent, uncontrollable" that,
while the characters might seek to dominate it, they also had to treat it
with respect.[20] The frontier setting "afforded Cooper a means of exploring

the social and moral ramifications of the historical process" of expansion,[21] but its landscapes were also "invested . . . with metaphorical import and used . . . as concrete instances of the frontier's crucible."[22]

Secondly, Cooper created the contradictory hero, variously called Hawkeye, Pathfinder, Natty Bumppo, and Leatherstocking. Cooper's central character was "a prototype of the uniquely American hero associated with the frontier and the opening of the West."[23] As John Cawelti points out, he embodies, in his frontiersman's dress, a mixture of nature and artifice, a "wilderness version of the settler's dress" ornamented with "buckskin fringes and porcupine quills 'after the manner of the Indians.'"[24] He condemns savagery but uses violence and is a man at home in nature whose gun is named "Kill-deer." His respect for and knowledge of the Indians is always marked by his emphasis on their racial difference; he is "a white hero who learns the ways of the savages so effectively that he can function simultaneously as their greatest friend and as their deadliest enemy."[25] Cooper helped to create the stereotypes of the Indian as the brutal or the noble savage, doomed to extinction, but his white hero was himself doomed, always moving with the frontier and driven ever westward by the civilization he protected and feared.

Crucially, Cooper's novels not only popularized the concept of the frontier but also developed a particular way of describing its landscapes. Lee Clark Mitchell points to the hero's keen vision and his ability to read the landscape through its smallest details. He links this to the strong emphasis on detailed description in Cooper's writing and to the way in which the protagonists so often halt in admiration or fear before a particularly striking terrain. Each novel begins with a panorama, "an eagle-eye view of native scenes that invokes the sublime," before moving into more detailed descriptions of particular scenes. These descriptions are not separate from the action but rather absorb narrative action into description; the hero has to adopt a watchful immobility in studying the landscape for the signs of activity, for small details that might reveal what the forest hides. Mitchell comments on how often in *The Last of the Mohicans* "activity . . . originates in stillness," episodes of violence being preceded by motionless, intense waiting. Mitchell suggests that this emphasis on reading the landscapes for narrative and thematic meaning encourages a particularly attentive approach not only in the hero but also in the reader. Cooper invites us, through his rhetoric, to admire the extensive passages of description that present the landscapes as "self-sufficient set pieces—indeed, as stage sets that draw attention to their own theatricality, or as self-consciously painted canvases."[26] At the same time, the descriptive passages require the reader, like the protagonists, to wait in suspense for the setting to come alive. The narrative of *The Last of the Mohicans*, therefore, while incorporating explosive bursts of action, relies on "still bodies and silent moments" as the characters pause attentively in highly composed settings; the novel ends with a final tableau in which the living and dead are held in "the ritual hush of death."[27] In the final novel of the sequence, *The Deerslayer*, Mitchell suggests that description is so dominant that it seems as if individual characters are "thrust into subsidiary roles attendant on the landscape [and] . . . figures seem absorbed by landscape."[28]

Other influential writers more directly linked to the western novel followed Cooper's use of lengthy descriptive passages to render the dominance of the landscape. Mitchell goes on to discuss Owen Wister's *The Virginian* and Zane Grey's *Raiders of the Purple Sage* and finds again a continual "shift between narrative and descriptive modes."[29] He argues that the best of this writing makes description active, a suggestion that has implications for analyzing the role of description in adaptations. Mitchell's account emphasizes deliberate sensory activity—listening and watching—undertaken by the reader as well as the hero, activity that is more strongly associated with the multimedia activity of cinema than with reading. As we have seen, those espousing media specificity in adaptation studies have stressed cinema's reliance on images. Cooper's long descriptive passages and the watchfulness they demand of the hero and reader suggest that cinema might carry this genre more effectively than the novel, using images to conjure up the external landscape. Film's "ability to show movement and record 'authentic' landscapes . . . seemed ideally suited to recording and restaging a historical West that was fast passing away."[30] This, combined with Mitchell's emphasis on the positioning of the novel reader as a viewer of landscapes, suggests, at last, that there is a possibility that an adaptation might not inevitably involve a diminution of the original.

There is one further aspect of Mitchell's account that will be pertinent. Mitchell considers the paintings of Albert Bierstadt, which were, like Cooper's novels, hailed as genuinely American art in the 1860s, and he finds in their "vast scale and exacting detail" the same emphasis on sublime description. Mitchell suggests however that Bierstadt's paintings lack a single viewing position from which the landscapes they depict can be understood and admired. Instead, different parts of the canvas offered "discrete *mise-en-scènes*, each with a physical integrity that seems convincing only in terms of itself." Shadows do not relate to the clouds above, mountains loom miles high, perspective is foreshortened, and the eye is compelled through "a disparate mix of realistic details, narrative enactments, and melodramatic sweep of landscape" that fails to cohere.[31] The paintings exceed the "faithful geography" they apparently promise and offer "conflicting perspectives, requiring a moving eye."[32] Like Cooper's lengthy descriptive passages, Bierstadt's paintings, in Mitchell's account, seem to require cinema for their fulfillment.

THE LAST OF THE MOHICANS
AND THE VANISHING NATIVE AMERICAN

Cooper's novel has been the subject of innumerable adaptations including children's abridged versions, films, comics, cartoons, and television series. Like the classics discussed in chapter 1, the story is more likely to be known through these different versions than through the original novel, and the 1992 film indeed credits the 1936 film adaptation as a source, largely following its version of the plot including the introduction of a story about the romance between the hero and one of the young women he is charged with protecting. It is not my intention, however, to look at the novel's different adaptations in a variety of formats, a task that Martin Barker and Roger Sabin undertook admirably in their book, *The Lasting of the Mohicans*. Instead, I want to focus specifically on the 1992 version and to begin this analysis by looking at the controversy that has surrounded its approach.

Before turning to this critical debate, it is worth noting that Mann, as part of the publicity for the film, took a deliberately provocative approach to his source. Far from expressing a wish to be faithful even to the spirit of the novel, Mann sets out to distance himself from the original. The first move in this process was a familiar one, a claim of greater realism that suggests to the potential audience that they are getting something closer to the truth. Here, Mann claims that the truth lies with himself and his earlier genre work rather than with the original author:

> The idea was to take this and make it the way it really must have been . . . and give it the same kind of edge that it would have had if I was making a contemporary thriller on the streets of L.A. or New York. The frontier was not this happy little place of log cabins. This was the lower east side of New York in the 18th century.[33]

The second move was to condemn the original's treatment of its Indian characters, but Mann's claims in relation to this proved to be more contentious. The press kit suggested that Mann "disliked Cooper's deeply conservative views on race, his mixing up of tribal names and iconography, and his indulging in poetic excesses."[34] He therefore suggested that his intention in this remake was to challenge the way Cooper "appropriated and discarded the entire history of the Northeastern Woodlands American Indians. What he took away was their power."[35] This was linked back to realism with the claim that the film would offer authentic representations of Native American life in terms of dress and weaponry that reflected the different tribal cultures in the film. In claiming greater realism and greater respect for Native American culture, Mann was positioning this version of *The Last of the Mohicans* as a revisionist adaptation.

The 1992 film has generated considerable anger among academic commentators who challenge Mann's claims. The film was released in the same year as the celebrations of the five hundredth anniversary of Columbus's "discovery" of America, and the film became part of a more general discussion of what was being celebrated. Jeffrey Walker mounts a swingeing attack on all the film adaptations of the book, suggesting that they "do a sterling job of presenting Cooper's *mise-en-scène*" but arguing that "none of the films accurately reproduce Cooper's plot, and few come close to understanding Cooper's theme."[36] The 1936 version demonstrates this by shifting the love interest to the hero, a "violation of the plot" that, Walker asserts, would have been "distasteful to Cooper."[37] He saves particular vitriol however for the "Michael Mann pot-boiler"[38] and comments that the damaging decision to turn it into a love story for commercial reasons means that it ignores "the essence of the Native American theme."[39] Walker objects to the way in which, following the 1936 version, *The Last of the Mohicans* (1992) involves Hawkeye in a romance; complains that the woman, Cora Munro, is white instead of mixed race (as she is in the novel); but then berates Hollywood for not going further than Cooper did by telling a story about "interracial relationships, independent men and women, Native Americans and the historical truth behind the real violence that generated American culture."[40]

Gary Edgerton, in a more measured article, takes up Mann's claimed intent of doing justice to the Native Americans and demonstrates that the film consistently "undercut his stated intentions to revise the negative stereotyping of Native Americans."[41] Edgerton argues that, although Hawkeye's upbringing as a Mohican is emphasized at first, the film moves him, particularly through his romance with Cora, into the position of a white character so that, by the end, his status as Chingachgook's son is overlooked. The Indian characters are both stereotyped and marginalized. Drawing on a detailed scene analysis, Edgerton argues that, from the opening deer-hunting episode, the presentation of Hawkeye as a dominant white action hero pushes to one side the more sympathetic Indian characters, Chingachgook and Uncas. Magua, although he is given a reason for his aggressive violence, is "still limited in status by his villainy" and meets a death that is "deserved, desired and justified."[42] The dubious spiritual qualities assigned to Chingachgook as a good Indian are illustrated by the "pure Hollywood hokum" of his speech (in English) at the end, and Edgerton suggests that the film does nothing to counter the myth that the Native American was doomed at this point in history.[43] The film accepts that the different races are, as Hawkeye says, "a breed apart"; the feeling expressed in the mutual looks between Uncas and Alice is "underdeveloped and a dead-end" so that "a multicultural union . . . is still inconceivable."[44] The hero has been brought up by his Indian father, but this is forgotten when Chingachgook declares himself "the last of the Mohicans," and Edgerton argues that "the characters behave as though genes are all that count in determining one's breeding."[45] In much of this, the film is faithful to the book. Like Walker and over the same issue, Edgerton wishes that this adaptation had taken the risk of unfaithfulness: "Keeping Cora a mixture of races and nationalities . . . and then linking her romantically with the cultural hybrid Hawkeye would be a bold and revisionist move for a Hollywood filmmaker today."[46] But he accepts that "the point is not so much to pass judgement on the filmmakers" as to understand that the film represents "another vivid reminder of how difficult it is in our culture to adequately imagine any credible solutions to the multiracial challenges that still confront us."[47]

Edgerton, unlike many commentators on film adaptations, analyzes image and editing as well as plot to make his critique. The same is true of a sophisticated account provided by M. Elise Marubbio, who begins with the promotion of this version as "a multicultural film dedicated to a more sympathetic and authentic reading of Native American cultures."[48] The film's failure is, she argues, the more disappointing at a time when the quincentenary had provoked an intense discussion about the realities of colonialism and racism that followed Columbus. Marubbio's argument falls into three strands. First, she argues that the film, far from critiquing the original, follows Cooper in "positioning Native American characters into racializing classificatory systems that reduce them to stereotypes which either idealize or debase them."[49] These "damaging representations (swarming, slaughtering, would-be rapists) are borrowed directly from Cooper and have become stock footage in film renditions of the story."[50] Order is achieved by reinforcing "a hierarchy of white racial and political dominance," an order that Mann's narrative, like Cooper's, achieves by "removing the most 'savage' and unruly elements from the setting."[51]

Second, Marubbio takes up the points at which the film differs from Cooper's novel, in particular the romance between Hawkeye and Cora. Like Edgerton, she argues that the focus on this relationship has the effect of pushing the Indian characters to the periphery. By making Uncas fall in love with the unobtainable Alice, rather than the mixed-race Cora of the original novel, the film calls up "past ideals of white purity."[52] While Hawkeye's upbringing gives him a certain exoticism for Cora and the audience, his role as Chingachgook's son is abandoned when he "chooses Cora . . . and her whiteness over his Indian family," and their union "effectively removes the possibility of an American future born of Anglo-Native blood and grounds America's mythic heritage in purely Anglo bloodlines."[53] This underlines the film's narrative alignment with the position of the colonial settlers in opposition to both the British and French rulers and the Indian savages. Cora's move toward Hawkeye and away from her Scottish father is expressed in her growing sympathy with Hawkeye's support for the colonialists' determination to defend their families and land, obscuring the contested ownership of the land and the colonial settlement as a cause of the vanishing of the Mohicans.

The third strand of the argument is Marubbio's discussion of the positioning of the spectator through visual organization and camera movement. Marubbio describes the first images of the film that give a panoramic view of the forest from above: "The cinematography . . . does not penetrate the landscape but gazes on its untouched entirety," and Marubbio suggests that the viewer is, in this way, put into the position of the early colonialists:

> Mann seductively draws us into a context in which we, as an extension of the camera's eye, take on the role of external surveyor of this American Eden. As the imperial eye, we take the first step in the colonial expansion process: We scout the seemingly untouched frontier wilderness—viewing its resources, its attributes—anticipating the cultivation of this Eden.[54]

This "colonial/imperial surveillance of a land suitable for exploit" is, Marubbio maintains, reinforced in the following scene of the deer hunt in which "the sequencing keeps us at a distance . . . which effectively positions us as a surveying neo-colonial presence attached to the camera eye,"[55] invited to classify the three men racially but also to voyeuristically objectify their physical appeal. Throughout the film then, Marubbio argues, "Mann positions the viewer as the neo-colonial eye of the camera,"[56] making it impossible for the film to represent the very different viewpoint of the Native American struggle and reviving "the romantic rhetoric of expansionism, imperialism and racial homogeneity" that informs the myth of the American frontier.[57] The revival of the frontier myth with its binary of the noble and vicious savages is, she suggests, not surprising at the politically charged time of the quincentenary. She reads the film's neo-colonial positioning of the viewer and the representation of Native Americans as "a group that must be ordered and silenced" as a political act, "a reaction to the rising activism of Native Americans since the 1960s."[58] At this point, though, at the end of the article, she backs away from the notion that this might be the conscious purpose of Mann as the director to whom she has consistently credited the organization of the film. Instead, the film reveals "the depth to which racism and colonialism are embedded in our culture";[59] whatever Mann's intentions, "the results are a neo-colonial sanctioning of white American supremacy that the viewer, including the Native American viewer, participates in reinforcing."[60]

This account of Cooper's importance to the development of the western and the discussion of the response that *The Last of the Mohicans* (1992) aroused in analysts of American culture opens up some avenues to be explored in the context of both the revisionist westerns discussed in this chapter. First of all, we have seen the way in which the concept of the frontier and the oppositions of wilderness and civilization, established by Cooper and elaborated by critics, have fed into the analysis of Mann's film by Edgerton and Marubbio. The stereotyping of the Indian characters, their association with savage death or doomed dignity, and the racial determinism that makes them "a breed apart" all stem from the metaphors that have sustained the western and that have been given a source of origin in Cooper's tales. This raises a problem about faithfulness that reverses the usual values of those adaptation critics for whom faithfulness to the original, to its plot or more vaguely to its spirit, is proposed as a way of warding off the effects of Hollywood's generic formulations. Here, though, the original novel is bound up with the creation of the genre, and faithfulness to the novel can no longer be offered as sufficient reason for the use of its racist tropes. The demand for the invention of new plot situations, even beyond the transformation of the central character, is an indication of how problematic the situation is, and both Edgerton and Marubbio come close to suggesting that Cooper's book is so tangled in racism that it cannot be filmed. Mann's claims that the answer could be found in the creation of a revisionist western, incorporating a self-aware acknowledgment of a problematic source, made his failure to produce such a film a source of anger.

If faithfulness does not provide a way out, then other elements need further examination. A second point, arising from this discussion, is the role of landscape in the western and its relationship to action. Cooper's emphasis on description and Mitchell's discussion of the western landscapes of painters such as Bierstadt place an emphasis on the pleasures of looking that seem highly pertinent to film. The viewing of landscape as a morally uplifting as well as an aesthetic experience is a tradition the western draws on, and the moral character of the hero is often related to the land over which he journeys. But, in writing about the relationship between landscape photography and the western, Buscombe has observed that "landscape in the cinema is never, or never for long, an object merely for contemplation."[61] We can ask therefore what does landscape signify in *The Last of the Mohicans* (1992), and indeed, in *Brokeback Mountain*, what is the relationship between description and action in the films' handling of narrative and characterization?

This leads us onto the third general point I want to explore—the question of the position of the viewer created by the film. Mitchell's account of Cooper's descriptions posits an alert, waiting viewer associated with a hero who values self-control and stillness, while the critics of *The Last of the Mohicans* (1992) argue that the film aligns the viewer with a particular set of racially defined positions involved with colonial exploitation. Marubbio suggests that the distanced overview, exemplified by the film's opening, sets up this problematic position, which is the more hard to resist because the film's depiction of landscape is "visually seductive."[62] This notion of a viewing position that relates visual organization (the view we are offered by camera position and editing) to the viewing position from which the narrative makes sense repays examination in both *The Last of the Mohicans* and *Brokeback Mountain*, two films in which the visual pleasure of landscape is overtly emphasized.

Finally, there is the question of romance. We have seen in other examples how Hollywood adds or plays up a romantic element in an original source and how consistently that is seen as a problem for a good adaptation. Walker follows this approach by viewing the romance between Hawkeye and Cora in *The Last of the Mohicans* (1992) as a flagrant misunderstanding of Cooper's hero. But Edgerton and Marubbio treat the romance as an ideological problem rather than a problem of adaptation, opening the way up for a discussion of the film on its own terms. For Pye, "Romance is central rather than marginal to the twentieth-century Western,"[63] and both *The Last of the Mohicans* and *Brokeback Mountain* have strong romance narratives. Far from being a distraction, these romances need to be analyzed in terms of the visual pleasures associated with the landscape and narrative action of the western.

ACTION AND LANDSCAPE IN *THE LAST OF THE MOHICANS*

Along with the controversial statements about righting Cooper's wrongs, the publicity provided for *The Last of the Mohicans* (1992) included an account by the director of the importance of the 1936 version to him: "*The Last of the Mohicans* [1936] is probably the first film I saw as a child. It was a black-and-white 16 millimeter print, and I must have been three or four—it's the first sense memory I have of a motion picture."[64] Mann's memory of this childhood screening has a double function at the beginning of this discussion. It signals a relationship with a childhood text that is both highly memorable—the first film—and inadequate—black-and-white, sixteen millimeter. It also offers a definition of a film not as the product of a visual medium but rather as a product of all the senses, a product that has to be imagined as well as seen—"a sense memory." It is worth bearing Mann's comments in mind at the beginning of a discussion of the film. He alerts potential audiences to his ambition to fulfill the promise and failure of the earlier version, to recreate that first excitement but this time through an overwhelming, sensory experience in which visual excitement is paralleled by a compelling soundtrack.

Marubbio begins her analysis of the film's colonial gaze with the panoramic opening whereby the viewer, unattached to any character, is invited to look over the blue hills and valleys, the mist blurring our view of the river below and the pulse of the music filling our ears. This is our first view of the landscape that will dominate the film; the final shot will parallel it and again give us a high view of the sky and hills, this time peopled by Hawkeye and Cora with Chingachgook standing beside them. I will return to these shots later, but first I want to suggest that the film is not marked by a consistent mode of viewing as Marubbio suggests but, more in the manner of Bierstadt's paintings, by a variety of positions that relate to different narrative threads. The position associated with the viewing of the landscape is the most complex experience but not the only one.

The clearest viewing position is associated with the political story. This is the story line in which Hawkeye is presented as a friend and supporter of the poor colonial settlers, in opposition to the British and French forces. Hawkeye supports the nascent political claims for independence and liberty, stands up to General Webb on the settlers' behalf, and helps them escape from Fort William Henry to go back to defend their homes. In scenes relating to this aspect of the story, the viewer is generally given establishing shots that offer a sense of place and space before the action of the scene gets going. An early example of this is the scene in which the settlers welcome Hawkeye, Chingachgook, and Uncas into their home. Although the camerawork and overlapping dialogue make parts of the scene hard to follow, it starts with establishing shots of the cabin in the open glade and the settlers moving to welcome the visitors, establishing that this is a friendly environment. The clarity with which the viewer is positioned is even stronger in the scenes that deal with the struggle between the British and French. The first shot, for instance, of the scene in which Montcalm and Munro negotiate the terms of the surrender has flat, open ground in front of the camera with Magua's Indians facing the camera in the background and a view of the river beyond. Either side of this landscape is filled by the marching soldiers from the two armies, and as the conversation takes place the camera is positioned between but slightly below the two leaders so their faces can clearly be seen. The action is accompanied by the diegetic military beating of drums. This is the classic expository viewpoint that allows us to understand the film's narrative. The viewer is positioned outside the debate but is able to follow the argument and the action. As Barker and Sabin indicate, this viewing position is not so much that of the colonial exploiter but rather of the colonized whites.

A different viewing position is offered in the romance narrative that follows the initial attraction between Hawkeye and Cora and their establishment as a couple. Scenes of dialogue between them are shot using shot–reverse shot conventions or a moving camera that provides balanced close-ups of one and then the other. Close-ups support important lines of dialogue, and lighting and framing confirm their status. This focus on the couple is maintained in scenes of confusion such as Magua's attacks on the army cohorts and the nighttime scenes in the besieged fort. Such scenes involve many characters and carry a number of story lines, but the romance story dominates through the music and editing. "I'm looking at you, Miss," Hawkeye tells Cora as she works in the hospital and the exchange of looks between them across battlefields and on the run clearly invites the viewer not only to understand this story line but also to feel its significance.

The political and the romance narratives are associated with viewing positions that allow clear narrative lines to emerge and engage our sympathy. Both however are bound into an adventure story of capture and escape that is repeated twice in the film. And here the viewing position becomes more complex. It is not it seems to me that of the fixed, appraising colonial gaze but rather of the partial, alert viewer immersed in the landscape, the reader Mitchell associates with Cooper's descriptive passages. Marubbio suggests that the hunting scene that follows the initial panorama is marked by the distant and appraising viewing position of the opening shots, but that surely is to overlook the very shock of difference that the cut from one to the other suggests. In the hunting scene, we are thrust into the middle of the action, and it takes time to realize what the three men are doing. As with many of the subsequent scenes of fighting or hiding, the viewer is deprived of an establishing shot, the camera is unstable, and there is no fixed position from which to view. Tree trunks, leaves, smoke, and bodies block sightlines so that the foreground is often blurred and the desired view obscured. The narrative point of such scenes tends to emerge well after the arresting close-up with which they often start, and significant action occurs in the background. For much of the film, we are presented not with a landscape to admire from afar but with fragmented glimpses of a terrain that we experience from the inside. The viewer has to learn to read it as Hawkeye, who is the product of this landscape, has.

This is reinforced by the use of sound, for this is not the silent wilderness that Mitchell finds in Cooper's novels. The aural track has to be understood just as Hawkeye listens for sounds that tell him what to expect in the wilderness. The human voice is often mumbled, hard to hear, and sometimes in a foreign language; in the scenes at the Indian council, the main statements are accompanied by the low murmur of rapid translation into French or English. Diegetic sounds often make us jump—the drums and the stamping of army boots on the earth, the war whoops, the blasts from the guns, and the banging of iron doors. The music accompanying the scenes of hunting, fighting, and pursuit is repetitive and rhythmical. The scenes at the waterfall exemplify the mix of sight and sound that animates the landscape but makes a fixed viewing position difficult. The water falling in front of the rock on which the group shelter blocks our sight while the roar of the falls dominates the soundtrack. Hawkeye has to shout his instructions, and the arrival of Magua is presaged by the faint glimmer of fire on the surface of the rocks.

I would suggest therefore that the landscape of *The Last of the Mohicans* (1992) is not coherently presented. There are points when we are given an overview that relates to the mythic landscape of the virgin West or shots that place the characters in telling compositions; there are also points when we are given a sufficient view from which to admire the exploits of Hawkeye, as, for instance, in the canoe episode when shots of Day-Lewis's body are cut with shots of the river and sky. But much of the time the viewing position is fragmented and partial, and there is a sense of being potentially at least overloaded by editing and sound. In publicity interviews for the launch of the film, Mann claimed that he had been influenced by Bierstadt's paintings,[65] and Mitchell's discussion of Bierstadt's "viewing position" is useful here. The film gives us "the moving eye," which, he argued, the paintings needed, but the elements are still not resolved into a whole; perspectives shift and the viewer can be put in the "wrong" position. This is neatly summed up in the initial hunting scene when Hawkeye shoots directly into the camera and therefore at the audience. The viewing position from which we have attempted to follow the action and perhaps admire the hero's body is, in this way, undermined, though, in this case, the experience is humorous as well as disconcerting. When a similar shot setup is repeated, toward the end, with Uncas's tomahawk swinging into the camera rather than at his foe, the effect is more visceral. But throughout the film, the mix of close-up detail, blocked-off perspectives, and wide overviews is not united into a single position. Instead, the audience is swept up in a struggle to keep up with sights and sounds that are continually on the move.

Cawelti argued that the western setting was particularly "expressive for portrayal of movement,"[66] and in this film movement is crucial to the role of Hawkeye and the construction of Daniel Day-Lewis as a star. The ability to move quickly and gracefully through the woods marks Hawkeye out as a natural man who shrugs off the demands of civilization. The easy, physical coordination between him, Uncas, and Chingachgook confirms his status as a Mohican and as a family member; it is demonstrated at the beginning in the hunting scene and is reprised several times, most crucially at the end in the urgent and desperate way the three run up the mountain toward Magua and the captive Alice. Movement is also intricately bound into Hawkeye's expression of feeling for Cora and his status as a romantic hero. At the fort, a lengthy pan follows his controlled and rhythmic lope through the fort as he moves to claim Cora. Similarly, in his long run on the battlefield, when bodies are flying and Hawkeye himself is killing, nothing can deflect him from his movement toward Cora; the contrast with Magua in a still, dramatic pose over Munro is striking, a contrast between love and death. And consistently, the running links the landscape to the action; Hawkeye runs across, down, and into the land-scape, so that looking at the view is not a contemplative, aesthetic act but rather an invitation into the action. It is in Hawkeye's dynamic move-ment, rather than in the plot changes or the representation of the Native Americans, that this adaptation moves furthest away from Cooper's Natty Bumppo.

But this movement is hard to maintain, and it threatens to fall back into stasis. Two drivers are associated with this: the doomed drive to death as-sociated with the Indian characters and the fixed status of achieved ro-mance. If the film's physical movement and sensory overload challenge Cooper's emphasis on "still bodies and silent moments," then the ending, with its falling bodies and frozen moments, returns the film not just to the landscape of the opening shots but also to the descriptive mode of the be-ginning. As the adventure narrative unwinds, bodies pile up, and Uncas, Alice, and Magua all fall to their deaths. Uncas's body slides over the rocks and then launches into the air as if flying. Alice's falling body is seen from below from a viewpoint only given to the audience and is then framed in a high shot, small and still in the greenery of the ravine. In the climactic moment of the fight between Chingachgook and Magua, the lat-ter's body is frozen against the sky as Chingachgook whirls into the final blow; there is a cut to ground level, and Magua's body falls to the ground, his rigid face on the hard rock filling the foreground of the screen. In each case, the moment of death is marked by the falling body, for a moment held between sky and ground, but in the end being absorbed back into the landscape. Movement ends in stillness.

But this stillness also affects Hawkeye and Cora despite their appar-ently happier ending. The final images refer back to other moments in the romance story when Hawkeye's movements have been stilled. In the fort, a highly composed shot on the ramparts marked the couple's sexual com-ing together; their bodies face the audience in a still embrace but look out in profile into unseen space. A similarly significant shot occurs when Cora learns that her father is dead. She and Hawkeye embrace and are held in silhouette against the light and movement of the waterfall, until a cut makes the water obliterate them. Both these images prefigure the final shot in which Hawkeye and Cora stand in silent embrace looking out on the sunset over the mountains while Chingachgook stands slightly to one side and the music wells up. Edgerton and Marubbio both point to the way in which Uncas has been replaced in the threesome and to the positioning of Chingachgook on the margin of the pair. But what has happened here is that all three have been positioned above the crevice in an aesthetic framing that signifies loss and immobility.

To understand this further, we need to go back to the romance narrative and the way it develops. Drawing on the conventions of the classic adaptation, Cora is presented as an independent-minded young woman, particularly when contrasted with Alice, who is reduced to silent shock by her ordeals. But her romance does not involve any suspense as to how either character will feel, and the outcome is quickly settled. Cora adopts Hawkeye's politics in defiance of her father and gives herself to him willingly; similarly, Hawkeye has no hesitation in staying in the fort for her sake rather than returning to the wilderness. The romance narrative is therefore resolved by the middle of the film and, despite Marubbio's assertion that Cora has chosen the Anglo bloodline and thereby marked out the American future as white, there is no subsequent discussion of the future, no plans for settlement. Cora does not imagine her future as her equivalent does in the 1936 film by declaring that the "new civilization" in America will need "spinning wheels" as well as rifles.

Alice's death, a "cliff-dive suicide," which Mann referred to as "a structural moment,"[67] gives us a clue as to what is going on here. Her movement from the path into the empty air is possibly her only deliberate act. She says nothing as Magua's bloodstained fingers beckon her but looks from him to the ravine and back again before we see her lean away. But Uncas had held her tenderly behind the waterfall, and it is possible to read her decision as an act of romantic love, following Uncas into the grave. Certainly, for Cora and Hawkeye, love is presented as transcendental and transformative, requiring extreme feelings. It is enough in itself, and it stops them in their tracks, high above the ravine with literally nowhere to go but into the landscape that has already claimed his brother and her sister. The descriptive shot and mournful music that end the film therefore has symmetry with the opening. Chingachgook mourns the end of his people; a more positive view of the Native American future has, as Edgerton declared, proved unimaginable. But so too is the future of Cora and Hawkeye, and the loss associated with them is also complex. There is the loss of masculinity often summoned up when the hero stops his wanderings at the end of a western. There is the loss of the virgin forest, the Eden presented in the first shots of the film, for a move in that direction would associate the couple with the despoliation and death that, the film has shown, occurs under the canopy of the trees. And there is the sense of loss associated with romantic love that can only be preserved, as a later cinematic couple found in *Titanic*, through death. No wonder it is better to stand still and be turned into myth.

Of course, it is possible to argue that Chingachgook and the Native American peoples deserved better than to be mixed up in this powerfully emotional but muddled ending and that a strong sense of loss is hardly sufficient recompense. Maltby argues that the transformation of the savage Indian into the Noble Savage in the revisionist western makes it impossible for the western's "classical imperial narrative of heroic repression" to be retold coherently—hence the "radical structural revisions" of this version.[68] Nevertheless, rather than offering the colonialist's perspective, the incoherence of the ending matches the instability of the viewing positions, the confused and overwhelming sensory experience of watching the film, and the incompatibility of the western and the romance. Mann claimed to have dealt with one set of Cooper's contradictions in his approach to the Native American. Instead, faced with the complex contradictions of American history and the myths used to tell it, the film comes to a frozen halt, rather than an ending. Its politics are visceral rather than rational. A future might be offered, but like the green light in another classic novel about America, F. Scott Fitzgerald's *The Great Gatsby*, it is already in the past; we know that the forest we are looking at no longer exists and, indeed, as the film has shown, never did exist as virgin land. Unable to move forward or back, the film offers not the colonialist gaze of exploitation but a past spectacle of the future that is already spoilt.

BROKEBACK MOUNTAIN

While *The Last of the Mohicans* (1992) trailed behind it a history of different versions, the film of *Brokeback Mountain* came from a short story, which its audience was not necessarily expected to know or have read. Yet, faithfulness to the original was important to the makers of *Brokeback Mountain*, and the film's status as an adaptation was consistently referred to in reviews. Spin-offs from the film provided not only a reissue of Proulx's short story collection with a cover featuring the film's stars but also a new book that featured the original short story and the screenplay, allowing the reader to see how faithfully the screenplay's dialogue and setting reflected the story. It also included brief articles by Proulx and the two scriptwriters, Larry McMurtry and Diana Ossana, which show how faithfulness was an issue for both parties. Proulx writes about the doubts she had when first approached since she "did not think this story could be a film."[69] However, the film gave her "as a writer . . . the rarest film trip: my story was not mangled but enlarged into huge and gripping imagery that rattled minds and squeezed hearts."[70] McMurtry argues that the story was a "literary masterpiece" that broke his general rule (another to add to the list given in the introduction) that strong books make weak films.[71]

Ossana tells of using the story as a blueprint for a script that aimed to retain the powerful emotions of the original. She describes the years of difficulty in finding "partners with the courage and passion" to make the film from their script (a further issue of faithfulness) and her deep satisfaction when finally seeing the film.[72] Her essay finishes with the statement, "*Brokeback Mountain* the film stands faithfully besides 'Brokeback Mountain' the short story."[73] In the DVD commentary, this emphasis continues with McMurtry commenting, "We used every bit of that story, virtually every sentence," while Ossana concludes, "It was Annie's story, we stayed true to her writing, we stayed true to her characters."[74]

It is important to note, however, that the film does not reference this commitment to being true to the original masterpiece. The function of the discourse of faithfulness is extratextual. It helps to make it possible, in a Hollywood film (albeit made by a studio specialist division, Focus Films), to tell a story of a homosexual relationship. Proulx's story had the reputation of being the best the *New Yorker* had ever published, and that respectability was important. In this film, faithfulness and progressive attitudes went hand in hand, and although this caused difficulties in the search for financial investment, it contributed to the critical success of the film. Ossana was annoyed that the script had been dubbed "'a story about gay cowboys,'" a reductive tag the film had to shake off to extend its appeal.[75] As *Brokeback Mountain* was launched and before it was clear that it was going to be a success, *Variety* referred to the film as "this ostensible gay Western" but countered the comment by noting that McMurtry and Ossana "have faithfully and perceptively retained the tone and the particulars of the tale in their screenplay" and that the film was "marked by a heightened degree of sensitivity and tact."[76]

Faithfulness to a literary masterpiece was not enough, though, and in contesting the label of gay cowboy movie the production team wanted to resist the association with the western genre as well. Proulx explained to those readers coming to her story via the film that she is "something of a geographic determinist, believing that regional landscapes, climate and topography dictate local cultural traditions and kinds of work."[77] The story drew on Proulx's understanding of contemporary western life, and its use as a source invoked some of the tropes of the western genre: the emphasis on the land and the characters and traditions shaped by it; descriptive passages that use a heightened vocabulary to make the landscape dynamic; and distinctive western characters whose taciturnity is leavened by tall stories and earthy dialect. But, since the western is no longer a popular film genre, the filmmakers endorse the realist detail of the story's take on the West but refuse the generic connections. Lee does describe the film as "a realistic western," and producer James Schamus emphasized how Proulx and the scriptwriters pay attention to the specificity of the West "to give the story the depth and grain of reality it needs."[78] But in the main, the film is hooked onto a more popular genre, the romance, and *Brokeback Mountain* presented as what the director Ang Lee called in many interviews "a universal and unique American love story." The film's tagline "Love is a force of nature" hinted at the western setting, but foregrounded romance and the similarity between its poster and that for *Titanic* provoked much comment on websites. This emphasis on transcendent love meant that *Premiere.com*, for instance, could reassure its readers that "it's a movie about romantic love, the most Romantic kind of romantic love—the kind you can never grasp long enough to even be vaguely satisfied by."[79] This kind of comment indicated that the producers had been successful in their purpose of aiming the gay, cowboy movie at straight, young women; a journalist from *The Hollywood Reporter* commented, "The initial marketing push is to women and younger moviegoers. 'You're looking for people who are empathetic,' says Schamus, 'and able to reach their emotions. And younger folks are way out ahead on this stuff. Overall, they are not worked up about gay issues.'"[80] The marketing of *Brokeback Mountain* worked hard to reposition the film as a love story and to ensure that audiences identified its genre correctly. I would argue, therefore, that the film is a revisionist western, but the revision relates not so much to the politics of representation, as *The Last of the Mohicans* attempts, but rather to the feelings that the film seeks to invoke and the attempt to create a viewing position more appropriate to an art house film than a traditional western.

In some ways, the setting of *Brokeback Mountain* fits much more clearly into the classic structures of the cinema's western than the forests of *The Last of the Mohicans*. The film establishes a frontier between civilization and wilderness, though this time it is not so much a matter of going westward as moving up into the mountains. The wilderness is a "retreat from the softness of civilization into the stoicism of the wilderness"[81] in which the heroes of the film, Ennis and Jack, can live a life of hardship and simplicity. In this version of the classic binary, the wilderness is a place of freedom and purity that challenges the protagonists to self-knowledge. The scenery is marked by the openness, the grandeur, and the extremes of light and climate that are associated with the setting of the western. The beauty and harshness of the mountain landscape, its imperviousness to the fragile camps that the men make on its fringes, and the huge vistas that render a human figure almost invisible is all, as Tompkins suggests of the western's desert landscapes, "so rhetorically persuasive that an entire code of values is in place, rock solid, from the outset, without anyone's ever saying a word."[82] As in the conventional western, the space is gendered, the contrast being made between the cold freedom of the mountains and the domestic and emotional clutter of life on the flat plains below in which women and children make complex demands.

Heath Ledger in Brokeback Mountain *(2005). The space in* Brokeback Mountain *is gendered as in conventional westerns, delineating between the freedom of the mountains and the domestic and emotional clutter of life with women and children in the plains.* Source: *Focus Features/The Kobal Collection*

In this modern rendering, though, there is no drive to people this emptiness with new settlements. This reflects the characters' uncertainty about their relationship, but it might also indicate a change in the possibilities associated with the concept of the frontier. In *Brokeback Mountain*, the landscape is preserved as a symbolic space in which their relationship is gradually fixed as impossible. Initially, it has a physical existence as a separate space in which they attempt to remake their relationship, but it

becomes more important as a space in their heads. And the setting becomes gradually more fixed as the relationship itself founders. In the last
meeting, when Jack protests at the difficulty Ennis is making about their
next meeting, he stands in front of the river against the distant mountains
in a static shot that is repeated several times. By this point, the setting,
though still beautiful, has ceased to be enabling; it fixes them rather than
allowing them to move on. Bitterly, Jack complains about their escapes to
the mountains, about the cold, the lack of ease, and the "high-altitude
fucks." The postcards Jack sends, with their secret, coded messages, are a
reminder of reality of the mountains, but as the pair grow older the reality recedes. When Lureen tells Ennis, after Jack's death, that she thought
Brokeback Mountain was one of his "pretend places" she speaks more
truly than Ennis, who responds by saying that it was a place where they
herded sheep one summer. And the final image of the film contrasts the
mountain peaks on the postcard with the plains' horizontal lines of flat
color, framed in Ennis's window.

Because of this emphasis on the symbolic function of the setting, there
is a sharp separation in *Brokeback Mountain* between the story and pictures, between "narrative and descriptive modes."[83] Although the setting
carries a range of meaning associated with the western as a genre, there is
a lack of integration between the landscape and the narrative action. In
classic westerns, the landscape shapes the story because it provides the
means by which the heroes test themselves and each other. As in *The Last
of the Mohicans* or indeed *Cimarron*, such narratives often concern a journey or pursuit in which the land itself is an obstacle that has to be overcome. Or the film might emphasize the hero's ease in the landscape, the
physical skills it encourages, and the power he draws from it. Tompkins
might exaggerate when she says that "in the end, the land is everything
to the hero. . . . He courts it, struggles with it, defies it, conquers it, and
lies down with it at night,"[84] but she is surely right to emphasize that the
land is at the heart of the story as well as central to the image of the western. But this is not true of Jack and Ennis. Jack and Ennis carry out the actions of cowboys in their riding, herding, and living on the land, but their
story is linked to the land only by its symbolic meaning. The mountains
provide some obstacles and some opportunities, but land is not their central concern. The landscape provides the setting for their story, but their
love is not dependent on how they stand up to its rigors or learn to read
its contours. The landscape is not animated by the story but is remote
from it. Brokeback Mountain stands for something other than itself and is
made abstract; it becomes description, a way of elevating the love story
into a symbolic spectacle and making it transcendent.

Although the landscape is not animated by narrative, the film does suggest, in the tradition of the western, that the characters of the two men are

formed by their environment. With the character of Ennis, in particular, the film draws on the western's traditional ways of representing masculine characters but revises them to acknowledge contemporary sexual politics. This fits the task of being faithful to the short story, and Proulx particularly praised Heath Ledger, "who knew better than I how Ennis felt and thought."[85] In the mountains, Ennis's wry comments and long silences fit the environment, and his character is expressed through his ease on a horse and at his work. Elsewhere, though, Ledger's laconic statements and tight-lipped, mumbling delivery emphasizes Ennis's embarrassment at being forced into speech. Such taciturnity is indeed "a prerequisite for the Western hero . . . part and parcel of his separateness, his loneliness, his superiority,"[86] and although there are western heroes who talk differently, spare, controlled dialogue is certainly a sign of a western to an audience no longer familiar with the genre. But Ennis is not superior, and his inability to communicate is offered instead as a painful flaw. Indeed, the film can be seen as an exemplification of the thesis that the western's conceptualization of masculinity is based on repression and loss. Ennis controls his emotion to such an extent that his body has to express the pain that he cannot articulate; he vomits at leaving Jack for the first time, physically fights with both Jack and Alma, and expresses his internalized rage nonverbally in unglamorized brawls with strangers. In this, he demonstrates the cost to the hero of the western's emphasis on control and self-containment.

The significance of Ennis's inability to express his feelings is underlined by the fact that when he does tell Jack about his harsh childhood, at the campfire on Brokeback, it is both a cause for comment ("Friend, that's more words than you've spoke in the past two weeks") and, in terms of the romance narrative, a sign of falling in love. In fact, both Jack and Ennis talk, albeit briefly, about their alienated relationships with their family, and their fathers in particular, in a way that offers a psychological explanation, more usual in a family melodrama, for their unease with their own feelings. Although the words are taken from the short story, they are repositioned in the context of the opening up of the short story by "fleshing out" the domestic background.[87] The taciturnity of the western seems even more inadequate in the intimate spaces of the home where the men's silence is associated with guilt and self-denial. This might explain why reviewers felt that *Brokeback Mountain* went beyond the usual female stereotypes associated with the western in its presentation of the two frustrated and angry wives, Alma and Lureen. Of the two, the characterization of Alma depends for its depth on Michelle Williams's performance, while Anne Hathaway's spirited sketch of Lureen's bitter assumption of a protective carapace is set against a depiction of family life in Texas that owes much to *Dallas* as well as *Giant*.

The film's examination of the codes of masculinity extends to its presentation of the cowboy, a form of address that the men consistently use to each other. Here the film draws on its appeal to realism, presenting the modern cowboy as a hired ranch hand and a failed rodeo rider. Even in the mountains, Jack and Ennis are not heroic cowboys, and they conform more to Mitchell's ironic description of real cowboys as "hired hands on horseback—in effect, a shepherd with a gun."[88] In addition, they are largely deprived of the action through which the western hero traditionally expresses himself. Even on the mountains, their herding activity is largely leisurely; they move slowly on horseback, and their basic task is to watch the sheep rather than physically battle with the cattle on the trail as the cowboys of *Red River* (Hawks, 1948) do. Subsequent visits to the mountains are spent mainly talking, and neither Ennis's laboring nor Jack's rodeo riding is shown in a way that emphasizes their physical power and control—nor indeed, after the initial sex scene, does the romance narrative offer physical activity. In some senses, then, the characters of *Brokeback Mountain* also experience the drive toward stasis, "the still bodies and silent moments," which Mitchell associates with the western.[89] Grundmann suggests that the "erotic rhythms" of their romance "echoes the kind of transience and mobility which constituted frontier life,"[90] but Jack is desperate to settle down. As with Hawkeye and Cora, perfect love relies on the moment being frozen. In his flashback at their final meeting, Jack reimagines being embraced by Ennis while standing still, "asleep on your feet like a horse." By the end, Jack is dead and Ennis has retreated into his ironically immobile mobile home.

Mitchell suggests that westerns present masculinity as both a natural, biological imperative and as a series of actions that can be learnt: "An achieved masculinity . . . is at once physical and based on performance that can be revealed."[91] Popular understandings have tended however to underestimate the performances required by the actors, and the association of masculinity with natural behavior is indicated by the strong association between actor and character. Actors in westerns do not win acting awards because it is assumed that John Wayne, Henry Fonda, and Clint Eastwood are playing some variant of themselves rather than performing learnt characteristics. What is striking about *Brokeback Mountain*'s reception is how much reviewers valued performance. This was undoubtedly fueled by the homophobic notion that it was courageous for a straight man to play a gay one. The production material goes out of its way to emphasize that Ledger and Jake Gyllenhaal are performing, not being, gay, and acting is strongly signaled as important. But this means that the actors are also praised for re-presenting the role of the western hero. According to the *New York Times*, "Mr. Ledger magically and mysteriously disappears beneath the skin of his lean, sinewy character" in a "great screen performance,"[92] which is compared with Marlon Brando, while for *Empire*, "Ledger's buttoned-down performance is a triumph of quiet complexity."[93] Ledger's self-containment is then not a natural consequence of his male personality but rather a deliberate performance of a particular kind of masculinity that no longer works in the modern world.

In the discussion of *The Last of the Mohicans*, we saw how the viewing position offered by the film had consequences for how the film could be understood. The discussion of setting and characterization here needs to be considered in the context of the viewing position offered, which has implications also for how *Brokeback Mountain* operates as both a western and a romance. In terms of the landscape, the film does not position the viewer in the setting in the manner of *The Last of the Mohicans* (1992) but encourages the viewer to appreciate the landscape aesthetically. This is apparent in the first trip into the mountains as Jack and Ennis herd the sheep up to the pastures. There is no dialogue, and plaintive guitar chords accompany a series of images showing the river and the landscape. The sequence starts with a low shot at ground level so that the viewer waits for the sheep to come into view as they move over the rise in ground. It flows through a series of long and medium shots that merge the activity and the setting and two distance shots in which the men and sheep can hardly be seen against the landscape. Although at various points the men are seen tending the sheep, there is no narrative tension in this task of shepherding animals through the terrain. Instead, the tone is reflective, allowing the viewer to stand back from the event. The sequence appears to finish with a shot of the two men lying on a grass valley at either side of the screen, watching the grazing sheep, but it then flows into a further wordless sequence, with orchestral music coming to the fore, in which the simple camp is made and the first night passes. Three spectacular landscape shots—of the clouds at sunset, the camp under moonlight, and the mountains at sunrise—are linked to Jack's experience of guarding the sheep but are not strongly linked to his viewpoint. There is little here that associates viewing the landscape with the cowboy's dominant vision,[94] nor do we know whether Jack and Ennis feel its awe-inspiring grandeur. The sequence offers the viewer, however, a coherent position as the appreciative and meditative observer of this landscape.

This distancing effect also characterizes the scenes in which Jack and Ennis return to the mountains after this initial experience. Such scenes often start with long shots of their activity in the landscape, and our first view of these temporary camps is a distanced one. The fourth meeting, for example, starts with a long shot of the mountain view that pans down to pick up the two men on horseback and then to a long shot of them by the mirrorlike river. Two shots of them crossing the river bring them nearer, but a dissolve returns to a more distant viewing position in which their

camp is seen from a low level at the other side of the river. As with the earlier sequences, this montage is accompanied by the guitar theme and the
sounds of the river. It is only after establishing this view of the pair as figures in an idyllic landscape that the story resumes again. Here, as is often
the case when narrative action is being played out, the scenes of Jack and
Ennis talking take place in the dark as if to remove the distraction of the
setting.

This sense of being positioned outside the situation and being given
time to observe it is not however confined to the presentation of the landscape. The characters are also presented for our observation in a context
that emphasizes aesthetic appreciation. Framing and composition are
drawn attention to from the start as two unnamed men are positioned
against the flat frontages of the small town.[95] Frequently, the first shot of
a sequence establishes the tone of the scene: a shot of Alma waiting with
the blank wall behind her, a black stripe on the table separating the coffee
cup and the sugar holder; Ennis eating apple pie in the brightly lit diner
with empty tables and chairs around him; and Jack's father rigidly domi-
nating the table in the cold, whitewashed parlor while his mother is unseen in the kitchen. Such shots offer aesthetic satisfaction, reinforce the art
house position of the viewer, and are often associated with enigma, regret,
and loss.

Such a positioning works with the western's emphasis on landscape
and setting, but I suggested earlier in my discussion of *The Last of the Mohicans* that a romance narrative can require a different kind of positioning
to convince the viewer of the importance of the relationship. In *Brokeback
Mountain*, the romance between Ennis and Jack is similarly underscored
by a shift in viewing position to one that emphasizes closeness and proximity. The scene in which the couple first has sex is filmed in close proximity to the characters with camera movement and editing following their
urgent movements. In the motel, without the physical restrictions of the
tent, the camera still stays tight, giving close-ups of their faces from the
front and side. Nevertheless, the camera in these scenes still tends to observe rather than dramatize the action, and arguably the more powerful
close-ups occur in the fight scenes. In the expansive scenery of Brokeback,
the fight scene is filmed close in with a moving camera and a devastating
cut underlining the effect of Ennis's punch. This fight is mirrored by that
at their final meeting when, after a struggle, Jack manages to hold Ennis
in an embrace and the close-ups show his tears and vulnerability. Early on
in the film, Ennis's response to a stranger who sees him crouched up in
pain at leaving Jack is "What the fuck are you looking at?"; it could be addressed to the viewer who comes too close.

Although the telling of the love story involves a viewing position that
is literally closer to the action, it is striking that the film does not draw on

the conventions of looking to engage the viewer in the lovers' desire. Jack and Ennis do watch each other but in a way that signifies loss as much as desire. We see Ennis's view as Jack rides back to the sheep, but he is a tiny figure on the mountain; a shot of Jack watching Ennis ride off after their first night together is followed by a cut that gives us not his view of Ennis but rather several shots of Ennis from the front and side, restored to the impersonal view of the camera. Indeed, the film refuses shots that might have implicated the spectator in their desire as, for instance, when we watch Jack determinedly not turn to look at Ennis washing naked by the river. This is in marked contrast to the exchange of looks that mark Jack's other encounters: with the clown whom he offers a drink at the rodeo; with Lureen when she picks him up; and with Randall on a night out with their wives. Instead, the shots that most clearly implicate the viewer in the relationship between Jack and Ennis are those in which our view is positioned with the voyeuristic (willing or otherwise) looking of others. A panning long shot of the camp that follows Jack and Ennis playfully wrestling becomes, with a reverse shot, the disapproving view through binoculars of their boss, Joe Aguirre. And even more powerfully the passionate, unstoppable embrace of the two men on their first reunion, seen at first in close-up, is repositioned so that the spectator shares Alma's view as she looks down from the apartment above. Grundmann suggests that "Lee uses the *mise-en-scène* of melodrama" to show the shocked, despairing look on Alma's face,[96] and it is striking that the powerful, shot–reverse shot conventions used to represent romantic desire are most forcefully used in this film to position the audience with the disgust and despair of those who cannot accept the relationship.

This is not to say that film does not work as a love story but rather that it offers a particular kind of identification with the romance. In its rendering of the setting as description, in offering a dominant viewing position based on observation and aesthetic appreciation rather than the shot–reverse shot that implicates the audience in desire, in rendering masculinity a performance the film invites us to reflect on rather than share the heroes' desire. The story is about a particular region and a particular couple, but the film refuses to position the viewer within the couple's shared looks and invites instead a distanced position of aesthetic appreciation of the men in the landscape. This seems to have encouraged a more generalized identification with lost love in which the symbolic space of Brokeback Mountain takes on a general meaning rather than a specific reality. This can clearly be seen in the website responses that use the film to share their own stories of relationships that are defined not so much by sexuality but rather by intensity and loss; the official websites invites those who have been moved by the film to "share your story": "Here's a place to share your feelings about the film, the connections you felt, and to share how watching it might have brought back memories of your own. After all, everyone has their own 'Brokeback Mountain.' Have you ever gone back to yours?"[97] In this way, the viewer is invited to substitute their own experience of transcendent romantic love for that of Jack and Ennis, with the specificity of place, language, and characterization discarded.

We have seen that the question of faithfulness to the source operates differently in these two films. Both films are westerns, attempting to work with genre conventions relating to character, landscape, and narrative action that have been discredited and fallen from audience favor. In the case of *Brokeback Mountain*, the fact of the adaptation from a literary source provided a way out of the problematic associations of the western. The story of a sexual relationship between two men both challenged the western's traditional handling of gender issues and provided a way of establishing the film as belonging to a different genre—a romance rather than a western. In this instance, declaring faithfulness to the source provided a way of explaining that the film's potentially problematic content belonged to its origin in a much praised short story. For *The Last of the Mohicans* (1992), there was no such escape. Cooper's work had been an important antecedent for the western, and controversy still surrounds his account of American society before independence, and in particular his representation of Native Americans. Mann therefore denounced his literary source, but the fact of adaptation meant that the film could not simply become a star vehicle and action movie. Genre and source combine here to render the film's revisionism impossible.

One of the less contentious consequences of drawing on the conventions of the western is the emphasis this places on setting and landscape. Both films offer landscapes as one of the spectacular pleasures of the films, though the viewing positions from which we are invited to experience them are different. In *The Last of the Mohicans* (1992), we are immersed in the sight and sound of the forest, while *Brokeback Mountain* offers a more distanced and knowingly aesthetic experience of the art film. In the former, watching the landscape and following the action are welded together, while, in the latter, narrative action and contemplation of the scenery are often separated. The films, therefore, offer examples of the different ways in which literary description can be adapted and handled in cinema. It is worth noting, though, since both films were praised for their spectacular scenery, that while faithfulness is an issue in the telling of the story, it is not a factor in assessing how the landscape described in the source is actually filmed. Both *The Last of the Mohicans* (1992) and *Brokeback Mountain* were made in the "wrong" place, *Mohicans* in North Carolina and *Brokeback* in Alberta, Canada. The implications of thinking about the adaptations required by location and set is the subject of the next chapter.

NOTES

1. Christian Metz, *Film Language*, trans. Michael Taylor (Oxford: Oxford University Press, 1991), 43.

2. Jack Nachbar, "Introduction: A Century on the Trail," *Journal of Popular Film and Television* 30, no. 4 (Winter 2003): 179.

3. Douglas Pye, "Introduction: Criticism and the Western," in *The Movie Book of the Western*, ed. Ian Cameron and Douglas Pye (London: Studio Vista, 1996), 9.

4. Ed Buscombe and Roberta Pearson, "Introduction," in *Back in the Saddle Again: New Essays on the Western*, ed. Ed Buscombe and Roberta Pearson (London: British Film Institute Publications, 1998), 3.

5. John R. Milton, *The Novel of the American West* (Lincoln: University of Nebraska Press, 1980), 62.

6. Jim Kitses, *Horizons West* (London: British Film Institute Publications, 2004), 21.

7. Rick Worland and Edward Countryman, "The New Western: American Historiography and the Emergence of the New Westerns," in *Back in the Saddle Again: New Essays on the Western*, ed. Ed Buscombe and Roberta Pearson (London: British Film Institute Publications, 1998), 185.

8. Lee Clark Mitchell, *Westerns: Making the Man in Fiction and Film* (Chicago: University of Chicago Press, 1996), 4.

9. Jane Tompkins, *West of Everything: The Inner Life of Westerns* (Oxford: Oxford University Press, 1992), 39.

10. Tompkins, *West of Everything*, 74, 66.

11. Tompkins, *West of Everything*, 121.

12. Pye, "Introduction: Criticism and the Western," 12.

13. Martin Pumphrey, "Why Do Cowboys Wear Hats in the Bath?" in *The Movie Book of the Western*, ed. Ian Cameron and Douglas Pye (London: Studio Vista, 1996), 52.

14. David Lusted, "Social Class and the Western as Male Melodrama," in *The Movie Book of the Western*, ed. Ian Cameron and Douglas Pye (London: Studio Vista, 1996), 66.

15. See David Lusted, *The Western* (London: British Film Institute Publications, 2003), 239–41, and Steve Neale, "Vanishing Americans: Racial and Ethnic Issues in the Interpretation and Context of Post-war 'Pro-Indian' Westerns," in *Back in the Saddle Again: New Essays on the Western*, ed. Ed Buscombe and Roberta Pearson (London: British Film Institute Publications, 1998), 8–28. I use the term "Indian" when referring to characters in particular films or to the way Native Americans are characterized in the genre.

16. Pat Dowell, "The Mythology of the Western Hollywood Perspectives on Race and Gender in the Nineties," *Cineaste* 21, nos. 1–2 (Winter–Spring 1995): 6.

17. Worland and Countryman, "The New Western," 187.

18. Milton, *The Novel of the American West*, 5.

19. Daryl Jones, *The Dime Novel Western* (Bowling Green, Ohio: Bowling Green University Popular Press, 1978), 23.

20. Martin Barker and Roger Sabin, *The Lasting of the Mohicans: History of an American Myth* (Jackson: University Press of Mississippi, 1995), 25.

21. Jones, *The Dime Novel Western*, 23.

22. Barry Keith Grant, "John Ford and James Fenimore Cooper," in *John Ford Made Westerns: Filming the Legend in the Sound Era*, ed. Gaylyn Studlar and Matthew Bernstein (Bloomington: Indiana University Press, 2001), 202–3.

23. Milton, *The Novel of the American West*, 8.

24. John G. Cawelti, *The Six-Gun Mystique* (Bowling Green, Ohio: Bowling Green University Popular Press, 1970), 45.

25. Patrick Brantlinger, "Forgetting Genocide: Or, the Last of *The Last of the Mohicans*," *Cultural Studies* 12, no. 1 (January 1998): 21.

26. All quotations Mitchell, *Westerns*, 32.

27. Mitchell, *Westerns*, 40

28. Mitchell, *Westerns*, 42.

29. Mitchell, *Westerns*, 8.

30. Gaylyn Studlar and Matthew Bernstein, "Introduction," in *John Ford Made Westerns: Filming the Legend in the Sound Era*, ed. Gaylyn Studlar and Matthew Bernstein (Bloomington: Indiana University Press, 2001), 4.

31. All quotations Mitchell, *Westerns*, 65.

32. Mitchell, *Westerns*, 68, 72.

33. Quoted in James Griffith, *Adaptations as Imitations: Films from Novels* (Newark: University of Delaware Press, 1997), 228.

34. Gary Edgerton, "'A Breed Apart': Hollywood, Racial Stereotyping, and the Premise of Revisionism in *The Last of the Mohicans*," *Journal of American Culture* 17, no. 2 (June 1994): 7.

35. Quoted in Edgerton, "'A Breed Apart,'" 13.

36. Jeffrey Walker, "Deconstructing an American Myth: Hollywood and *The Last of the Mohicans*" (1992), reprinted in *Hollywood's Indian: The Portrayal of the Native American in Film*, ed. Peter C. Rollins and John E. O'Connor (Lexington: University Press of Kentucky, 1998), 171.

37. Walker, "Deconstructing an American Myth," 173.

38. Walker, "Deconstructing an American Myth," 170.

39. Walker, "Deconstructing an American Myth," 173.

40. Walker, "Deconstructing an American Myth," 183.

41. Edgerton, "'A Breed Apart,'" 13.

42. Edgerton, "'A Breed Apart,'" 9, 13.

43. Edgerton, "'A Breed Apart,'" 11.

44. Edgerton, "'A Breed Apart,'" 11.

45. Edgerton, "'A Breed Apart,'" 14.

46. Edgerton, "'A Breed Apart,'" 13.

47. Edgerton, "'A Breed Apart,'" 16.

48. M. Elise Marubbio, "Celebrating with *The Last of the Mohicans*: The Columbus Quincentenary and Neocolonialism in Hollywood Film," *The Journal of American and Comparative Culture* 25, nos. 1 and 2 (Spring and Summer 2002): 139.

49. Marubbio, "Celebrating with *The Last of the Mohicans*," 142.

50. Marubbio, "Celebrating with *The Last of the Mohicans*," 145.

51. Marubbio, "Celebrating with *The Last of the Mohicans*," 140–41.

52. Marubbio, "Celebrating with *The Last of the Mohicans*," 146.

53. Marubbio, "Celebrating with *The Last of the Mohicans*," 146.

54. Marubbio, "Celebrating with *The Last of the Mohicans*," 140.

55. Marubbio, "Celebrating with *The Last of the Mohicans*," 141.

56. Marubbio, "Celebrating with *The Last of the Mohicans*," 144.

57. Marubbio, "Celebrating with *The Last of the Mohicans*," 148.

58. Marubbio, "Celebrating with *The Last of the Mohicans*," 148.

59. Marubbio, "Celebrating with *The Last of the Mohicans*," 148.

60. Marubbio, "Celebrating with *The Last of the Mohicans*," 144–45.

61. Ed Buscombe, "Inventing Monument Valley: Nineteenth Century Photography and Western Film," reprinted in *The Western Reader*, ed. Jim Kitses and Gary Rickman (New York: Limelight Editions, 1998), 127.

62. Marubbio, "Celebrating with *The Last of the Mohicans*," 139.

63. Pye, "Introduction: Criticism and the Western," 14.

64. Quoted in Edgerton, "'A Breed Apart,'" 1.

65. Mann suggested that Bierstadt's paintings were an influence on the film "in terms both of compositions and of what the place looked like." See Gavin Smith, "Wars and Peace," *Sight and Sound* 2, no. 7 (November 1992): 10.

66. Cawelti, *The Six-Gun Mystique*, 42.

67. Smith, "Wars and Peace," 12.

68. Richard Maltby, "A Better Sense of History: John Ford and the Indians," in *The Movie Book of the Western*, ed. Ian Cameron and Douglas Pye (London: Studio Vista, 1996), 49.

69. Annie Proulx, "Getting Movied," in *Brokeback Mountain: Story to Screenplay*, ed. Annie Proulx, Larry McMurtry, and Diana Ossana (London: Harper Perennial, 2006), 133.

70. Proulx, "Getting Movied," 137.

71. Larry McMurtry, "Adapting *Brokeback Mountain*," in *Brokeback Mountain: Story to Screenplay*, ed. Annie Proulx, Larry McMurtry, and Diana Ossana (London: Harper Perennial, 2006), 140.

72. Diana Ossana, "Climbing Brokeback Mountain," in *Brokeback Mountain: Story to Screenplay*, ed. Annie Proulx, Larry McMurtry, and Diana Ossana (London: Harper Perennial, 2006), 147.

73. Ossana, "Climbing Brokeback Mountain,"151.

74. Larry McMurtry and Diana Ossana, in "From Script to Screen" feature on DVD.

75. Ossana, "Climbing Brokeback Mountain," 147.

76. Todd McCarthy, "*Brokeback Mountain*," *Variety*, September 3, 2005.

77. Proulx, "Getting Movied," 129.

78. Ang Lee and James Schamus, in "From Script to Screen" feature on DVD.

79. Glenn Kenny, "*Brokeback Mountain*," *Premiere.com*, September 12, 2005, www.premiere.com/moviereviews/2428/brokeback-mountain.

80. Anne Thompson, "Anne Thompson Asks, What Took Hollywood So Long? Ang Lee's '*Brokeback Mountain*' explores 'Last Frontier,'" www.thebookstandard

.com/bookstandard/community/commentary_display.jsp?vnu_content_id=1001
478879.

81. Buscombe, "Inventing Monument Valley," 128.

82. Tompkins, *West of Everything*, 74.

83. Mitchell, *Westerns*, 8.

84. Tompkins, *West of Everything*, 81.

85. Proulx, "Getting Movied," 137.

86. Sarah Kozloff, *Overhearing Film Dialogue* (Berkeley: University of California Press, 2000), 142.

87. McMurtry, in "From Script to Screen" feature on DVD.

88. Mitchell, *Westerns*, 25. This relates also to the class position of the two men who operate on the fringes of the world they long to belong to.

89. Mitchell, *Westerns*, 40.

90. Roy Grundmann, "*Brokeback Mountain*," *Cineaste* 31, no. 2 (Spring 2006): 51.

91. Mitchell, *Westerns*, 155.

92. Stephen Holden, "Riding the High Country: Finding and Losing Love," *New York Times*, December 9, 2005.

93. Damon Wise, "Brokeback Mountain," *Empire*, www.empireonline.com/reviews/review.asp?FID=9981.

94. See Tompkins, *West of Everything*, 74–76, for a discussion of the relationship between scanning the landscape and power over the land.

95. Anthony Lane compares the first scene to the enigmatic opening of *Once Upon a Time in the West* (Leone, 1968). See "New Frontiers," New Yorker, May 12, 2005.

96. Grundmann, "*Brokeback Mountain*," 50.

97. www.brokebackmountain.com.

6

Space, Setting, and Mobility in Old New York

The Heiress, The House of Mirth, *and* Gangs of New York

Throughout this book, I have argued that one of the features of an adaptation is a sense of doubleness, of a relationship between the film and other manifestations, relationships that the film itself triggers and that we are often reminded of in the publicity processes that surround it. While this relationship can be connected to some memory of the original source, it is not necessarily grounded in the written text. We might find it in visual references to Dickens's London, in the crisscrossing of generic references, or in the adoption of a theatrical acting style. In this chapter, I want to look at another source of doubleness, the use of locations and settings and in particular locations and settings that are set in the urban past. In doing so, I want to consider a number of questions: what kind of possibilities and resonances are raised by the different use of locations and sets? how is space organized in terms of the mobility of characters and their access to the city? and how are ideas about faithfulness and adaptation worked through when we focus on the physical appearance of a set that aims to represent the past? Overall, this chapter looks at how set design and the discourses that accompany it can also be thought about in terms of adaptation and transformation.

This chapter brings together three films that are set in old New York. Their setting therefore involves a historical set of references to the city, and for Charles Tashiro this immediately puts the audience into a different relationship with what is on the screen, taking us out of an unproblematic reliance on realism:

> We know the past did not look the way the present does. We know because other disciplines equally dependent on surface appearance—art

history and archaeology—lay substantial claims to our sense of historical truth. Our knowledge that our reality does not appear as it does on the screen immediately marks the historical image as stylised, thus fictional.[1]

Tashiro considers film to "be dependent on surface appearances," which means that a film set in the past has to present a "look" of the past; representation of a change in time is achieved through a representation of place. This chapter explores how place is created, and its focus on the filmed city engages us with two different sets of discourses that are used to analyze the films. The first is the language of production design, which, with its emphasis on authenticity and its references to other sources, echoes some of the assumptions of adaptation theory. The second develops out of work on the city and urban spaces, which emphasizes not just physical geography but also the mediated images and experiences that contribute to our understanding of the city and how to live in it. In such work, New York operates as an extreme version of the modern metropolis, providing, as one anthropologist puts it "a permutation of physical, social and iconic characteristics that presents dramatic contrasts better than lesser cities."[2]

I want to dwell a little further on the issues raised by these different discourses. In terms of production design, the building and dressing of the set and location is intended both to create an imagined world for the narrative and to provide ways of making it meaningful; as Jane Barnwell puts it, "Not only might a designer be required to invent individual buildings, spaces, cities and worlds, but also to provide them with a history, with a connection to the film's narrative and to endow them with meaning."[3] This involves a double process that can be contradictory. In the building of the imagined world, there is a strong emphasis on accuracy and on a faithful reproduction of the period. As James Sanders illustrates, the Hollywood studios built up reference libraries of photographs, drawings, films, and descriptions to serve their production designers and art departments,[4] and the demise of such resources has made it even harder to carry out the research deemed necessary for a period film. All this work might seem excessive, given that an object that took months to find might appear on the screen only for fleeting seconds, but the research is not done just to avoid being caught out by more knowledgeable members of the audience. A manual on production design stresses the need in a period film "to address the specificity of the time period the film will visually project" and adds that a film that gives only a generalized impression of the period "does an injustice" to those who are knowledgeable about the period and those who are not; in the case of the former, "the specific design violates the trust between the filmmaker and the audience member, and in the other, it cheats the viewer out of a historically accurate experience."[5] The language here (like that of some adaptation criticism) elevates accuracy to a moral duty and sees sloppy or "generalized" design as a betrayal. In addition, however, the production designer and others in the art team are involved in and responsible for the concept of the look that makes visible the overall theme of the film so that "décor becomes the narrative's organising image."[6] Such a concept might use paintings and other visual stimuli to provide an overall motif or might develop the design through a series of contrasts (country/city, light/darkness, day/night) that pull together the different aspects of the film. Articulating the design concept as the film is made often involves simplification or stylization so that settings and props fit the overall design; this attempt to embed the concept in the décor might conflict with the drive toward detail associated with authenticity.

Running across these approaches is a debate between the merits of studio sets and locations and about the different sense of place that they create. At first sight, this would appear to hinge on the difference between the realism of location and the artificiality of the studio set, but the distinction is more subtle than this. Eugene Lourie, art director in Hollywood after his arrival from France in 1941, claimed that using sets actually involved a greater commitment to reality: "We didn't want to eliminate reality . . . the designer could make the sets much more expressive than real locations. They could become more real than real. A poetic reality, a reality with soul."[7] Generally, though, location shooting is deemed more likely to fulfill the quest for authenticity, but its spaces also need to be worked on. British designer, Stuart Craig, commented, "Every time you pick a real location you better make sure it's saying what you want it to say and you better try to eliminate anything extraneous, because the real world is confusing, it sends out conflicting signals all the time."[8] The use of location is further complicated by the fact that frequently one location has to be made to stand for another, and the trend for Hollywood to move productions to locations and sets elsewhere in a search for "cheap, distinctive and authentic locations"[9] is now very marked.

Vincent LoBrutto offers some guidelines for disguising the fact that you are "shooting at one location for another." They include maxims like "utilize confined areas. . . . Control your design illusion by limiting the scope of each shot. The wider the shot, the harder it is to create the intended illusion."[10] But again the difference between location shooting and shooting on set in this respect is sometimes exaggerated. As Sanders notes, the blocks of Hollywood's New York Street set "had a gentle bend midway in their length, or met each other in T-shaped intersections—very unlike the real city"; such geographical adaptation was necessary to close down the vistas that would otherwise be both difficult and expensive to fill.[11] And Barnwell suggests that, despite the use on location of real rooms in low-budget 1990s British films, the limitations on camera position and the re-dressing of the same space to stand for different settings produces "a kind of visual coherence . . . reminiscent of the system of recycling sets in the traditional studio."[12]

Location and studio settings, used and reused, accrue resonances and layers of meanings. Prosaically, Barnwell points to the fact that objects are hired out by prop houses to successive productions and can become familiar and indeed "tired" in the process,[13] while Sanders comments on the reuse of permanent New York studio sets, which were modified, built on, and added to as if in a real city.[14] But beyond these practicalities, both types of setting carry less tangible resonances. Geoffrey Nowell-Smith celebrates film's rootedness in a sense of place by suggesting that "locations, however carefully researched, are impure,"[15] while Daniel Day-Lewis muses that "when you work on location . . . it's always imbued with some kind of spirit. . . . In a studio, there is nothing unless you are interested in the ghosts of other movies . . . there's no inherent life in those places."[16] But the "ghosts of other movies" also have resonances, and Sanders captures brilliantly his disorientating experience of walking through the New York Street sets built by the major studios: "Seventy feet wide, forty feet high, standing under the bright Californian sun." They evoke a New York that is familiar but strange and, having no interiors, turn out to be "false fronts, propped up with bracing" through which the blue sky can be seen.[17] The sets are literally doubles and offer ghostly references not only to the films previously made there but also to the city they seek to stand for.

We have noted how Hollywood publicity has long drawn attention to the work behind the elaborate settings created for films like *Cimarron* and *The Good Earth*. This emphasis on the process of creation has been made available in a different way by the technological resources of the DVD. Barbara Klinger has noted how the "capstone element of the [DVD] supplement is unquestionably the section devoted to visual effects,"[18] but for films set in the past the information about locations and costume have a similar status to the information about special effects in a science fiction film. The DVD extras seek to privilege the process of production, but for audiences they are part of the reception process, working to direct the audience to a particular kind of understanding. These glimpses behind scenes attempt to fix the film's meaning by offering explanations premised on the act of creation; they emphasize both the quest for authenticity and the craft skills that help to disguise the inevitable compromises of filmmaking. The supplements offer an "insider" view of the processes of making a film set in the past, throwing emphasis on setting rather than narrative and opening up the discourses of location, sets, and costume by identifying the stately homes used as locations and having the designers comment on their work. In addition, the director's commentary often gives extensive detail about production, usually dwelling on the difficulties involved; the story behind the film almost inevitably becomes one in which the director continually struggles to get his vision on screen. As we shall see in this chapter, directors Terence Davies and Martin Scorsese provide a mass of information in their DVD commentaries about how they struggled with locations and sets to build up and represent the complexity of old New York. But, in providing what seems to be the definitive account, they use metaphors and analogies that can themselves be analyzed and that offer highly suggestive terms for thinking about the implications of this kind of adaptation. So, we can look at both the supplements and the commentary, not as the final word on the film, but rather as further elements of the text that add more layers of doubling, reference, and analogy.

The commentaries and features offered by the DVD can also be seen as part of the process of recall that helps to fix a film as an adaptation. Just as adaptations, if they are to function as adaptations, have to make their audiences *"recall* the adapted work, or the cultural memory of it,"[19] so these glimpses behind scenes make us aware of the period film's claim to authenticity and its relationship with a historical environment. In these adaptations, therefore, the transformation involves not just the original sources but also the re-presentation of the physical world through the adaptation of locations so that they can stand for a past society or the transformation of a built set into a version of a real world. The DVD extras often follow in the traditions of Hollywood publicity by emphasizing the painstaking artificiality with which authentic settings are created. By celebrating the processes of building and dressing, the discourse of art direction, as we shall see, both celebrates and exposes the transformations of cinema itself.

We will look further at the implications of this in the analysis of the films under discussion, but I also want to consider ways in which thinking about the city might also inform that analysis. Sanders comments, in his invaluable study of films set in New York, that filming in the city at the beginning of the twentieth century established that we should look at the city as an urban place in which the spaces between the buildings, with their sidewalks, traffic, and crowds of people, were even more important than the distinctive architecture. Using panoramic swivels and moving platforms, the short, silent documentary films made in New York provided glimpses of "the solid matter of the city giving way to movement and energy."[20] More generally, Peter Madsen argues that the city offers different points from which to view: the bird's-eye view of the map, the planner's perspective; the horizontal view of the skyline, from appropriately distanced vantage points; and the local view of the person in the street.[21] These points combine to generate restless movement and an ever-changing juxtaposition of people and activities.

Writing about New York as "Empire City" in the mid-nineteenth century, historian David Scobey comments,

> Victorian observers stressed again and again . . . that the new metropolis was divided against itself. New York was a vast melodrama of "sunshine and shadow," as popular journalists put it, counterposing wealth and destitution, virtue and vice. These contrasts were inscribed in the built environment itself, making the Manhattan grid a mosaic of grandeur, congestion and decay. . . . Space was at once fractured and boundariless in Victorian New York and the city streets became a theater of class distance, class friction, and persistent civil violence during the mid-nineteenth century.[22]

This emphasis on the city as fractured and interlocking is evident in a more abstract account by Peter Marcuse of New York as the "layered city."[23] In his model, the different residential quarters of the city, which are linked to different kinds of employment and services, appear to carve out the city into separate spaces. The rich occupy "luxury areas," which they can move in and out of at will, and they work in similarly flexible spaces, often at the top of buildings. The "gentrified city" of the professional is in proximity to spaces of consumption, urbanity, and culture as well as to professional work, while the suburban city is centered on the home with an emphasis on physical security and escape from the relentless energy of the city. "Tenement city" is the city of unskilled workers whose power, such as it is, is based on their status as essential workers who keep the city functioning. The "abandoned city" is the city of the homeless, the transient, and the poor whose forced rootlessness is an ironic counterpoint to the mobility of the very wealthy.

These different versions of the city occupy definable spaces in terms of specific areas on the ground, types of housing, and work premises and levels within buildings. But Marcuse suggests that what one can see as "patterns of presence" when mapped out as separate quarters actually work as "transparencies overlaid on one another."[24] This layering means that the same space can have different meaning at different times of day and that modes of accessing and occupying the similar spaces can be very different. The offices during the day occupied by young professionals are taken over by cleaning staff at night; a wall serves to exclude or entrap, depending on whether it surrounds a gated community or a housing project; the entrance to a smart shop can be an access point or an uncertain shelter for the homeless; and the space at the top of buildings might house a penthouse suite, a smart nightclub, or a family on welfare, all having, physically and metaphorically, different means of access. Within the layered city, different groups will seek to differentiate themselves from those below while inevitably meeting them on their journeys through the streets. "The picture," Marcuse concludes, "is of New York City as a city divided in quarters spatially, residentially and economically, in which quite different spaces are occupied by different groups at different times, and often, and increasingly, with walls between them. In short, a quartered, walled and layered city."[25]

Marcuse's metaphor of layers and transparencies for understanding the city is suggestive in thinking about adaptations set in New York, and indeed *Celluloid Skyline* offers many examples of how similar insights might be used.[26] In this chapter, this model of the layered city is set alongside the contrasting use of location and studio, to inform an analysis of the use of space and place in three adaptations that seem highly conscious of New York as a "quartered, walled and layered city." *The Heiress* (Wyler, 1949) is an adaptation of Henry James's short story *Washington Square* and was filmed on an elaborate set in Paramount Studios; *The House of Mirth* (Davies, 2000) is an adaptation of Edith Wharton's novel of the same name, filmed on location in Scotland; and *Gangs of New York* (Scorsese, 2002) is an adaptation of a little-known "informal history of the underworld" first published in 1927 that was made at the Cinecittà Studios on a specially built set.

THE HEIRESS—THE BOUNDARIES OF HOME

The credits of *The Heiress* set the film firmly in the past ("100 years ago") and in a place that has been reimagined since it is presented to us through a series of tapestry-work scenes first of a woman indoors, then of the exterior of the house with its architectural details. The sequence concludes with an embroidered version of the square with a plate in front that identifies it as a particular place in "the Common Council of the City of New York." A dissolve animates the square, bringing the venue to life as an elaborate studio set with carriages and horse-drawn delivery vans, nursemaids, and a child feeding white birds. The credits remind us of the source in adaptation: the film is in fact based on the play *The Heiress* whose authors have written the screenplay, and both film and play appear to be "suggested by the Henry James novel 'Washington Square.'" So, although *The Heiress* does not refer to its location in its title, the credits suggest a narrow focus on a particular place, Washington Square.

The design concept of the film was based on the set of the house in which Dr. Sloper and his daughter Catherine live. The layout of the house was, as Sanders illuminatingly demonstrates, an adaptation of the standard New York row house with two main rooms and a wide hall running past them, a staircase going up from the hall, and an elaborate front door that can be observed from the stairs as well as the hall and that marks the formal interaction of house and street. The doctor's office is below. The addition of a library, winter garden, and staircase at the back in a less classical style served the practical purpose of providing settings for particular scenes but also demonstrated Dr. Sloper's attachment to the past and to the memory of his dead wife, Catherine's mother. The designer, Harry Horner, won an Oscar for this work and reflecting on it for *Hollywood Quarterly* commented that it was "not a house of one period, but of many." "It must give the feeling of having gone through several styles," he went on, "thus making that first phase of his life which existed only in his memory stand out and become visible to us."²⁷ So, the period style of decoration not only reflects the architecture of the past but also fulfills the designer's brief to provide the buildings and spaces of the film "with a history, with a connection to the film's narrative, and to endow them with meaning."²⁸

The solidity of the house-as-set is matched by the artificiality and functionality of the exterior scenes. Filming in the square itself is restricted to the area in front of the house, and although the trees, grass, and benches are "real," the composition and framing suggest a created space in which a character can be briefly out of the house and therefore offstage. The party at which Catherine first meets Morris is held in a garden that functions as a room decorated with lights and is organized for dancing and display. The garden at the back of the house is walled, and its rather medieval, gothic style provides a quasitheatrical setting for a romantic liaison. And the street in which Catherine buys fish and says goodbye to her guests is also clearly a set. These are exterior settings that lack fresh air; they suggest not only that, as Sanders observes,²⁹ the city creates public rooms out of outdoor spaces but also more specifically that wherever Catherine goes the boundaries of the house in Washington Square metaphorically surround her. She lives within a walled and quartered city.

The restrictions that the set literally and the house metaphorically place on the characters do not mean that mobility and access are not issues in understanding the film. Sanders draws attention to the crucial way in which the set of *The Heiress* is organized around public and private spaces. He observes that this distinction is not just between the street outside and the house inside but also lies in the gradations of outside and inside, front and back. We can see a distinction between the front exterior and the back. While the steps, pillars, and arch of the former indicate a public area where entry deliberately courts being seen, the back door and small garden are public areas that achieve some privacy by being hidden from view. Entry this way belongs to the inmates of the house, including the servants, and to those claiming such intimacy, as Catherine's lover, Morris Townsend, does. Crossing into the house from the outside does not in itself constitute a move from the public to private world. The doorstep, the hall, and the drawing room all have a public demeanor and a form of public access, while the back parlor, the library, and the bedrooms require various degrees of private access. The spaces associated with the work of keeping house and with the lowest layers of the social hierarchy are not made visible to us. A maid comes up the stairs from the basement to answer the main door, and the cook is reported to be suffering with her rheumatism in bed, but we do not see either the kitchen or the servants' private quarters. The ground floor offers the most flexible space: we see the hall from the main rooms and the staircase; the sliding pocket doors between the front and back parlor can be opened and closed to change the nature of the space and to assert or grant privacy.

Different characters have access to different spaces, and the film uses this as a metaphor to underpin the romantic story of Catharine's thwarted love. Again, it is worth noting that the servants' access does not indicate power but rather the lack of it. Like office cleaners, they occupy space at a different time (early in the morning, last thing at night), or their presence is sanctioned by permission of the room's occupier. In terms of the other characters, it is the battle over access to the house that gives physical expression to Catherine's love affair. Movement within this space and the capacity to change its shape or function indicates the dynamics of the relationships between the three main characters—Catherine, her father Dr. Sloper, and Morris.

Dr. Sloper, at least until the crisis over Catherine's defiance, has the most settled relationship with the house and uses its spaces most actively to define public and private. He is regularly seen on his own in the library, which acts as his study and is where the picture of his late wife is kept on his desk. He makes decisions about where particular conversations are to be conducted. For instance, when Catherine waits up for him to break the news of her engagement to Morris, she falls asleep in the wrong place on a sofa in the hall; waking, she baldly tells her father, "I am engaged to be married," but he invites her into the back parlor to continue the discussion. The following morning he interviews Mrs. Montgomery, Morris's sister, in his study, probing her for her brother's weaknesses and the truth of his feelings for Catherine; when Catherine is invited into the room to meet Mrs. Montgomery, she is immobilized in a shot that has the two of them seated in the foreground with Sloper between them in the background. Sloper uses the flexibility of the ground-floor rooms to reiterate the distinction between public and private space. When Morris arrives to request the father's permission for the engagement, Sloper slides the doors shut to create the back parlor for a private discussion with his sister and sister-in-law; he opens them again to walk through and greet Morris, and shuts them behind him, indicating that Morris will stay in the most formal part of the house and that in his dealings with his daughter's suitor he will take no notice of her aunts' pleadings. Although Sloper uses and values his own privacy, he blocks off knowledge of the depths of his subjectivity, refusing to understand the damage his devotion to the past is doing. Catherine's refusal to go to his bedroom when he is dying is not only revenge but also a demonstration that she has learnt from him the power that comes from keeping rooms separate and refusing entry to those that are most private.

Catherine's other teacher is Morris, and from him she learns different lessons about control of the house. Rather ironically, Dr. Sloper, as he goes back to work after the dinner at which Morris has been a guest, orders Catherine and her aunt to "extend the honors of the house to Mr. Townsend." This is a dangerous invitation since Morris is a man who does not maintain boundaries, and the house is the site of his most flagrant attempts to breach them. In the week following their first meeting at the party, Morris is reported to have visited the house so frequently that Catherine goes out to avoid the apparent impropriety. In the long scene of the visit that follows her return, Morris's wooing is accompanied by an invited move from the doorstep into the hall and the front parlor and then a move initiated by himself into the intimacies of the back parlor and the piano. The camerawork and acting also make us aware that Morris breaches the customary distance between people; he leans toward Catherine so that she has to lean backward to maintain a suitable distance from him. In this way, Morris ignores the established meanings of particular spaces and reworks space to his own ends. It is striking that his proposal of marriage to Catherine and his lengthy kissing of her take place in the front room and then in the hall as he departs, the formal public nature of these spaces indicating both the risk he is taking of discovery and the way he pushes against the boundaries of appropriateness.

Once Sloper dismisses him as a suitor, Morris's status in the house becomes both ambiguous and furtive. The inappropriate intimacy he demands is confirmed by the scene in which he makes himself at home, while Catherine and her father are in Europe, playing backgammon with Aunt Lavinia and sitting firmly back in his chair as he confirms his liking for the house. His lingering presence is discovered on their return by the use he has made of brandy and cigars. From then on, his access is either denied or misunderstood. He lurks under the arch at the back of the house until Catherine initiates their long conversation in the back garden. After Dr. Sloper's death, Aunt Lavinia invites him to the house, an invitation that Catherine first countermands and then allows. But Morris, who has always tried to use the house on his own terms, does not understand the terms on which he is now invited in. Standing under the arch between the front and back rooms, poised on one of the blurred lines between public and private space, he tells Aunt Lavinia, "I'm home, really, truly home." But his claim expresses a profound misunderstanding of the nature of his presence in that set. Catherine controls his access, a fact she demonstrates by agreeing to elope again with no intention of complying. The film ends with Morris at the front door once again, barred from the house by Catherine.

Catherine's access to the house is more complex. First of all, she lives as a young girl under the control of her father, with her own private spaces represented by a scene in her bedroom early in the film in which we see a freer, livelier, and more spontaneous Catherine than the woman we see in public. She is involved in running the house but is overseen by her father, who comments on the inappropriateness of her carrying fish from the stall and himself gives the servants orders about the organization of the household. Catherine can receive her own visitors, but Aunt Lavinia is supposed to be chaperoning her, and she is made vulnerable when her matchmaking aunt leaves her alone with Morris.

Catherine's desire for Morris is linked with her need to escape the house. As she waits to elope with him for the first time, she throws open the window of the formal front room and reflects, "I may never see Washington Square again, never be in this house again." When Morris fails to arrive, she retreats back into the house, first, weeping, to the back of the front parlor as her aunt shuts the door against the audience and then, stony-faced, trudging with her packed bags up the stairs. But after this bitter disappointment, Catherine begins to claim the house. After her father's death, she refuses to leave the house for a holiday, telling her Aunt Elizabeth, "I like the square." Her embroidery frame dominates the front parlor, she deals with the servants ("Maria, you are as free in this house as I am"), and she chooses whether she is "at home" to Morris or not. But this assertion of control has a cost. Catherine has slipped the control of her father and asserted her own authority in the house, but she is also controlled by it. If Morris cannot come in, she cannot go out.

Generically, *The Heiress* can be linked to the woman's film of the 1940s and in particular that group of films that Mary Ann Doane called the "'paranoid women's films.'"[30] She pinpoints the start of the cycle with *Rebecca* (Hitchcock) in 1940 and sees it coming to an end in the late 1940s when these narratives emerge in another form, the gothic paperback. *The Heiress* does not share the narrative structure of these films in which a woman fears that she is in mortal danger from her husband, a fear that makes her doubt her own sanity and understanding. Catherine, however deeply distressed, does not fear murder—nor, despite her difficulty in "reading" Morris and her father, does she hesitate in trusting her own judgment about what to do. But *The Heiress* does share the paranoid woman's film's use of the "paradigmatic woman's space—the home"—to explore the psyche and the "mapping of gender-differentiated societal spaces onto the film."[31] Doane discusses the significance of doors, staircases, and windows in the home, of the boundaries on which the outside threatens the inside. Very often the resolution of the film results in the destruction of the home—by fire in *Rebecca*, *Jane Eyre* (Stevenson, 1944), and *Secret beyond the Door* (Lang, 1948)—so that a new relationship between husband and wife can be established.

Recognizing this generic overlapping also helps to identify that, in *The Heiress*, the father causes the trouble by overengaging with the home. The great fear of the heroine of the paranoid woman films is that her husband is still in love with his first wife. Sloper takes up this structural position in the narrative of *The Heiress* even though he is a father, not a husband. The same kind of obsession drives him, and although he seems to be concerned and kindly toward his daughter and even to the servants, his interest in the minutiae of Catherine's world is overintense. He has taken over not just the relationship the home has with the outside world but also its inner workings. In the private world of the home, he acts out the role of the dead mother, commenting on Catherine's dress, providing her with a chaperone, and overseeing her shopping. Like Morris, he has too much invested inside the house, but his concern for household management conceals his real feelings. In the crisis generated by Morris's incursions, he cannot respond intuitively to his daughter, and her exposure to what she understands as his dislike leads to the final act in which she excludes both men and immures herself in the house.

Critics have related Catherine's growing power in the film and her assertion of control to the position of women after the Second World War. But it is worth considering the ambivalence of the ending in the light of the overt commitment to democracy and equality during and after the Second World War. *The Heiress* was "sluggish"[32] in terms of audience figures, and Mike Chopra-Gant has suggested that the most popular films of the immediate postwar period actually expressed optimism about American values and "reinvigorate the myth of America as a classless, democratic society."[33] The huge, fixed set of *The Heiress* represents the opposite of this, its hierarchies and boundaries reaffirming class as well as gender positions. Morris not only offered romance but also a different set of class relationships, connections with the people outside the house exemplified by his sister and nieces and nephews living on Second Avenue. In that context, Catherine's walk up the stairs at the end of the film involves turning her back on the possibilities of the city, of freezing Washington Square into the patterns of her last piece of tapestry rather than opening herself up to the juxtapositions of status and class that moving out of the house might involve.

THE HOUSE OF MIRTH—THE PERILS OF MOBILITY

In moving from *The Heiress* to *The House of Mirth*, we move from the grandeur of the studio system to the exigencies of independent filmmakers in the UK. When making his adaptation of Edith Wharton's *The Age of Innocence* (1993), even Martin Scorsese had found the absence of support from studio system difficult: "We no longer have the studios that have all the props and sets,"[34] he commented, though his passion for authenticity was reflected in a budget of over thirty million dollars and locations in Troy, New York, and Philadelphia that were "more in keeping with the nineteenth century than the streets of New York City."[35] Terence Davies thought *The Age of Innocence* "a masterpiece,"[36] and scenes in *The House of Mirth* are reminiscent of the earlier work. But *The House of Mirth* was shot on location mainly in Glasgow and in period houses elsewhere in Scotland. Davies has discussed the difficulties of this in interviews given during and after the shoot and in his self-effacing DVD commentary draws specific attention to the inventive practicalities of turning Glasgow at the end of the twentieth century into New York at the beginning. In contrast to *The Age of Innocence*, this film, while aiming for plausibility, did not look to authenticity as the rationale for its use of setting and décor. Instead, the layering of an imaginative version of one past city onto the physical remnants of another provide an overall metaphor for the process of filmmaking that is reinforced by the film's use of space and mobility in the story of its heroine, Lily Bart.

The use of Glasgow was necessary because of the financial arrangements that produced the film's low budget of 7.5 million dollars.[37] The money was painstakingly put together from sources of subsidy, which included the Scottish Arts Council, and Glasgow's Film Office advised on locations. An abandoned upstairs room in a public house becomes the scene for the Dorsets' dinner party in Monte Carlo; the billiards room in a gentlemen's club is transformed into Aunt Peniston's reception room. Other scenes take place on rundown doorsteps in noisy Great Western Road as well as in the restored marble of Glasgow's city chambers and the stately homes of Gosford House (East Lothian) and Manderston (the Borders), which, though both dated back to the 1790s, had been heavily restored in the nineteenth and twentieth century. From Glasgow to New York is a long stretch, but if New York's title was "Empire City," Glasgow had claimed to be the "Second City of the Empire" whose wealth in the eighteenth century was built on tobacco trade with the American colonies and whose workshops and dockyards later in the industrial revolution produced both goods for export and ships to transport them. If the exquisite society that rejected Lily Bart was built on the products of capital, then Glasgow, which by the time of the shoot had spent over a decade restoring its monumental Victorian architecture, was an appropriate place to tell her story. And certainly Glasgow, too, had the melodramatic contrast of extreme wealth and desperate destitution that made New York "a mosaic of grandeur, congestion and decay."[38]

Davies's commentary on the DVD emphasizes the transience of location shooting in terms of both time and space. He draws attention to the constrictions placed on many shots by the need to avoid glimpses of what cannot be dressed or is not there. He tells of the silver banister at Manderston that could be touched only by Gillian Anderson with her gloves on and of the dereliction that surrounded the marbled hall at Gosford House, which was used as the scene for a society wedding reception; he comments on the restrictions of the budget, which meant that only one end of a large room could be dressed, restricting where he could put the camera; he delights in the patch of real wallpaper that gave a bronzed richness to a close-up of Sam Rosedale; and he indicates how summer in a great house could be evoked by the shot of a sunlit conversation under a tree. Time, too, limits the settings, and Davies comments several times on how a particular location, such as the Theatre Royal for the opera scenes, was available for only a day. While the commentary emphasizes the pressure and tiredness that result from this, the limited availability also creates a sense of evanescent interiors with setups being crammed in before the access runs out and the location disappears. The pressure of time is also a matter of the weather, since Glasgow and the West of Scotland are known for rain. Limited access to locations crams the setups in, and poor weather leaves acres of wasted time with shots snatched when the sun finally flickers at the end of a long day.[39]

In such circumstances, lighting and sound are used to extensive effect to direct the eye and to suggest a sense of place when the set cannot be fully dressed or the light is going. The gloomy interiors of Aunt Peniston's mansion are lost in shadow, the lacy patterns of curtains filter light and block the (nonexistent or inappropriate) view at the windows, and the light from the unseen stage shines on a layer of gilded boxes at the opera. The heat and sensuousness of the South of France are signified by the luminous canvas sheets, rippling with the breeze, which protect those on the yacht from the full light of the sun and so disguise the fact that the scenes are being filmed in a studio setup in Glasgow with the help of some computer-generated imagery (CGI). The soundtrack creates a sonic landscape that contributes to our understanding of space and setting. Take the scene in which Lily returns home from her disastrous visit to the opera. The camera is placed in the hall, and Lily's shadowy figures is seen against the glass as she opens the door; she then moves through the hall and rapidly goes up the staircase before being summoned by Aunt Peniston.

But much of the texture of the brief scene is provided by sound: the sound of horses' hooves indicating the unseen carriage moving away; the chimes of the clock resonate in the grandiose arch of the hall; Lily's shoes make a hollow, thudding sound on the hall floor that is replaced by lighter, more urgent taps and the susurration of her skirt as she half runs up the staircase; Aunt Peniston's voice is preceded by the sound of the opening of a door to the left, offscreen; and as Lily moves into her aunt's room the sound of doors closing indicates not only her movement but also that of Grace, who has been deliberately spying on Lily's return.[40]

It is possible to explain the use of location in *The House of Mirth* in terms of budget, but the impact feeds right into the film's representation of the layers of New York society. The transient locations have an impact on how the city and its society are represented in exterior and interior scenes. The blocking off of what has to remain off camera reinforces the way in which the homes and pleasures of society are separate from the rest of the city. The city is not presented as a geographical entity but rather as a social one. We see not a particular district or quarter but "the residences of the wealthy [that], while located in clearly defined residential areas, are at the same time non-spatially bound."[41] Given the easy mobility of the rich, this includes not only town houses and restaurants in the city but also places

Gillian Anderson in The House of Mirth *(2000). In* The House of Mirth, *lighting and sound are used to direct the eye and to suggest a sense of place when the set cannot be fully dressed or the light is going.* Source: *Granada/Arts Council/Film 4/The Kobal Collection/Jaap Buitendijk*

like the Trenors' country home, Belmont, and the streamlined luxury of the Dorsets' yacht. Behind such venues lurks the city as "a location of power and profit,"[42] the city in which Gus Trenor and Rosedale make money out of the speculative, unseen deals of the financially mobile. In the homes of the rich, we see how the wealth created in this way is rendered solid, and their arches, galleries, and corridors display objects of beauty. Lily wants and needs to be part of this display, and the film's use of her in a *tableau vivant* is only the formal version of a number of shots that see her posed for the watching gaze inside and outside the film.[43] But her problem is that she also needs to use these spaces for her own subterfuges, only to find that they offer precarious protection. A conversation with Gus Trenor about her "investments" takes place in the darkened frame of an alcove, but Rosedale discusses the secret in the open richness of the marbled galleries so Lawrence Selden can hear. Similarly, the curved framing of a stone bench at Belmont seems to protect her kiss with Selden from watching eyes, but she is unknowingly exposed to Trenor's gaze when she moves quickly away up the stone steps.

As Lily's hold on her position in society become more tenuous, the film offers instances when her access to social spaces is marked as different from that of others even when she is in the same room, as if she were an overlaid transparency that could be removed simply by lifting her out. We can see this most clearly in the scene of the dinner in Monte Carlo just before Bertha Dorset makes her move to oust Lily from that layer of society. The dinner party that for others is a social occasion becomes for Lily a test of her place in society; she and Selden sit at the end of the table furthest away from the Dorsets. In their two-shots, the background is dark and blurred, while reverse shots show the other guests against the solid background of furniture. Similarly, when Lily is in the restaurant with Mrs. Fisher, the Trenors behave as if she were invisible until they are forced to drag their eyes round to her by Lily's greeting, and the Dorsets' butler blocks her entry to their house, leaving her standing on the doorstep against the blurred background of the trees.

But, well before Lily begins to find her presence in the luxury areas unwelcome, moving between them has been a problem for her. She does not control her own transport systems, and as a woman on her own, moving about represents a risk and a danger for her. At first, she is willing to go with the risks and to use the unpredictable encounters for her own purpose as in her unwise hailing of Lawrence Selden on the station platform when she misses her train, which leads to her visit to his rooms at the Benedick. When she resumes her journey, Mr. Rosedale and the cleaner meet her on the stairs, and these encounters catch up with her later in the film. The train journey to Belmont brings her the reward of meeting the rich Percy Gryce, but after the visit two scenes of transport involve a closed-carriage encounter with Gus Trenor, who deviously offers to invest her money, and an open one with Aunt Peniston and Grace in which Lily's lightness of tone is misunderstood as flippancy by her aunt. For Lily, the map of New York's acceptable social spaces is marked by the difficulty of moving between them.

Lily's story is one of a woman who wants the luxury, in every sense, of a secure place in society but fails to achieve it in the only way she thinks she can, through marriage. Prone to poor judgments and let down by a succession of men, her fading beauty means that she is no longer a desirable commodity, and the film traces her downward movement in social standing and status. She becomes a social secretary to Mrs. Hatch and thereby loses the security of her own space as her employer enters Lily's bedroom to give her orders. Another slide takes her into what might be described as the "tenement city" in which Lily becomes one of the essential workers who maintains the superstructure of the city since, when dress and décor mark the boundary lines of class, millinery is an essential industry for those who live in the luxury areas of New York. Only at this point, when she has no means of transport beyond walking, does Lily begin to come into contact with the streets and crowds of New York. Her relationship with the city is still fleeting, but it sets her in a different context, a geographical context in which we see how people move from place to place. A CGI exterior shows us the crowds, bridges, and stairways of the station that had previously been excluded from her path. The busy streets and the overseen rooms of the milliner's workshop bring her into contact with the working poor; the sounds of the street permeate the tenement room in which she finally takes her own life.

Like *The Heiress*, *The House of Mirth* ends with the heroine immobile. Davies tells us in the commentary that he had intended to end the film with shots of prints of New York, scenes that would have placed her fate in the context of the city. Instead, the credits come up over a freeze-frame of Lily languidly sleeping into death while Selden kneels beside her; the red of the chloral is gradually lost as color bleaches away from the image and the screen goes dark. Critics, particularly those who have emphasized the film's use of the gaze and Lily's position as to-be-looked-at, have seen this as a fetishization of Lily's beauty in death. But the immobility of this frame fits the pattern of movement and mobility in the film as if Lily had sunk through the layers of the city to its bedrock. The deathbed scene, reminiscent of nineteenth-century melodramas, shows that, while movement involves risk, lack of it certainly leads to death; by implication, it looks back on all the posed beauties earlier in the film. It engages us with reflections on cinema itself and its reliance on movement, color, and light. Critical to this is the astonishing sequence that, earlier in the film, takes the narrative and Lily on the journey from New York to Monte Carlo and involves the audience in the complex processes of cinematic transformation. The movement of the camera is out of darkness to light, out of the shrouded room, skirting the high walls through the thickening rain, following the movement of water that indicates the journey across the ocean, and around the bays of the Mediterranean; the sequence takes us from the reality of soft (Scottish) rain to the fake sunshine of "Monte Carlo in downtown Scotland," as Davies puts it in the commentary. Lily has in fact moved from one luxury area to another, and the move only confirms her downward fall. But as the sequence briefly asserts the hope as well as the risk in her dramatic move so this transitional shot reminds the audience of the possibilities and risks of a rootless cinema, possibilities that are fleeting and evanescent because they rely on capturing a moment that is endlessly moving on. The Scottish locations of this New York film, even when they go unrecognized, make a major contribution to that understanding.

GANGS OF NEW YORK—"IN ITALY, I WAS LIVING IN NEW YORK"

The Heiress and *The House of Mirth* can be seen as adaptations of their source novels in the manner of others discussed in this book. *The Heiress*, like *Pride and Prejudice* (1940) and *The Good Earth*, used classic Hollywood's strategies of streamlining the narrative of the novel via a theatrical adaptation, while *The House of Mirth* has the visual self-consciousness of the art film.[44] Both films can and have been discussed in terms of their faithfulness to their sources. No such discussion accompanies analysis of the film of *Gangs of New York*, despite the frequently told tale of how the film was inspired by Herbert Asbury's book of the same name, which Scorsese chanced upon in a friend's bookcase. What *Gangs of New York* takes as its source is more ambitious; with this film, the debates about faithfulness, accuracy, and being true to the spirit of the text are shifted from the source novel to history itself.

Scorsese, in interviews about the film and in the DVD commentary, describes himself as being, from his teenage years, "fascinated by our history, particularly by the East Coast and how America was formed."[45] His aim is to make his audience aware of a history of New York that is as crucial to the shaping of the United States as the Revolutionary War and the founding fathers but that has been forgotten and covered over. In unearthing this history, Scorsese is concerned to show how debates about immigration were fought on the streets and how a multicultural America was an integral part of a struggle for democracy. A commitment to historical accuracy is referenced in the comments on the years of research put into the project; the employment of an historical advisor, Luc Sante; the use of contemporary material—engravings, photographs, press reports, and histories—in designing the sets and costumes; and the use of a recording of Walt Whitman speaking as a source for Daniel Day-Lewis's accent. The supplementary features on the DVD place a particular emphasis on history in the discussion of the sets and the costume design, and in the feature "The History of the Five Points," Sante discusses the problematic nature of sources such as the lurid *Police Gazette* and the difficulty of knowing historically about the lively culture of the streets. Accuracy is important to the film, and Scorsese claims, for instance, that the film is "historically accurate to the nature of the anarchy and chaos."[46]

Nevertheless, Scorsese also tells us, early in the DVD commentary, that the film is about the myth of America, and in his discussion of the use of historical material he draws on the same vocabulary of compression and reorganization as is used in discussions of adaptations. He refers to his habit of calling up Sante to "ask him what would be happening" but also "could we take license?" Scorsese and the actors acknowledge the characters to be composites, and historical facts about their originals are rearranged: Bill "The Butcher" is based on a real person, but his name is changed and he dies later in the film. Historical facts are, in Scorsese's unusual phrase, "moved up" so that they take place earlier than they did in fact. So, the fire that destroyed Barnum's famous museum takes place in the film during the draft riots rather than two years later; the Chinese Pagoda and indeed the presence of the Chinese themselves in New York can be accurately dated to 1870 but are "moved up" to the early 1860s for the purposes of the film; and Paradise Square, the film's geographical center, is moved closer to the water.[47] In this way, Scorsese describes his film as being inspired by his obsession "with historical fact and imagination."

The importance of this is the link to the elaborate set that allowed Scorsese to try to put this historical world on screen. Much of the prepublicity for the film centered on the budget and the set. A screening of a twenty-minute sequence at the Cannes Film Festival in 2002 gave "a sense of how vivid and spectacular a world the money has been spent on."[48] The DVD also takes the set as the major attraction of the film, offering an interview with production designer Dante Ferretti, the astonished response of a number of the actors to the reality of the set, and a feature called "Exploring the Set of *Gangs of New York*," with the invitation to activate 360-degree shots of the set at particular points on the tour. The emphasis is on not only the scale of the set but also its intricacy, the fact that the sets have interiors you can go into and the detail of the reconstruction. At several points in the features and the DVD commentary, Scorsese and the actors underline the overwhelming nature of the set when they remark that, although they were in Italy when making the film, they were living in New York.

So what are the consequences for the film's representation of space and place, of this emphasis on history and myth, and of the use of huge, purpose-built studio set? They can be described in the terms of quarters, layering, and mobility, which I used to discuss *The Heiress* and *The House of Mirth*, but they operate very differently. In terms of Marcuse's model, *Gangs of New York* focuses on "the abandoned city," the city of the very poor, the excluded, and the homeless. Marcuse does not relate the abandoned city to a particular form of work, or indeed to the criminality that is the form of work undertaken by the gangs in the film, but his emphasis on this city as a space of "abandoned manufacturing buildings" and "the most polluting and environmentally detrimental components of the urban infrastructure"[49] does chime with the prominence of the old brewery that had been abandoned when the film starts and the general sense of "some sort of medieval society where a breakdown of civilization has occurred."[50] From this emerges the film's emphasis on geography, mobility, and layering from the bottom up.

Unlike *The Heiress* and *The House of Mirth*, *Gangs of New York* works to give the viewer a specific sense of the geography. The overall space of the set is laid out clearly at the beginning when "Priest" Vallon leads his followers out to battle through the underground caves, up into the old brewery, and out into Paradise Square. The moving camera gives us sliding snapshots of the people and spaces of the brewery and then a panoramic shot of the square itself. This early emphasis on making the space comprehensible is reinforced at various points in the film by shots that pull back to show the relationships the different buildings have to the street, the square, and each other: "Monk" looks down from his barber's shop, Bill strides out into Paradise Square, and the revived Dead Rabbits gang group themselves against the church. The viewer is given the means to map the set. In addition, the film early on shows the district of the Five Points, with Paradise Square at its center, in relation to the rest of New York. After the first battle and the death of "Priest" Vallon, the camera pulls up to show the layout of the district as a map within lower Manhattan and then dissolves into a shot of the same area, sixteen years later, showing the infilling of the streets and expansion of the city. Another dissolve and a further move back in perspective shows us the full length of Manhattan and its position as an island between two rivers. Through these shots, New York is shown as a geographical entity that is very familiar (a map) and one that changes over time. Both this familiarity and the theme of change are picked up at the end when the film closes with another very familiar reference, the New York skyline, and shows it changing through a series of dissolves from the 1860s to the skyscrapers of 2001.

Gangs of New York thus emphasizes the relationship between spaces by mapping them, but it also stresses mobility, the relationship between people and places. So, although there is a good deal of discussion in the film and in the DVD commentary about the importance of territory, the tribalism of the gangs, and the difference between Five Points and the houses of the rich on Fifth Avenue, what we see is mobility and mixing. Johnny introduces Amsterdam Vallon to the different gangs and identifies them through their costume and criminal inclinations, but all are parading through Five Points, jostling through the area that is also occupied by reformers, politicians, beggars, and pigs. The well-to-do Schermerhorn family and the campaigning newspaper editor, Horace Greeley, are shown around Paradise Square and greeted by Butcher Bill in his most genteel voice. Amsterdam and Jenny can travel uptown on the horse-drawn omnibus and walk alongside Central Park. Jenny, with the advantage of gender, is the most mobile of them all; disguised as a maid, she slips through the French windows of a rich house and invisibly moves up the grand staircase to "rob [them] blind." No wonder, her dream is to keep moving and to take Amsterdam out of Five Points by getting a boat to San Francisco.

If the film emphasizes mobility and access, juxtapositions that create tension and drama, then also its set calls attention to history as a process of layering. The set is indeed a visual model of that process. Scorsese asserts that the caves of the film are based on fact and likens the viewing of the film to an excavation; he comments that he wanted to "give you the impression, as if you lift up a stone or if there's an excavation going on and you look below and you discover a whole world and it's all alive." He refers to the set design's use of photographs of "buildings on outcrops of rock," to the concept of a "place being built with no plan," as if it emerged organically. The film indeed offers a metaphor of history being written from the bottom up, of "old New York seeping out of the ground." The art direction's central concept is of a "place being built with no plan" in which buildings perch on outcrops of rock and tree roots break through the walls of a bar. The caves form the lowest part of the set, and beneath their floors Amsterdam and Jenny hide the mementoes of their parents. The rocks of the cave push above the surface, intruding like a reminder of the past, into Bill's lair in the old brewery, and into the square itself. The makeshift rooms of the brewery are laid on top of one another with long galleries offering vantage points for what is happening below. This layering of living space provides another form of access since it means that secret liaisons can always be overheard or spied on. The Chinese Pagoda is a maze of secret rooms, but rough doors and windows allow for secret viewing points. Even Jenny's room, the most settled and decorated room in the set, is accessible to Bill and has a glass roof that makes it vulnerable to a gaze from above. And of course the moving camera regularly provides overhead shots that allow the viewers a different form of access, denied to the inhabitants of the created world below.

The physical reality of the set provided a space in which Scorsese claims to find stories rather than impose them. The set becomes a metaphor for what the film could be—an endless series of stories that shape the history of New York and that arise out of life there. The set weathers like a real city and is improved by being acted on by the passage of time; "The more the weather hit us the better the buildings looked, the mud got worse, the pigs got bigger." Scorsese comments on the way in which the set itself inspired his imagination, remarking humorously in the light of the film's lengthy shooting process, that "I could still be shooting the film. I could keep going down the street, 'Let's do a scene in this building, let's do a scene in that building.'" But at a certain point the layering of history had to stop, and the film finished. The foreground story of the romance between Amsterdam and Jenny and their significance for the future of America was a way of trying to impose a single story on the stories that emerged from the layering of physical geography and national history that the studio set embodied.

The DVD commentary reflects Scorsese's ambitions for the set of *Gangs of New York* and his sense of failure. His ambition in his film is to give an impression of what it was like to live there ("We felt this was our place," he says), but it is an impossible task. His use of all the resources of filmmaking still cannot quite achieve what he desires, the reality of time and place; in a mumbled comment about costumes, he confesses, "We've highlighted the fantasy of the place, but there's no doubt about it; whatever we do on a film, there's probably much more, who knows, much more intense —— [mumbled word], if we had been there." And his very use of this enormous and elaborate set is haunted by the sense that, with the arrival of CGI, this might be "the last set of its kind." Cinema itself is changing, is no longer interested in this very physical representation of things as things. At the end of his commentary, Scorsese tells the story of a publicity event for television in which he and Leonardo DiCaprio were taken to visit the real Five Points in a New York snowstorm. Only two points are left anyway, but "the snow was so thick and fast," Scorsese comments, "I couldn't see a thing." But it had to be done that day, and so they filmed nothingness, an apt metaphor perhaps of the impossibility of fixing history by an attempt to reconstruct the space in which it took place.

In their use of space and setting, all these films reflect not only on the past that they are trying to create but also on how cinema itself can effect those transformations. We can see *The Heiress* as a declaration of cinema's ability to create solidity and "thereness" out of detailed research, make-believe sets, and artificial streets; ironically, this confidence in the studio system was misplaced since it was already beginning to enter its period of long decline. *The House of Mirth* affirms the ability of cinema to make a virtue out of rootlessness and to catch reality on the wing, through movement, editing, and light. *Gangs of New York* rather sadly tells us of the ambition and impossibility of cinema's project of creating an imaginary world that is real enough to live in. In all three films, the process of adaptation involved rendering the city visible by establishing the separated quarters of the city but also offering instances of how crossing those boundaries is a necessary precondition of drama. It is that movement that creates the juxtapositions of melodrama, the counterpoint of "wealth and destitution, virtue and vice" that Scobey reminds us underpinned understandings of the city. Catherine immured in her great house, Lily dead in her tenement room, and Bill killed on the cobbled streets of Five Points all demonstrate how lives are shaped and ended by the social clashes that the films present in their very different handling of the city setting.

Examining these adaptations through an analysis of their use of sets and locations offers another instance of the way in which questions of faithfulness and authorship go well beyond a discussion of the translation of the book to the screen. In these films, faithfulness to the source is in different ways overridden by a commitment to be accurate about the social mores of a historical city that can be best expressed through the use of setting. *Gangs of New York* takes to an extreme the commitment to authenticity evident in many period films that can work with or against the adaptation's discourse of faithfulness to the source. The audience's understanding of that discourse, previously underpinned by the kind of publicity that emphasized the painstaking art direction of *Cimarron* and *The Good Earth*, can now be found in the DVD supplements. The material in such supplements adds other layers of meaning, other voices that claim attention for the care with which costume, sets, and locations have been rendered. But, in case such voices become too distracting, the now well-established use of the director's commentary gives him the last word. In this respect, *House of Mirth* and *Gangs of New York* offer a further extension of the process at work in the modernist adaptations discussed in chapter 2. In those adaptations, the author of the original source and the director of the film were often held in balance in the extratextual material that worked to position audiences' understanding of the adaptation. With the DVD commentary, the authentic voice of truth about the film becomes, however inaccurately or tendentiously, that of the director. And it is significant that these commentaries concern themselves not with the adaptation from the original sources but rather with the battle to transform physical reality into a satisfactory rendering of the past city.

NOTES

1. Charles S. Tashiro, *Pretty Pictures: Production Design and the History Film* (Austin: University of Texas Press, 1998), 64.

2. James A. Clapp, "Are You Talking to Me? New York and the Cinema of Urban Alienation," *Visual Anthropology* 18, no. 1 (January–February 2005): 5.

3. Jane Barnwell, *Production Design: Architects of the Screen* (London: Wallflower, 2004), 21.

4. James Sanders, *Celluloid Skyline: New York and the Movies* (New York: Alfred A. Knopf, 2001).

5. Vincent LoBrutto, *The Filmmaker's Guide to Production Design* (New York: Allworth Press, 2002), 103.

6. Charles Affron and Mirella Jona Affron, *Sets in Motion: Art Direction and Film Narrative* (New Brunswick, N.J.: Rutgers University Press, 1995).

7. Quoted in Sanders, *Celluloid Skyline*, 80–81.

8. Quoted in Barnwell, *Production Design*, 15.

9. The quotation is from the back cover of a book of academic essays on the phenomenon, *Contracting Out: Hollywood Runaway Productions and Foreign Location Shooting*, ed. Greg Elmer and Mike Gasher (Lanham, Md.: Rowman & Littlefield, 2005).

10. LoBrutto, *The Filmmaker's Guide*, 153.

11. Sanders, *Celluloid Skyline*, 176.

12. Barnwell, *Production Design*, 120.

13. Barnwell, *Production Design*, 75, 86.

14. Sanders, *Celluloid Skyline*, 70–71.

15. Geoffrey Nowell-Smith, "Cities: Real and Imagined," in *Cinema and the City*, ed. Mark Shiel and Tony Fitzmaurice (Oxford: Blackwell, 2001), 103.

16. Daniel Day-Lewis, in the "Set Design" feature on the *Gangs of New York* DVD.

17. Sanders, *Celluloid Skyline*, 143–44.

18. Barbara Klinger, *Beyond the Multiplex: Cinema, New Technologies, and the Home* (Berkeley: University of California Press, 2006), 70.

19. Catherine Grant, "Recognising Billy Budd in *Beau Travail*: Epistimolgy and Hermaneutics of Auteurist 'Free' Adaptation," *Screen* 43, no. 1 (Spring 2002): 57.

20. Sanders, *Celluloid Skyline*, 29.

21. Peter Madsen, "Introduction," in *The Urban Lifeworld*, ed. Peter Madsen and Richard Pluntz (London: Routledge, 2002), 30–31.

22. David Scobey, *Empire City: The Making and Meaning of the New York City Landscape* (Philadelphia: Temple University Press, 2002), 7.

23. Peter Marcuse, "The Layered City," in *The Urban Lifeworld*, ed. Peter Madsen and Richard Pluntz (London: Routledge, 2002): 94–114.

24. Marcuse, "The Layered City," 106.

25. Marcuse, "The Layered City," 106.

26. As an example, see Sanders's discussion of the use in New York films of the apartment-house canopy that occupies a liminal space between the inside of the building and the outside of the street (*Celluloid Skyline*, 197–99).

27. Harry Horner, "Designing *The Heiress*," *Hollywood Quarterly* 5, no. 1 (Fall 1950): 1. I am indebted to Sanders's discussion of the film as well as to that of Laurence Raw in "Reconstructing Henry James: *The Heiress* (1949)," *Literature/Film Quarterly* 30, no. 4 (2002).

28. Barnwell, *Production Design*, 21.

29. Sanders, *Celluloid Skyline*, 177.

30. Mary Ann Doane, *The Desire to Desire: The Woman's Film of the 1940s* (Bloomington: Indiana University Press, 1987), 124.

31. Doane, *The Desire to Desire*, 134, 136.

32. Raw, "Reconstructing Henry James," 246.

33. Mike Chopra-Gant, *Hollywood Genres and Postwar America: Masculinity, Family, and Nation in Popular Movies and Film Noir* (London: I. B. Tauris, 2006), 152.

34. Martin Scorsese, *Scorsese on Scorsese* (London: Faber, 1989), 187.

35. Charles H. Helmetag, "Recreating Edith Wharton's New York in Martin Scorsese's *The Age of Innocence*," *Literature/Film Quarterly* 26, no. 3 (July 1998): 164.

36. Quoted in Linda Costanzo Cahir, "*The House of Mirth*: An Interview," *Literature/Film Quarterly* 29, no. 3 (July 2001): 168.

37. See Rae Graham, "*The House of Mirth* Navigates a Vicious Circle," *American Cinematographer* 82, no. 2 (February 2001), for comments by the cinematographer Remi Adefarasin on the budget and set design.

38. Scobey, *Empire City*, 7.

39. Davies comments that they shot both the scene between Lily and Gus at the shore and the scene between Lily and Rosedale in the street late in the day because of the lack of light.

40. I am grateful to Mark Brownrigg for his insight into the use of sound in *The House of Mirth*.

41. Marcuse, "The Layered City," 94.

42. Marcuse, "The Layered City," 95.

43. See Julianne Pidduck, *Contemporary Costume Film* (London: British Film Institute Publications, 2004), for a discussion of this aspect of Lily's presentation.

44. See Wendy Everitt, *Terence Davies* (Manchester, UK: Manchester University Press, 2004), for an analysis along these lines.

45. Ian Christie, "Manhattan Asylum," *Sight and Sound* 13, no. 1 (January 2003): 21.

46. Martin Scorsese, in the commentary feature on DVD. Unless otherwise indicated all other comments from Scorsese come from this source

47. "Exploring the Set of *Gangs of New York*" feature on DVD.

48. Nick James, "*Gangs of New York*," *Sight and Sound* 12, no. 7 (July 2002): 17.

49. Marcuse, "The Layered City," 97.

50. Scorsese quoted in Christie, "Manhattan Asylum," 21.

Conclusion

I argued in the introduction that there was no one model that could be applied to screen adaptations. I chose the studies that make up this book to illustrate particular approaches to analyzing adaptations, but they do not themselves make up a method that will fit all adaptations. Nevertheless, some general conclusions can be drawn from these case studies. In outlining them here, I want to point to the more open approach that is already implicit in my more detailed film analyses that arises out of my unwillingness to restrict analysis to a comparison between film and source.

As the introduction indicated, the appeal to intertextuality has been specifically developed as a methodological challenge to the fidelity model. Recent collections that I have drawn on show how productively intertextual approaches have gained ground in U.S. and European work in this area.[1] In such studies, the central task becomes "the study of the intertextual universe," and there is a deliberate attempt "to avoid even the appearance of a tendency to reinscribe the superiority of the literary source."[2] But the claim of intertextuality is the beginning not the end of the matter. As Dimitris Eleftheriotis has pointed out in a similar debate about the importance of hybridity in genre criticism, "The fact that everything is hybrid [or intertextual] . . . should not be a point of arrival but a point of departure in the investigation of different conditions and forms."[3] And the process of departure involves a more flexible approach to the concept of adaptation and accepting the consequences of the insight that the most important thing about an adaptation might precisely not be its adaptation status.

This is difficult. Even a highly intertextual critic, who defines adaptation as a "practice of cultural intertextuality" in which the movement is not simply from literature to film, still maintains as one of his broad principles that an adaptation is "always a reading of the source text."[4] Or as Robert Stam puts it, summarizing his rallying cry for an intertextual approach, "The source text forms a dense informational network, a series of verbal cues which the adapting film text can then selectively take up, amplify, ignore, subvert, or transform."[5] Giving agency to the film text here does not disguise the fact that Stam's emphasis on intertextuality still puts the source text first and maintains that the task of looking at adaptations is to continue the comparison between literature and screen. Intertextuality makes this into a more even exchange with an emphasis on dialogism, but the initial impulse to start with the source text still remains and frames the analysis. My decision to remove the original book or play from the analysis is a necessary step in examining how adaptations can be understood without the crucial emphasis on literary origin.

In the analysis of the films discussed in this book, therefore, I have deliberately tried to change the framework, to shake up the kaleidoscope so that different elements are brought to the fore and seen as important in the process of recall I referred to in the introduction. The intention has been that the established conventions of popular cinema—the interplay of genres, the organization of space and time through editing and camerawork, the presentation of performers as stars, the handling of landscape and setting, and the practices of reviewing and publicity that surround many films—are understood at the beginning of the analysis, not wheeled in as explanations for failure. Generic frameworks have proved particularly important for developing this approach, whether they work with or in contradiction to the conventions being brought in from the literary sources or from other screen versions. I am not suggesting that genres have been ignored in debates about intertextuality but rather that testing out their importance has been limited by the tendency to associate them with the commercial imperatives of mainstream cinema.

One of the striking features of theoretical work on adaptations is the use of metaphors as an explanation of the process of adaptation. Among other things, adaptations are deemed to borrow, transform, translate, hold a conversation with, and provide a reading of. Kamilla Elliott has brilliantly extended these metaphors in her discussion of modes of adaptation, but the most influential of recent metaphors has been Stam's "ongoing whirl of intertextual reference and transformation, of texts generating other texts in an endless process of recycling, transformation and transmutation, with no clear point of origin."[6] This is a dramatic metaphor that emphasizes endless, circular movement and the impossibility of fixing a clear, if temporary, point at which one engages with a text. Stam does, of course, use other metaphors, including, a page later, the notion that "film adaptations can be seen as a kind of multileveled negotiation of inter-texts."[7] With this metaphor, Stam moves toward the notion of a more sta-ble layering of elements, something Dudley Andrew also suggests in his account of the difference between adaptations and other films:

> The celluloid of an adaptation resembles that of other films: meaning rises from images and sounds inscribed on its surface. However, the value of an adaptation's meaning . . . depends on an additional dimension, the dimen-sion of depth provided by the substrate text that supports what is on the cel-luloid. A palimpsest, we might say, but a peculiar one, in that the surface layer engages, rather than replaces, a previous inscription.[8]

This comment plays with the double meaning of the world "film"—as a textual work and as a layer itself. The metaphor is a productive one, which, for Andrew, does not depend on the original text being the "sub-strate text" and which allows for layers of different thickness and signifi-cance. Like the transparencies used in art design, a thin, gauzy layer al-lows for much to be seen through it, while a more opaque sheet attempts to substitute its own presence for the layers that lie behind. Generally, though, thinking about adaptations in terms of layering at least allows for the possibility of seeing through one film (in both senses) to another and acknowledges that the effect of simultaneity might draw on understand-ings built up through time and knowledge. The layering process involves an accretion of deposits over time, a recognition of ghostly presences, and a shadowing or doubling of what is on the surface by what is glimpsed behind.

In analyzing the layering that takes place in the films I have examined, I have identified a number of different instances when this metaphor might be suggestive. Generic referencing is particularly important in un-derstanding how screen adaptations take on meaning. In one mode, generic referencing occurs when one genre is anticipated or referenced be-cause of its closeness to another. This might be a welcome or fruitful lay-ering, such as that between the maternal melodrama and the woman's film, or it might be more problematic as in the case of the art film and the heritage film. Our understanding of the film depends on how we under-stand these generic hints; attitudes to Dr. Sloper in *The Heiress*, for in-stance, might take on a more sinister inflection if his position in the house-hold recalls the problematic husbands of the paranoid woman's film. Generic referencing also involves genres that are not normally considered to be close but that are brought into a relationship through the adaptation. In films like *Cimarron* (1931), the interaction can be found in the original novel, but the balance is changed because of cinema's different invest-ment in the western and the woman's film. Or, as in *Oliver Twist*, the screen adaptation might itself draw in very different generic modes that are not referenced in the original source. The reception of the film depends on how these generic layers are evaluated and in what context.

The layering process of adaptations also affects how changing social attitudes are presented and understood so that modern attitudes are seen through references to previous understandings. This is most marked in the representation of race and gender as we have seen with the feminist and postfeminist heroines of classic adaptations and in the interaction between Edna Ferber's progressive views and the more regressive cinema she was being adapted for. It can also mark the points where the invocation of faithfulness is overridden by the need to avoid accusations of sexist or racist attitudes. We have seen how adaptations of *Oliver Twist* were affected by this fear in relation to the character of Fagin and how *The Last of the Mohicans* (1992) was challenged over its representations of Native Americans. Adapting social attitudes can involve contradictory approaches in the same film. Terence Davies was against modernizing the women characters in *The House of Mirth* because "they're not modern women. . . . You cannot apply the same feminist principles."[9] Nevertheless, he removed the anti-Semitic characterization of Wharton's Sam Rosedale because "I simply could not bring myself to write it or to direct an actor to do it."[10]

Performance and setting offer complex layers that bring to the fore different elements of an adaptation. The layering of roles has long been considered essential to the creation of a star image. In adaptations, the layering of performances takes on additional resonances in which one performance references another in relation to how it creates a particular character. The character (Oliver, Elizabeth Bennet, Hawkeye, and Stanley Kowalski) is the same, but the adaptation enables us to see how the same character is performed in different ways and contexts. Something similar happens with the use of setting and landscape; the place might be familiar (Victorian London, the American West, the grid of New York), but it can be understood in terms of different generic associations and different uses of location and set.

The layering of different kinds of media is also characteristic of adaptations and indeed can be used to draw attention to the process of adaptation. The referencing of books and writing is common in classic and modernist adaptations, but we could also include here the referencing of theatrical performance and sets in the Tennessee Williams adaptations, the use of landscape as description in *Brokeback Mountain*, and of references to artworks and pictorial qualities in films as different as *The House of Mirth* and *The Good Earth*. In addition, adaptations use literary references and publicity promotion to suggest connections with the author of the original source, but they also complicate questions of authorship. Cinema is not traditionally associated with authorship, though art cinema and, more recently, the concept of the director's cut have, in different ways, proposed that, even in the collaborative and industrial modes of cinema, interpretation can be assisted by establishing the director as some kind of author. In this way, the original author and the film director are brought into a relationship that can shape how the film is interpreted, as we saw in chapter 2, but writers, designers, and stars can also add an individual signature that serves to make meaning. Adaptations layer one kind of author over another; more than other films, they equate meaning with authorial intention, but in doing so they also set the author in the context of a many-layered construction.

Emphasizing the various ways in which elements are layered into an adaptation helps to put the question of faithfulness into context. For faithfulness is only another element that can be drawn on differently depending on the status and type of adaptation. Referencing the original source and claiming a faithful relationship with it is but one approach; the film might also claim to be faithful to a particular period setting or a particular relationship with contemporary reality. However faithfulness is referenced, it is only ever one of the many layers that create a screen adaptation.

In the introduction, I agreed with Catherine Grant that there could be no such thing as a "secret adaptation,"[11] and in the analysis I have examined the various ways in which the work of drawing attention to a source is carried out in extratextual activity: in the publicity practices, reviewing conventions, and DVD commentaries that accompany the films. In drawing attention to the layering that sustains so many adaptations, I am suggesting that there are other more subtle ways in which adaptations make themselves visible and claim our attention. The doubling that is a feature of adaptations might be inspired by the movement between adaptation and source but is not confined to it. The complex textual referencing of many adaptations, their layering of genres, performances, and settings, provides evidence for how they work as films, not as versions of another form, nor as a whirl of references without their own shape. In the end, theoretical models are only fruitful if they help us share an understanding of the particular films we are subjecting to analysis. The worth of the more film-centered and open approach I have outlined here must lie with the analyses of the individual films that have formed the basis of this study.

NOTES

1. Robert Stam and Alessandra Raengo, eds., *A Companion to Literature and Film* (Oxford: Blackwell, 2004); Robert Stam and Alessandra Raengo, eds., *Literature and*

Film: A Guide to the Theory and Practice of Film Adaptation (Oxford: Blackwell, 2004); and Mireia Aragay, ed., *Books in Motion: Adaptation, Intertextuality, Authorship* (Amsterdam: Rodophi, 2005).

2. Mireia Aragay, "From Reflection to Refraction: Adaptation Studies Then and Now," in *Books in Motion: Adaptation, Intertextuality, Authorship*, ed. Mireia Aragay (Amsterdam: Rodophi, 2005), 24, 26.

3. Dimitris Eleftheriotis, *Popular Cinemas of Europe* (New York: Continuum, 2001), 100–101.

4. Pedro Javier Pardo Garcia, "Beyond Adaptation: Frankenstein's Postmodern Progeny," in *Books in Motion: Adaptation, Intertextuality, Authorship*, ed. Mireia Aragay (Amsterdam: Rodophi, 2005), 240, 238.

5. Robert Stam, "Introduction: The Theory and Practice of Adaptation," in *Literature and Film: A Guide to Theory and Practice of Adaptation*, ed. Robert Stam and Alessandra Raengo (Oxford: Blackwell, 2004), 46.

6. Robert Stam, "Beyond Fidelity: The Dialogics of Adaptation," in *Film Adaptation*, ed. James Naremore (London: Athalone Press, 2000), 66.

7. Stam, "Beyond Fidelity," 67.

8. Dudley Andrew, "Adapting Cinema to History: A Revolution in the Making," in *A Companion to Literature and Film*, ed. Robert Stam and Alessandra Raengo (Oxford: Blackwell, 2004), 190–91.

9. Quoted in Wendy Everett, *Terence Davies* (Manchester, UK: Manchester University Press, 2004), 215.

10. Linda Costanzo Cahir, "*The House of Mirth*: An Interview," *Literature/Film Quarterly* 29, no. 3 (July 2001): 169.

11. Catherine Grant, "Recognising Billy Budd in *Beau Travail*: Epistemology and Hermeneutics of Auteurist 'Free' Adaptation," *Screen* 43, no. 1 (Spring 2002): 57

Filmography

The Age of Innocence (United States, Martin Scorsese, 1993)
Antonia's Line (Netherlands, Marleen Gorris, 1995)
L'Avventura (Italy, France, Michelangelo Antonioni, 1960)
Bend It Like Beckham (UK, Germany, United States, Gurinder Chadha, 2002)
The Bicycle Thief (Italy, Vittorio De Sica, 1948)
Billy Liar (UK, John Schlesinger, 1963)
Bride and Prejudice (UK, United States, Gurinder Chadha, 2004)
Bridget Jones's Diary (UK, France, Sharon Maguire, 2001)
Brief Encounter (UK, David Lean, 1945)
Brokeback Mountain (United States, Ang Lee, 2005)
La Captive (France, Belgium, Chantal Akerman, 2000)
Cat on a Hot Tin Roof (United States, Richard Brooks, 1958)
A Christmas Carol (UK, Brian Desmond Hurst, 1951)
A Christmas Carol (United States, Richard Williams, 1971)
A Christmas Carol (United States, Stan Phillips, 1997)
Cimarron (United States, Wesley Ruggles, 1931)
Cimarron (United States, Anthony Mann, 1960)
Clueless (United States, Amy Heckerling, 1995)
The Color Purple (United States, Steven Spielberg, 1985)
Come Back, Little Sheba (United States, Daniel Mann, 1952)
The Covered Wagon (United States, James Cruze, 1923)
Crouching Tiger, Hidden Dragon (Taiwan, Hong Kong, Ang Lee, 2000)
Dances with Wolves (United States, Kevin Costner, 1990)
David Copperfield (United States, George Cukor, 1935)

The Death of Nancy Sykes (United States, Mabel Fenton and Charles Ross, 1897)
East Is East (UK, Damien O'Donnell, 1999)
8½ (Italy, France, Frederico Fellini, 1963)
Gangs of New York (United States, Martin Scorsese, 2002)
Giant (United States, George Stevens, 1956)
The Good Earth (United States, Sydney Franklin, 1937)
Grease (United States, Randal Kleiser, 1978)
Great Expectations (United States, Alfonso Cuarón, 1998)
Harry Potter and the Sorcerer's Stone (UK, United States, Chris Columbus, 2001)
The Heiress (United States, William Wyler, 1949)
Henry V (UK, Laurence Olivier, 1945)
Home from the Hill (United States, Vincente Minnelli, 1960)
The House of Mirth (UK, France, Terence Davies, 2000)
Howards End (UK, James Ivory, 1992)
Hulk (United States, Ang Lee, 2003)
Imitation of Life (United States, John M. Stahl, 1934)
The Iron Horse (United States, John Ford, 1924)
Jane Eyre (United States, Robert Stevenson, 1944)
Jeanne Dielman, 23 Quai du Commerce, 1080 Bruxelles (Belgium, France, Chantal Akerman, 1976)
The Kid (United States, Charlie Chaplin, 1921)
The Last of the Mohicans (United States, George B. Seitz, 1936)
The Last of the Mohicans (United States, Michael Mann, 1992)
The Lord of the Rings: The Fellowship of the Ring (New Zealand, United States, Peter Jackson, 2001)
The Lord of the Rings: The Return of the King (New Zealand, United States, Peter Jackson, 2003)
The Lord of the Rings: The Two Towers (New Zealand, United States, Peter Jackson, 2002)
Madame Bovary (United States, Vincente Minnelli, 1949)
Manhunter (United States, Michael Mann, 1986)
Mansfield Park (UK, Patricia Rozema, 1999)
Mildred Pierce (United States, Michael Curtiz, 1945)
Mrs. Dalloway (UK, United States, Netherlands, Marleen Gorris, 1997)
My Beautiful Laundrette (UK, Stephen Frears, 1985)
Notorious (United States, Alfred Hitchcock, 1946)
Notting Hill (UK, United States, Roger Michell, 1997)
Now, Voyager (United States, Irving Rapper, 1942)
Oliver! (UK, Carol Reed, 1968)
Oliver Twist (United States, Frank Lloyd, 1922)
Oliver Twist (UK, David Lean, 1948)

Once upon a Time in the West (Italy, United States, Sergio Leone, 1968)
On the Waterfront (United States, Elia Kazan, 1954)
Les Parents Terribles (France, Jean Cocteau, 1948)
Pride and Prejudice (United States, Robert Z. Leonard, 1940)
Pride and Prejudice (UK, France, Joe Wright, 2005)
Purab Aur Pachhim (India, Manoj Kumar, 1970)
Question of Silence (Netherlands, Marleen Gorris, 1982)
Rebecca (United States, Alfred Hitchcock, 1940)
Red River (United States, Howard Hawks, 1948)
Rome Open City (Italy, Roberto Rossellini, 1945)
Room at the Top (UK, Jack Clayton, 1959)
A Room with a View (UK, James Ivory, 1985)
The Rose Tattoo (United States, Daniel Mann, 1955)
Saratoga Trunk (United States, Sam Wood, 1945)
Saturday Night and Sunday Morning (UK, Karel Reisz, 1960)
Secret beyond the Door (United States, Fritz Lang, 1948)
Sense and Sensibility (United States, UK, Ang Lee, 1995)
Show Boat (United States, Harry A. Pollard, 1929)
Show Boat (United States, James Whale, 1936)
Show Boat (United States, George Sydney, 1951)
Spellbound (United States, Alfred Hitchcock, 1945)
Stella Dallas (United States, King Vidor, 1937)
A Streetcar Named Desire (United States, Elia Kazan, 1951)
Swann in Love (France, Germany, Volker Schlöndorff, 1984)
Sweet Bird of Youth (United States, Richard Brooks, 1962)
A Tale of Two Cities (United States, Jack Conway, 1935)
This Sporting Life (UK, Lindsay Anderson, 1963)
Time Regained (France, Italy, Portugal, Raoul Ruiz, 1999)
The Tin Drum (Germany, France, Volker Schlöndorff, 1979)
Titanic (United States, James Cameron, 1997)
Ulysses (UK, United States, Joseph Strick, 1967)
Unforgiven (United States, Clint Eastwood, 1992)
Vertigo (United States, Alfred Hitchcock, 1958)
West Side Story (United States, Robert Wise, 1961)
The Wings of the Dove (UK, United States, Iain Softley, 1997)
Written on the Wind (United States, Douglas Sirk, 1956)
Wuthering Heights (United States, William Wyler, 1939)

TELEVISION

Bleak House (UK, BBC, Ross Devenish, 1985)
Bleak House (UK, United States, BBC, WGBH Boston, Justin Chadwick and
   Susanna White, 2005)

Dallas (United States, Canada, Lorimar Television for CBS, Michael Preece and others, 1978–1991)

David Copperfield (UK, 20th Century Fox Television, NBC, Delbert Mann, 1969)

David Copperfield (UK, United States, BBC, WGBH Boston, Simon Curtis, 1999)

David Copperfield (United States, Hallmark Entertainment, Peter Medak, 2000)

Goodness Gracious Me (UK, BBC, Gareth Carrivick and Nick Wood, 1998–2000)

The Kumars at No. 42 (UK, BBC, Lissa Evans and Nick Wood, 2001–)

Oliver Twist (UK, United States, Claridge Productions, Grafton Productions, Clive Donner, 1982)

Oliver Twist (United States, Walt Disney Television, Tony Bill, 1997)

Oliver Twist (UK, Diplomat Films, HTV, WGBH Boston, Renny Rye, 1999)

Our Mutual Friend (UK, BBC, Peter Hammond, 1976)

Our Mutual Friend (UK, BBC, Julian Farino, 1998)

Pride and Prejudice (UK, BBC, Simon Langton, 1995)

Seinfeld (United States, Castle Rock Entertainment, West-Shapiro, Andy Ackerman and others, 1990–1998)

A Streetcar Named Desire (United States, Keith Barish Productions for ABC, John Erman, 1984)

Selected Bibliography

Affron, Charles, and Mirella Jona Affron. *Sets in Motion: Art Direction and Film Narrative*. New Brunswick, N.J.: Rutgers University Press, 1995.

Altman, Rick. *Film/Genre*. London: British Film Institute Publications, 1999.

Andrew, Dudley. "Adapting Cinema to History: A Revolution in the Making." In *A Companion to Literature and Film*, edited by Robert Stam and Alessandra Raengo, 189–204. Oxford: Blackwell, 2004.

Aragay, Mireia, ed. *Books in Motion: Adaptation, Intertextuality, Authorship*. Amsterdam: Rodophi, 2005.

———. "From Reflection to Refraction: Adaptation Studies Then and Now." In *Books in Motion: Adaptation, Intertextuality, Authorship*, edited by Mireia Aragay, 11–34. Amsterdam: Rodophi, 2005.

Baer, William. *Elia Kazan: Interviews*. Jackson: University Press of Mississippi, 2000.

Ballio, Tanio. *Grand Design: Hollywood as a Modern Business Exercise, 1930–1939*. New York: Scribner, 1993.

Barker, Martin, and Roger Sabin. *The Lasting of the Mohicans: History of an American Myth*. Jackson: University Press of Mississippi, 1995.

Barnwell, Jane. *Production Design: Architects of the Screen*. London: Wallflower, 2004.

Baron, Cynthia. "Crafting Film Performances: Acting in the Hollywood Studio Era." In *Screen Acting*, edited by Alan Lovell and Peter Krämer, 31–45. London: Routledge, 1999.

Basinger, Jeanne. *A Woman's View: How Hollywood Spoke to Women, 1930–1960*. London: Chatto & Windus, 1993.

Bazin, André. "Theater and Cinema—Part One." In *What Is Cinema?* translated by Hugh Gray, 76–94. Berkeley: University of California Press, 1971.

———. "Theater and Cinema—Part Two." In *What Is Cinema?* translated by Hugh Gray, 95–125. Berkeley: University of California Press, 1971.

Belton, Ellen. "Reimagining Jane Austen: The 1940 and 1995 Film Versions of *Pride and Prejudice*." In *Jane Austen on Screen*, edited by Gina Macdonald and Andrew Macdonald, 175–96. Cambridge: Cambridge University Press, 2003.

Belton, John. *American Cinema/American Culture*. New York: McGraw Hill, 1994.

Bluestone, George. *Novels into Film*. Baltimore: Johns Hopkins University Press, 1957.

Bobo, Jacqueline. "*The Color Purple*: Black Women as Cultural Readers." In *Female Spectators Looking at Film and Television*, edited by E. Deirdre Pribram, 90–109. London: Verso, 1992.

Bordwell, David. "The Art Cinema as a Model of Film Practice" (1979). Reprinted in *The European Cinema Reader*, edited by Catherine Fowler, 94–102. London: Routledge, 2002.

———. *Narration in the Fiction Film*. London: Methuen, 1985.

Brantlinger, Patrick. "Forgetting Genocide: Or, the Last of *The Last of the Mohicans*." *Cultural Studies* 12, no. 1 (January 1998): 15–30.

Brownlow, Kevin. *David Lean*. London: Richard Cohen Books, 1996.

Brustein, Robert. "The New Hollywood: Myth and Anti-myth." *Film Quarterly* 12, no. 3 (Spring 1959): 23–31.

Buscombe, Ed. "Inventing Monument Valley: Nineteenth Century Photography and Western Film." Reprinted in *The Western Reader*, edited by Jim Kitses and Gary Rickman, 115–30. New York: Limelight Editions, 1998.

Buscombe, Ed, and Roberta Pearson. "Introduction." In *Back in the Saddle Again: New Essays on the Western*, edited by Ed Buscombe and Roberta Pearson, 1–7. London: British Film Institute Publications, 1998.

Byars, Jackie. *All that Hollywood Allows: Re-reading Gender in 1950s Melodrama*. London: Routledge, 1991.

Byron, Stuart, and Martin L. Rubin. "Elia Kazan Interview." *Movie* 19 (Winter 1971–1972): 1–13.

Cahir, Linda Costanzo. "*The House of Mirth*: An Interview." *Literature/Film Quarterly* 29, no. 3 (July 2001): 166–71.

Campbell, Donna. "'Written with a Hard and Ruthless Purpose': Rose Wilder Hare, Edna Ferber, and Middlebrow Regional Fiction." In *Middlebrow Moderns: Popular American Women Writers of the 1920s*, edited by Lisa Botshon and Meredith Goldsmith, 25–44. Boston: Northeastern University Press, 2003.

Cardwell, Sarah. *Adaptation Revisited: Television and the Classic Novel*. Manchester, UK: Manchester University Press, 2002.

Cartmell, Deborah, I. Q. Hunter, Heidi Kaye, and Imelda Whelehan, eds. *Classics in Film and Television*. London: Pluto Press, 2000.

Cartmell, Deborah, and Imelda Whelehan. "*Harry Potter* and the Fidelity Debate." In *Books in Motion: Adaptation, Intertextuality, Authorship*, edited by Mireia Aragay, 37–49. Amsterdam: Rodophi, 2005.

Cawelti, John G. *Adventure, Mystery, and Romance*. Chicago: University of Chicago Press, 1977.

———. *The Six-Gun Mystique*. Bowling Green, Ohio: Bowling Green University Popular Press, 1970.

Chatman, Seymour. "What Novels Can Do That Films Can't (and Vice Versa)." *Critical Inquiry* 7, no. 1 (Autumn 1980): 121–40.

Chopra-Gant, Mike. *Hollywood Genres and Postwar America: Masculinity, Family, and Nation in Popular Movies and Film Noir*. London: I. B. Tauris, 2006.

Christie, Ian. "Manhattan Asylum." *Sight and Sound* 13, no. 1 (January 2003): 20–23.

Churcher, Mel. *Acting for Film: Truth 24 Times a Second*. London: Virgin Books, 2003.

Ciment, Michel. *Kazan on Kazan*. New York: Viking Press, 1974.

Clapp, James A. "Are You Talking to Me? New York and the Cinema of Urban Alienation." *Visual Anthropology* 18, no. 1 (January–February 2005): 1–18.

Cohan, Steven. *Masked Men: Masculinity and the Movies in the Fifties*. Bloomington: Indiana University Press, 1997.

Conn, Peter. *Pearl S. Buck: A Cultural Biography*. Cambridge: Cambridge University Press, 1996.

Corrigan, Timothy. *Film and Literature*. Upper Saddle River, N.J.: Prentice-Hall, 1999.

Courtney, Susan. *Hollywood Fantasies of Miscegenation*. Princeton, N.J.: Princeton University Press, 2005.

de Beauregard, Raphaelle Costa. "*A Streetcar Named Desire* (1947/1952) as a Freaks Show." In *A Streetcar Named Desire: Tennessee Williams—Elia Kazan*, edited by Dominique Sipière, 106–17. Nantes, France: Editions du Temps, 2003.

DeBona, Guerric. "Dickens, the Depression, and MGM's David Copperfield." In *Film Adaptation*, edited by James Naremore, 106–28. London: Athalone Press, 2000.

Doane, Mary Ann. *The Desire to Desire: The Woman's Film of the 1940s*. Bloomington: Indiana University Press, 1987.

Dowell, Pat. "The Mythology of the Western Hollywood Perspectives on Race and Gender in the Nineties." *Cineaste* 21, nos. 1–2 (Winter–Spring 1995): 6–10.

Edgerton, Gary. "'A Breed Apart': Hollywood, Racial Stereotyping, and the Promise of Revisionism in *The Last of the Mohicans*." *Journal of American Culture* 17, no. 2 (June 1994): 1–20.

Eleftheriotis, Dimitris. *Popular Cinemas of Europe*. New York: Continuum, 2001.

Elliott, Kamilla. *Rethinking the Novel/Film Debate*. Cambridge: Cambridge University Press, 2003.

Elmer, Greg, and Mike Gasher, eds. *Contracting Out: Hollywood Runaway Productions and Foreign Location Shooting*. Lanham, Md.: Rowman & Littlefield, 2005.

Elsaesser, Thomas. "Tales of Sound and Fury: Observations on the Family Melodrama" (1972). Reprinted in *Home Is Where the Heart Is*, edited by Christine Gledhill, 43–69. London: British Film Institute Publications, 1987.

Forbes, Jill. "*Germinal*: Keeping It in the Family." *Sight and Sound* 4, no. 5 (May 1994): 24–26.

Frank, Stanley. "Sure-Seaters Discover an Audience (1952)." In *Moviegoing in America*, edited by Gregory A. Waller, 255–58. Oxford: Blackwell, 2002.

French, Philip. *Westerns*. Manchester, UK: Carcenet Press, 2005.

Garcia, Pedro Javier Pardo. "Beyond Adaptation: Frankenstein's Postmodern Progeny." In *Books in Motion: Adaptation, Intertextuality, Authorship*, edited by Mireia Aragay, 223–42. Amsterdam: Rodophi, 2005.

Geraghty, Christine. "Jane Austen Meets Gurinder Chadha: Hybridity and Intertextuality in *Bride and Prejudice*." *South Asian Popular Culture* 4, no. 2 (October 2006): 163–68.

Giddings, Robert, and Keith Selby. *The Classic Serial on Television and Radio*. Basingstoke, UK: Palgrave, 2001.

Gledhill, Christine. "The Melodramatic Field: An Investigation." In *Home Is Where the Heart Is*, edited by Christine Gledhill, 5–39. London: British Film Institute Publications, 1987.

Graham, Rae. "*The House of Mirth* Navigates a Vicious Circle." *American Cinematographer* 82, no. 2 (February 2001): 12–14.

Grant, Barry Keith. "John Ford and James Fenimore Cooper." In *John Ford Made Westerns: Filming the Legend in the Sound Era*, edited by Gaylyn Studlar and Matthew Bernstein, 193–219. Bloomington: Indiana University Press, 2001.

Grant, Catherine. "Recognising Billy Budd in *Beau Travail*: Epistemology and Hermeneutics of Auteurist 'Free' Adaptation." *Screen* 43, no. 1 (Spring 2002): 57–73.

Griffith, James. *Adaptations as Imitations: Films from Novels*. Newark: University of Delaware Press, 1997.

Grundmann, Roy. "*Brokeback Mountain*." *Cineaste* 31, no. 2 (Spring 2006): 50–52.

Hanks, Pamela Anne. "Must We Acknowledge What We Mean? The Viewer's Role in Filmed Versions of *A Streetcar Named Desire*." *Journal of Popular Film and Television* 14, no. 3 (Fall 1986): 114–22.

Harbord, Janet. *Film Cultures*. London: Sage, 2002.

Hatch, Kristen. "Movies and the New Faces of Masculinity." In *American Cinema of the 1950s: Themes and Variations*, edited by Murray Pomerance, 43–64. Oxford: Berg, 2005.

Heilman, Jeremy. "La Captive." *MovieMartyr*, August 5, 2002. www.moviemartyr.com/2000/lacaptive.htm.

Helmetag, Charles H. "Recreating Edith Wharton's New York in Martin Scorsese's *The Age of Innocence*." *Literature/Film Quarterly* 26, no. 3 (July 1998): 162–65.

Hendler, June. *Best Sellers and Their Film Adaptations in Postwar America*. New York: Peter Lang, 2001.

Higson, Andrew. *English Heritage, English Cinema: The Costume Drama in the 1980s and 1990s*. Oxford: Oxford University Press, 2003.

———. "Film Acting and Independent Cinema." *Screen* 27, nos. 3–4 (May–August 1986): 110–32.

Hill, John. *British Cinema in the 1980s*. Oxford: Clarendon Press, 1999.

———. *Sex, Class, and Realism: British Cinema 1956–1963*. London: British Film Institute Publications, 1986.

Hitt, Jim. *The American West from Fiction (1823–1976) into Film (1909–1986)*. Jefferson, N.C.: McFarland, 1990.

Hoban, James L. "Scripting *The Good Earth*: Versions of the Novel for the Screen." In *The Several Worlds of Pearl S. Buck*, edited by Elizabeth J. Lipscomb, Frances E. Webb, and Peter Conn, 127–44. Westport, Conn.: Greenwood Press, 1994.

Horner, Harry. "Designing *The Heiress*." *Hollywood Quarterly* 5, no. 1 (Fall 1950): 1–7.

James, Nick. "Magnificent Obsession: Interview with Chantal Ackerman." *Sight and Sound* 11, no. 5 (May 2001): 20–23.

Johnson, Albert. "*Cat on a Hot Tin Roof*." *Film Quarterly* 12, no. 2 (Winter 1958): 21–35.

Jones, Daryl. *The Dime Novel Western.* Bowling Green, Ohio: Bowling Green University Popular Press, 1978.

Kaplan, Deborah. "Mass Marketing Jane Austen: Men, Women, and Censorship in Two Film Adaptations" (1996). Reprinted in *Jane Austen in Hollywood*, edited by Linda Troost and Sayre Greenfield, 177–87. Lexington: University of Kentucky Press, 1998.

Kenaga, Heidi. "Edna Ferber's *Cimarron*, Cultural Authority, and 1920s Western Historical Narratives." In *Middlebrow Moderns: Popular American Women Writers of the 1920s*, edited by Lisa Botshon and Meredith Goldsmith, 167–201. Boston: Northeastern University Press, 2003.

Kirby, Lynne. *Parallel Tracks: The Railroad and Silent Cinema.* Durham, N.C.: Duke University Press, 1997.

Kitses, Jim. *Horizons West.* London: British Film Institute Publications, 2004.

Klinger, Barbara. *Beyond the Multiplex: Cinema, New Technologies, and the Home.* Berkeley: University of California Press, 2006.

———. *Melodrama and Meaning: History, Culture, and the Films of Douglas Sirk.* Bloomington: Indiana University Press, 1994.

Kouvaros, George. "Improvisation and the Operatic: Cassavetes' *A Woman under the Influence.*" In *Falling for You: Essays on Cinema and Performance*, edited by Lesley Stern and George Kouvaros, 49–71. Sydney: Power Publications, 1999.

Kozloff, Sarah. *Overhearing Film Dialogue.* Berkeley: University of California Press, 2000.

Kuhn, Annette. *Women's Pictures: Feminism and Cinema.* London: Routledge and K. Paul, 1982.

La Place, Maria. "Producing and Consuming the Woman's Film: Discursive Struggle in *Now, Voyager.*" In *Home Is Where the Heart Is*, edited by Christine Gledhill, 138–66. London: British Film Institute Publications, 1987.

Leff, Leonard J. "And Transfer to Cemetery: The 'Streetcars Named Desire.'" *Film Quarterly* 55, no. 3 (Spring 2002): 29–37.

Leff, Leonard J., and Jerold L. Simmons. *The Dame in the Kimono: Hollywood Censorship and the Production Code from the 1920s to the 1960s.* New York: Grove Weidenfeld, 1990.

Leitch, Thomas. "Twelve Fallacies in Contemporary Adaptation Theory." *Criticism* 45, no. 2 (Spring 2003): 149–71.

Leong, Karen J. *The China Mystique.* Berkeley: University of California Press, 2005.

Lev, Peter. *Transforming the Screen, 1950–1959.* New York: Charles Scribner's Sons, 2003.

Liao, Kang. *Pearl S. Buck: A Cultural Bridge across the Pacific.* Westport, Conn.: Greenwood Press, 1997.

LoBrutto, Vincent. *The Filmmaker's Guide to Production Design.* New York: Allworth Press, 2002.

Lusted, David. "Literary Adaptations and Cultural Fantasies." *Journal of Popular British Cinema* 4 (2001): 72–80.

———. "Social Class and the Western as Male Melodrama." In *The Movie Book of the Western*, edited by Ian Cameron and Douglas Pye, 63–74. London: Studio Vista, 1996.

———. *The Western.* London: British Film Institute Publications, 2003.

Lye, Colleen. *America's Asia: Racial Form and American Literature 1893–1945*. Princeton, N.J.: Princeton University Press, 2005.

Macdonald, Gina, and Andrew Macdonald. "Introduction." In *Jane Austen on Screen*, edited by Gina Macdonald and Andrew Macdonald, 1–8. Cambridge: Cambridge University Press, 2003.

MacKinnon, Kenneth. "The Family in Hollywood Melodrama: Actual or Ideal?" *Journal of Gender Studies* 13, no. 1 (March 2004): 29–36.

Madsen, Peter. "Introduction." In *The Urban Lifeworld*, edited by Peter Madsen and Richard Pluntz, 1–41. London: Routledge, 2002.

Maltby, Richard. "A Better Sense of History: John Ford and the Indians." In *The Movie Book of the Western*, edited by Ian Cameron and Douglas Pye, 34–49. London: Studio Vista, 1996.

Marcuse, Peter. "The Layered City." In *The Urban Lifeworld*, edited by Peter Madsen and Richard Pluntz, 94–114. London: Routledge, 2002.

Margolyes, Miriam. "Playing Dickens: Miriam Margolyes. A Conversation with John Glavin." In *Dickens on Screen*, edited by John Glavin, 104–9. Cambridge: Cambridge University Press, 2003.

Marubbio, M. Elise. "Celebrating with *The Last of the Mohicans*: The Columbus Quincentenary and Neocolonialism in Hollywood Film." *The Journal of American and Comparative Culture* 25, nos. 1 and 2 (Spring and Summer 2002): 139–54.

McFarlane, Brian. *An Autobiography of British Cinema*. London: Methuen, 1997.

———. "It Wasn't Like That in the Book." *Literature/Film Quarterly* 28, no. 3 (2000): 163–69.

———. *Novel to Film*. Oxford: Clarendon Press, 1996.

McMurtry, Larry. "Adapting *Brokeback Mountain*." In *Brokeback Mountain: Story to Screenplay*, edited by Annie Proulx, Larry McMurtry, and Diana Ossana, 139–42. London: Harper Perennial, 2006.

Mercer, John, and Martin Shingler. *Melodrama: Genre, Style, Sensibility*. London: Wallflower, 2004.

Metz, Christian. *Film Language*, translated by Michael Taylor. Oxford: Oxford University Press, 1991.

Milton, John R. *The Novel of the American West*. Lincoln: University of Nebraska Press, 1980.

Mitchell, Lee Clark. *Westerns: Making the Man in Fiction and Film*. Chicago: University of Chicago Press, 1996.

Nachbar, Jack. "Introduction: A Century on the Trail." *Journal of Popular Film and Television* 30, no. 4 (Winter 2003): 178–80.

Naremore, James. *Acting in the Cinema*. Berkeley: University of California Press, 1990.

———. "Introduction: Film and the Reign of Adaptation." In *Film Adaptation*, edited by James Naremore, 1–16. London: Athalone Press, 2000.

Neale, Steve. "Art Cinema as Institution." *Screen* 22, no. 1 (Spring 1981): 11–40.

———. *Genre and Hollywood*. London: Routledge, 2000.

———. "Vanishing Americans: Racial and Ethnic Issues in the Interpretation and Context of Post-war 'Pro-Indian' Westerns." In *Back in the Saddle Again: New Essays on the Western*, edited by Ed Buscombe and Roberta Pearson, 8–28. London: British Film Institute Publications, 1998.

Newman, Kim. *"Cimarron."* In *The BFI Companion to the Western*, edited by Ed Buscombe, 255. London: Andre Deutsch, 1988.

Noriega, Chon. "'Something's Missing Here!': Homosexuality and Film Reviews during the Production Code Era." *Cinema Journal* 30, no. 1 (Autumn 1990): 22–41.

Nowell-Smith, Geoffrey. "Cities: Real and Imagined." In *Cinema and the City*, edited by Mark Shiel and Tony Fitzmaurice, 99–108. Oxford: Blackwell, 2001.

Ossana, Diana. "Climbing Brokeback Mountain." In *Brokeback Mountain: Story to Screenplay*, edited by Annie Proulx, Larry McMurtry, and Diana Ossana, 143–52. London: Harper Perennial, 2006.

Palmer, Augusta. "Seven Questions with Marleen Gorris." *indieWIRE*, February 23, 1998. www.indiewire.com/people/int_Gorris_Marleen_980223.html.

Palmer, R. Barton. "Tennessee Williams and the Evolution of the Adult Film." In *Cambridge Companion to Tennessee Williams*, edited by Matthew C. Roudané, 204–31. Cambridge: Cambridge University Press, 1997.

Phillips, Gene D. *The Films of Tennessee Williams*. London: Associated Universities Press, 1980.

Pidduck, Julianne. *Contemporary Costume Film*. London: British Film Institute Publications, 2004.

Pointer, Michael. *Charles Dickens on the Screen: The Film, Television, and Video Adaptations*. Lanham, Md.: Scarecrow Press, 1996.

Powrie, Phil. "Marketing History: *Swann in Love.*" *Film Criticism* 12, no. 3 (Spring 1988): 33–45.

Price, James. *"Ulysses."* *Sight and Sound* 36, no. 3 (Summer 1967): 144–45.

Proulx, Annie. "Getting Movied." In *Brokeback Mountain: Story to Screenplay*, edited by Annie Proulx, Larry McMurtry, and Diana Ossana, 129–38. London: Harper Perennial, 2006.

Pumphrey, Martin. "Why Do Cowboys Wear Hats in the Bath?" In *The Movie Book of the Western*, edited by Ian Cameron and Douglas Pye, 50–62. London: Studio Vista, 1996.

Pye, Douglas. "Introduction: Criticism and the Western." In *The Movie Book of the Western*, edited by Ian Cameron and Douglas Pye, 9–21. London: Studio Vista, 1996.

Radway, Janice A. *Reading the Romance: Women, Patriarchy, and Popular Literature*. Chapel Hill: University of North Carolina Press, 1984.

Raw, Laurence. "Reconstructing Henry James: *The Heiress* (1949)." *Literature/Film Quarterly* 30, no. 4 (2002): 243–48.

Reader, Keith. *"Time Regained*—Review." *Sight and Sound* 10, no. 1 (January 2000): 61.

Richards, Jeffrey. *Films and British National Identity: From Dickens to Dad's Army*. Manchester, UK: Manchester University Press, 1997.

Romano, John. "Writing after Dickens: The Television Writer's Art." In *Dickens on Screen*, edited by John Glavin, 89–94. Cambridge: Cambridge University Press, 2003.

Romney, Jonathan. "Masque of the Living Dead." *Sight and Sound* 10, no. 1 (January 2000): 30–33.

Rosenbaum, Jonathan. "The Sweet Cheat." *Chicago Reader*, 2000. www.chicagoreader.com/movies/archives/2000/0700/000721.html.

Sanders, James. *Celluloid Skyline: New York and the Movies.* New York: Alfred A. Knopf, 2001.

Schatz, Thomas. *Hollywood Genres.* New York: Random House, 1981.

Schlueter, June. "Imitating an Icon: John Erman's Remake of Tennessee Williams' *A Streetcar Named Desire.*" *Modern Drama* 28, no. 1 (Spring 1985): 139–47.

Scobey, David M. *Empire City: The Making and Meaning of the New York City Landscape.* Philadelphia: Temple University Press, 2002.

Sconce, Jeffrey. "Dickens, Selznick, and *South Park.*" In *Dickens on Screen*, edited by John Glavin, 171–87. Cambridge: Cambridge University Press, 2003.

Scorsese, Martin. *Scorsese on Scorsese.* London: Faber, 1989.

Segar, Linda. "Creating Workable Adaptations." *Creative Screenwriting* 4, no. 2 (Summer 1997): 87–89.

Smith, Gavin. "Wars and Peace." *Sight and Sound* 2, no. 7 (November 1992): 10–15.

Smith, Grahame. *Dickens and the Dream of Cinema.* Manchester, UK: Manchester University Press, 2003.

Smyth, J. E. "*Cimarron*: The New Western History in 1931." *Film and History* 33, no. 1 (January 2003): 9–17.

Stam, Robert. "Beyond Fidelity: The Dialogics of Adaptation." In *Film Adaptation*, edited by James Naremore, 57–76. London: Athalone Press, 2000.

———. "Introduction: The Theory and Practice of Adaptation." In *Literature and Film: A Guide to the Theory and Practice of Film Adaptation*, edited by Robert Stam and Alessandra Raengo, 1–52. Oxford: Blackwell, 2004.

———. *Literature through Film: Realism Magic and the Art of Adaptation.* Oxford: Blackwell, 2005.

Stam, Robert, and Alessandra Raengo, eds. *A Companion to Literature and Film.* Oxford: Blackwell, 2004.

———, eds. *Literature and Film: A Guide to Theory and Practice of Adaptation.* Oxford: Blackwell, 2004.

Stanfield, Peter. *Hollywood, Westerns, and the 1930s.* Exeter, UK: University of Exeter Press, 2001.

Studlar, Gaylyn, and Matthew Bernstein. "Introduction." In *John Ford Made Westerns: Filming the Legend in the Sound Era*, edited by Gaylyn Studlar and Matthew Bernstein, 1–22. Bloomington: Indiana University Press, 2001.

Tashiro, Charles S. *Pretty Pictures: Production Design and the History Film.* Austin: University of Texas Press, 1998.

Tompkins, Jane. *West of Everything: The Inner Life of Westerns.* Oxford: Oxford University Press, 1992.

Tucker, Patrick. *Secrets of Screen Acting.* London: Routledge, 2003.

Vincendeau, Ginette. "*The Captive.*" *Sight and Sound* 11, no. 5 (May 2001): 45.

———, ed. *Film/Literature/Heritage.* London: British Film Institute Publications, 2001.

Viviani, Christian. "Who Is without Sin? The Maternal Melodrama in American Film, 1930–39." In *Home Is Where the Heart Is*, edited by Christine Gledhill, 83–99. London: British Film Institute Publications, 1987.

Wake, Bob. "David Copperfield (2000)." *Culturevulture*. culturevulture.net/Television/DavidCopperfield(2).htm.

Walker, Jeffrey. "Deconstructing an American Myth: Hollywood and *The Last of the Mohicans*" (1992). Reprinted in *Hollywood's Indian: The Portrayal of the Native American in Film*, edited by Peter C. Rollins and John E. O'Connor, 17–186. Lexington: University Press of Kentucky, 1998.

Wexman, Virginia Wright. *Creating the Couple: Love, Marriage, and Hollywood Performance*. Princeton, N.J.: Princeton University Press, 1993.

Worland, Rick, and Edward Countryman. "The New Western: American Historiography and the Emergence of the New Westerns." In *Back in the Saddle Again: New Essays on the Western*, edited by Ed Buscombe and Roberta Pearson, 182–96. London: British Film Institute Publications, 1998.

Young, Jeff, ed. *Kazan on Kazan*. London: Faber and Faber, 1999.

Index

About the Author

Christine Geraghty is professor of film and television studies at the University of Glasgow, Scotland, UK. She taught for many years on adult evening classes for the British Film Institute before becoming a full-time academic at Goldsmiths College, University of London. She has written extensively on film and television and is the author of *Women and Soap Opera* (1991) and of *British Cinema in the Fifties: Gender, Genre and the "New Look"* (2000). With David Lusted, she coedited *The Television Studies Book* (1998), and she has contributed to a range of journals including *Screen*, *International Journal of Cultural Studies*, and *European Journal of Cultural Studies*. Her study of the British film *My Beautiful Laundrette* was published in 2005.